SEALED IN PARCHMENT

I0887621

Frontispiece, *Le Conte del Graal*
Paris, Bibliothèque Nationale, MS fr. 12596, fol. 1

SEALED IN PARCHMENT

Rereadings of Knighthood in the Illuminated Manuscripts of Chrétien de Troyes

SANDRA HINDMAN

THE UNIVERSITY OF CHICAGO PRESS

Chicago & London

SANDRA HINDMAN is professor of art history at Northwestern University. She is the author of *Text and Image in Fifteenth-Century Illustrated Dutch Bibles* and of *Christine de Pizan's "Epistre Othéa": Painting and Politics at the Court of Charles VI* and editor of *Printing the Written Word,* among other publications.

THE UNIVERSITY OF CHICAGO PRESS, CHICAGO 60637
THE UNIVERSITY OF CHICAGO PRESS, LTD., LONDON

© 1994 by The University of Chicago
All rights reserved. Published 1994
Printed in the United States of America

03 02 01 00 99 98 97 96 95 94 1 2 3 4 5
ISBN: 0-226-34155-0 (cloth)
0-226-34156-9 (paper)

Publication of this book has been aided by a grant from the Millard Meiss Publication Fund of the College Art Association.

MM

Library of Congress Cataloging-in-Publication Data

Hindman, Sandra, 1944–
Sealed in parchment : rereadings of knighthood in the illuminated manuscripts of Chrétien de Troyes / Sandra Hindman.
p. cm.
Includes bibliographical references and index.
1. Chrétien de Troyes, 12th cent.—Manuscripts. 2. Chrétien de Troyes, 12th cent.—Illustrations. 3. Illumination of books and manuscripts, Medieval—France. 4. Illumination of books and manuscripts, French. 5. Knights and knighthood in literature. 6. Arthurian romances—Illustrations. 7. Knights and knighthood in art. 8. Romances—Illustrations. I. Title.
PQ1448.H56 1994
841′.1—dc20 93-5300
CIP

The paper used in this publication meets the minimum requirements of the American National Standard for Information Sciences—Permanence of Paper for Printed Library Materials, ANSI z39.48-1984.

For my students:
Vicki
Jean
Anne D.
Michael
Véronique

CONTENTS

ILLUSTRATIONS

PREFACE

THIS BOOK HAS GERMINATED FOR A LONG TIME. SHORTLY AFTER I FINISHED WORKING ON CHRISTINE DE PIZAN'S *EPISTRE OTHÉA* (1986), I WANTED TO UNDERSTAND BETTER ONE ILLUMINATED text of Christine's, a courtly romance, *Le Livre du duc des vrais amans,* and so I set out to uncover the conventions of romance illustration. Finding that virtually nothing had been published on the subject, I began a project that examined the earliest illustrations of romance in a large group of thirteenth-century vernacular manuscripts, including those of Chrétien de Troyes, the *romans réalistes,* Marie de France, and Adenet le Roi. Since the project as originally conceived proved far too vast, I eventually concentrated on the romances of Chrétien de Troyes. Ironically, as this book was being finished, I returned to Christine and completed a study of *Le Livre du duc des vrais amans,* which now casts it as a kind of antiromance. My book on Chrétien is much more than an attempt to uncover the pictorial conventions of romance, however. It represents my thinking on how the study of manuscripts as primary documents can lead to a richer understanding of the complexities of the society and culture of the Middle Ages in the interrelated areas of literature, history, and art.

Begun in Paris in 1987 while I was on leave from Northwestern University, this book was completed in Chicago and Paris under the tenure of a National Endowment for the Humanities Fellowship in 1990–91, for which I am most grateful. I also thank the staff of the Newberry Library, especially the Center for Renaissance Studies, where I intermittently enjoyed the benefits of an appointment as research associate while writing a draft of this book.

The project has benefited from discussions with many individuals. These include many of my graduate students, especially Laura Weigert, Kristin Sazama, and Danielle Fox, among others who took two seminars on medieval romance at Northwestern University. At a very early but important stage over dinner in Paris, Cynthia Hahn posed a series of questions that helped unleash the contents of chapters 1 and 2. Peggy McCracken graciously read and commented on the entire manuscript with her usual generosity and intelligence; my readings owe a lot to our dialogue. At a later stage, Sylvia Huot's comments helped me refine the final version. Gabrielle Spiegel's sensitive and profound input went well beyond the scope of the romances treated in this book. For many other lively discussions that helped shape my thinking at various stages, I also thank Roberta Krueger, Mary Beth Rose, David Hult, Michael Camille, Paul Gehl, Douglas Kelly, John Baldwin, and Karl Werckmeister. My debt of gratitude to my parents, Adriana Pencin and James Clark Hindman, who always help in many diverse ways, is immeasurable.

Paris, France
September 1992

INTRODUCTION

And all those who travel the road can still see the story there,
sealed in parchment.

Manessier's Continuation to *Le Conte del Graal*[1]

CHRÉTIEN DE TROYES, THE TALENTED AUTHOR OF THE FIRST ARTHURIAN ROMANCES AND THE MEDIEVAL FRENCH POET MOST PROMINENT TODAY, REMAINS ELUSIVE.[2] THE LITTLE WE KNOW FOR CERtain comes mostly from piecing together bits of information from his own writings, which date roughly between 1170 and 1183. He was perhaps originally from the cathedral town of Troyes (he names himself "Chrétien de Troyes" in *Erec et Enide*), capital of the counts of Champagne, who encouraged its celebrated medieval fairs, attracting tradesmen from all over the world. Chrétien may have been a returning crusader who distinguished himself in the Holy Land, or possibly even a converted Jew—Troyes having been a renowned talmudic center from the eleventh century—which would account for his odd first name.[3] However mysterious his origins, he most likely worked in Troyes during the 1170s at the refined court of Marie, daughter of the remarkable Queen Eleanor of Aquitaine and herself countess of Champagne. In the prologue of *Le Chevalier de la charrette (Lancelot)*, he acknowledges that he composed the poem, a daringly explicit tale of the adulterous love of Queen Guinevere and Lancelot, at Marie's request. He may eventually have left Champagne to go to the court of Philip of Alsace, count of Flanders. Dedicated to Philip, the unfinished *Le Conte del Graal (Perceval)*, about the making of a youthful knight who is perhaps meant to recall the count himself, breaks off in midsentence, presumably because of the poet's death.

In all, Chrétien wrote five captivating verse romances, unusually vivid stories full of marvelous adventures and keen psychological insight, which he probably composed in the following order: *Erec et Enide* (ca. 1170), *Cligès* (ca. 1176), *Le Chevalier de la charrette (Lancelot)* (ca. 1177), *Le Chevalier au lion (Yvain)* (ca. 1177), and *Le Conte del Graal (Perceval)* (ca. 1182).[4] *Erec et Enide* recounts the coy romance of a couple who are so engrossed in their love for each other that they forget their duties. *Cligès* tells of the secret love of a Greek prince, Cligès, for Fenice, wife of the emperor of Constantinople, who manages to deceive her husband with a magic potion. And *Le Chevalier au lion* narrates the fulfillment of the love between the Arthurian knight Yvain and Laudine after a series of awesome quests. Other writings by Chrétien have not survived. At the beginning of *Cligès* he reveals that he also translated Ovid's *Remedia amoris* from Latin into French, wrote adaptations of Ovid's *Metamorphoses,* and composed a version of the Tristan story (*Conte du roi Marc et d'Iseult la Blonde*). His authorship of the pious adventure story *Guillaume d'Angleterre,* written by a certain Chrétien, remains disputed. Conversant with the Latin literature of the day, he was probably trained as a cleric, although certain curious turns of phrase suggest that he may have been a minstrel, borrowing from oral traditions and even adapting his own verses for performance (Vitz 1990).

Tantalizingly scant contemporary documentation makes the surviving manuscripts of Chrétien's romances all the more precious for the evidence they preserve about the poet and the reception of his works. Forty-four manuscripts of his romances are extant.[5] Of these, thirty-two are either complete manuscripts or substantial fragments, and the rest are smaller fragments. For a twelfth-century author, this number is sizable and affirms his popularity. Although certain medieval texts such as the *Roman de la Rose* survive in hundreds of manuscripts, other courtly romances composed in verse, like Chrétien's, have in fact come down to us in astonishingly few copies. For example, among the writings of Chrétien's contemporary Marie de France, her lays are extant in four manuscripts, of which only one is "complete," and her fables in twenty-four.[6] Or of the so-called *romans réalistes,* most are preserved in a single copy or at most two copies.[7] How many more romances must there have been that have not survived at all? As with most twelfth-century writers, none of the manuscripts of Chrétien's romances are contemporary with the author's lifetime; instead, most date from nearly a century later, about 1275 to about 1325. Whereas Chrétien probably worked mainly in Champagne, most of the manuscripts can be localized in Picardy and Flanders. Virtually none date later than the early fourteenth century. This brief overview of the group of surviving manuscripts immediately raises two pertinent questions: Why were the manuscripts so popular in the geographically circumscribed area of Picardy and Flanders? And why did their popularity apparently cease in the early fourteenth century?

About a third of the complete or nearly complete manuscripts, totaling ten copies, are illustrated—some very sparsely, others profusely—with either historiated initials or independent miniatures. In statistical terms alone this relatively high percentage of illuminated romances is noteworthy. Once again, comparison with the works of Marie de France is telling. None of the manuscripts of her lays and only three manuscripts of her fables are illustrated. By contrast, for Chrétien there are two illustrated copies of *Erec et Enide* (with one and three miniatures),[8] no illustrated copies of *Cligès,* two illustrated copies of *Le Chevalier de la charrette* (with one and three miniatures, the latter incomplete),[9] two illustrated copies of *Le Chevalier au lion* (with seven and ten miniatures, the former incomplete),[10] and five illustrated copies of *Le Conte del Graal* and its continuations (with fifty-one, fifty-two, fifty-four, twenty-six, and fifty miniatures).[11] In addition, two manuscripts were apparently planned to include illustrations, but they were never executed.[12] Because of the large number of illuminated versions of Chrétien's texts, any study of the reception of the manuscripts will thus have to take into account readings presented by these illuminated copies.

Certain unexpected characteristics of the physical appearance of some of these manuscripts are singular. Even though many were evidently luxury productions—including miniatures composed with extensive gold leaf and lapis lazuli, which were costly materials—they are most often transcribed on crudely prepared, discolored parchment that has been torn, then mended. The corners of their pages are limp and dog-eared from extensive use, their luxurious miniatures now rubbed and worn. Food stains occasionally spot the pages. These factors have led art historians, typically attracted by deluxe, high quality works produced in the emerging court environment of the Parisian capital, to turn away from Chrétien's manuscripts instead of taking them seriously as cultural artifacts and asking the relevant question: What can the now shabby condition of these manuscripts, coupled with other evidence provided by their texts and illustrations, tell us about their original use?

Other peculiarities of the manuscripts, such as their makeup as anthologies, also bear directly on the question of their use. Few of the extant manuscripts of Chrétien's writings include entirely independent copies of his romances. Rather, most include Chrétien's romances, either singly or as a kind of collected works, bound together with other writings, which might include antique romances, other Arthurian tales, epic romances or chansons de geste, genealogies, and religious or didactic works. Strikingly, none of the illuminated manuscripts includes any prose writings, nor is prose commonly compiled with verse in any of the unillustrated copies. This suggests, particularly since the composition of the prose Arthurian romance cycles predates the surviving manuscripts of Chrétien, that readers made a clear-cut distinction on a discursive level between verse and prose. Such compilation is not uncommon in manuscripts of thirteenth-century vernacular works, although editions of individual texts rarely even specify this extratextual character of the work. Marie de France's lays and fables, for example, are embedded in a vast *recueil,* or anthology, that includes other poems, recipes, and even music in what is generally taken to be the editio princeps of her work.[13] A fuller appreciation of the use of Chrétien's texts, including eventually a richer understanding of the sharp division between verse and prose, emerges out of a study of the compilations that include them.

Arguing from the perspective that we can best recover medieval readings of Chrétien's romances from a close scrutiny of the actual manuscripts, I take as my point of departure the illuminated manuscripts of his texts. In my investigation of the individual manuscripts, I consider diverse evidence. This evidence includes the physical characteristics of the manuscripts: size, nature of the parchment, and evidence of use. It also includes their textual content: significant textual variations in Chrétien's works, as well as the identity, number, and order of other texts originally bound together with them. It likewise includes their pictorial content: the number, placement, subjects, and types of illuminations in the different manuscripts, including texts other than Chrétien's. And it includes a consideration of their *mise en page:* the organization on the page of the text and pictures for the reader, including the nature and content of any rubrics. Not all sorts of evidence end up being relevant for every manuscript, but taken together the evidence enables me to develop fresh rereadings of Chrétien's writings in their sociopolitical and cultural milieus.

Considerable previous research on the manuscripts of Chrétien de Troyes—even if no work is specifically devoted to his illuminated manuscripts—provides a useful foundation for further study.[14] Literary historians, especially Micha (1939), have examined the manuscripts, briefly describing their overall textual content and dividing them into philological families. Struck by the prevalence of *recueils* and noting the unusual features of some of the compilations, however, Micha puzzled over the question of audience without really attempting to resolve it. He was also forced to conclude, based on many idiosyncratic textual features of individual manuscripts, that the manuscripts do not fit easily into families. Since Micha's fundamental monograph, the discovery of other fragments has done little to change the overall picture of Chrétien's literary production. Editions by Foerster,[15] Hilka,[16] and Roques[17] for the manuscripts of

Chrétien's romances and by Williams, Oswald,[18] and Roach[19] for the four continuations of *Le Conte del Graal*, while contributing to and building on Micha's study, have also made Chrétien's stories readily accessible in printed form. Numerous modern translations guarantee the continuing availability of the romances to an ever wider public.

The complicated textual problem exhibited by the widely diverse manuscripts of Chrétien's romances has, however, provoked considerable controversy (see Reid 1976; Hunt 1979). On one hand, a group of scholars favors a philologically traditional approach by which the establishment of an ideal Ur-text provides the basis for an edition, which in turn permits comparison for the purpose of classifying an even wider range of variants (for the two perspectives, see Hult 1986, 1989; Utti and Foulet 1988). On the other hand, a rival camp of critics gives priority to the reading presented by a single manuscript, such as the famous "Guiot" copy, thought to be nearest to Chrétien's own intentions and produced in Champagne closer to his origins than other manuscripts. For this latter group there is no one "correct" reading of Chrétien's texts, in part because scribes, working within an oral tradition, felt little restraint about changing their exemplars. Their spirit of innovation leads to an understanding of authorship that itself precludes the recovery of poetic individuality, as Zumthor (1972, 65–79; 1981; 1984, 110 15), Zink (1985), and more recently Hult (1988), among others, underscore. In differing respects these critics stress that it is the scribe's treatment of the text that constitutes its interpretation, much as the minstrel interprets the text in its oral transmission (they thus distinguish between the *acteur*-scribe-minstrel and the *auteur*-author in medieval vernacular writings; see Hult 1986, esp. 853–55).

My approach similarly gives priority to the reading of each individual manuscript—its transcription and its illustration—as a means of retrieving its reception. I also offer a different sort of evidence, derived primarily from the pictures, that reinforces the idea of the effacement of the *auteur*-author in Chrétien's writings. In an effort to privilege the interpretations of individual manuscripts particularly in light of their social functions, my book, like the work of the critics cited above, contributes to the "new philology," itself a cornerstone of the "new medievalism" (see Nichols in Brownlee, Brownlee, and Nichols 1991, 1–26, Nichols 1988, and Busby 1993).

As Micha's work provides a basis for all the ensuing discussion of the texts, the research of certain art historians, especially Loomis, provides a basis for considering the miniatures. In fact the Loomises (Loomis and

Loomis 1938) gathered together in a kind of encyclopedic visual corpus large numbers of representations of the Arthurian legend from diverse manuscripts, not to mention from caskets, combs, and wall paintings. Concentrating first on the prose romances, Stones has also assembled much little-published material and has begun to formulate new questions for it, touching primarily on production. Noting that the same ateliers were responsible for vernacular, biblical, and liturgical manuscripts, she has started to explore the relation between the secular and the sacred, particularly with regard to the models used to create miniatures for these diverse texts (Stones 1970, 1976, 1977, 1991). But so focused is she on style and workmanship that she has not been able to see beyond what she refers to as the "qualitative difficulty," the "general lack of artistic accomplishment," of Chrétien's illuminated manuscripts (the great author illustrated by not-so-great pictures), and in concluding that much of the Arthurian material does not "measure up," she regrettably misses the point and ignores the interrelated questions of audience and function (Stones 1991, esp. 23–24). Recently, with Busby, Nixon, and Walters, Stones has undertaken a monumental corpus that for the first time makes available the illustrations, including decoration, for all the manuscripts (Busby et al. 1993).

Few studies, however, attempt to analyze the miniatures to determine what they might reveal about reception. In one exception, which is misleading because it is based on a misidentification of the subjects of some of the miniatures, it has even been suggested for manuscripts of the Perceval story that the pictures, having nothing to do with the text and occurring at regular intervals, simply represent "performance" breaks in the text because it was felt that the "reader appreciated regular visual entertainment" (Busby 1988). In contrast, I argue that, far from merely offering visual diversion, the miniatures, when read with their texts, prompt distinctive and sometimes highly inventive readings. Manuscripts that have been dismissed as having little interest for the text tradition—because, say, they are full of errors or lacunae or present relatively late transcriptions—thus reemerge as important documents for the rereadings their pictures offer.

A few isolated studies of vernacular manuscripts of this period hold out promise for an approach that relies overwhelmingly on the evidence each manuscript can yield. Touching on the romances of Chrétien, Sylvia Huot (1987) has inventively employed the evidence of thirteenth- and fourteenth-century manuscripts to arrive at an understanding of poetics in the genre of lyric, especially in the works of Guillaume Machaut and Richard de Fornival. Lori Walters (1985) has convincingly shown how scribes of certain manuscripts of Chrétien de Troyes embedded extratextual meaning in their stories by compiling them with Wace's *Brut* to offer a sort of realistic testimony on the reign of Arthur. Hans Runte (1989) has outlined, with some unexpected results, how even the decorated initials can structure the readings of Chrétien's romances. But such studies, besides being few and far between, offer no systematic analysis of the illuminated manuscripts of Chrétien's works.

Focusing on the reception of Chrétien's illuminated romances in Picardy and Flanders, my book outlines two interrelated hypotheses about their audience, one sociopolitical and the other cultural. First, I reread the romances as a timely commentary on the crisis the northern aristocracy experienced during the period, as statements about the disempowerment and social mobility of various social groups. Second, I reread them as evidence of a crisis in reading, as examples that show the uneasy coexistence of oral and literate—performative and nonperformative—modes of thought in a transitional cognitive culture where verse was also giving way to prose. For me these rereadings, which consider the manuscripts as representations of cultural change, help answer the key questions posed earlier both about the peculiar geographic aspect of the reception of the romances in Picardy and Flanders and about their oddly circumscribed time frame between 1275 and 1325.

As sociopolitical commentary on the crisis of the aristocracy of this period, manuscripts of Chrétien's romances participate in a general phenomenon that, following on the work of Georges Duby,[20] among others, is by now widely acclaimed and well documented. Briefly stated, the rising strength of the centralized Capetian monarchy, especially under Philip Augustus, who died in 1220, gradually eclipsed the power and prestige of the northern nobility. The strength of the monarchy made itself felt not only in ideological terms, as it developed a powerful profile of divine kingship, but in material terms, as it wrested juridical, administrative, political, and ultimately social autonomy from local nobles. In the rise of vernacular prose historiography, under the direct sponsorship of these Picard and Flemish nobles around the year 1200, Spiegel (1984 and esp. 1993) has understood a response to their threatened status as they sought to recapture, even to invent, a usable past. For Spiegel, the use of prose for historiography becomes a discursive strategy whereby the nobility staked its claim through the truth-telling authority of this discourse.

Our manuscripts, dating in the last quarter of the century and written in verse, document differently a later stage of the same impulse. Written and illustrated for the descendants of these northern nobles, they address the enduring crisis, which remains perceptible at numerous social levels as the aristocracy continued to resist the erosion of its status in regional terms, when it simultaneously faced difficult socioeconomic problems that threatened its very stability on home grounds.[21]

A word should be said here about Erich Köhler's thesis, which may on the surface seem close to my own.[22] Köhler set out to cast the writings of Chrétien, not their reception in manuscript form, as a response to a crisis in feudal society in the late twelfth century, developing the idea of the quest as a search for autonomous identity on the part of the chivalric class and of Arthur as a kind of anti–Philip Augustus. Grounded in a later period and based on a different body of evidence, my own interpretation does not so much run counter to Köhler's as it elaborates on the manuscripts as vehicles of a process of cultural change that responded to different sociopolitical circumstances in a distinctive milieu.

As evidence of a crisis of reading, manuscripts of Chrétien's romances also participate in a general development, which is so far better described for the twelfth century than for the thirteenth. Ong (1982), Clanchy (1979), Stock (1983, 1984), and Godzich and Kittay (1987; Kittay 1988), among others, have studied in different ways the changing use of writing during the period, calling attention to the interim status of the written text as transcribed speech at the time when oral and written modes of thought still coexisted. Others, specifically concerned with the romance genre, such as Green (1986; see also Scholz 1980) have also pointed out how written texts continued to be used in performance, creating "hearing" as a middle ground in the axis between oral "seeing" and literate "reading."

I will show that, in all sorts of complex ways that include the construction and use of their illustrations, the manuscripts of Chrétien's romances occupy this middle ground, used in a culture unlike our own that was not yet accustomed to individual or silent reading of vernacular texts. My hypothesis about reading helps to account for other peculiarities of Chrétien's manuscripts mentioned earlier. For example, it makes it easier to understand the popularity of the compilation—a group of texts used by more than one person in a household or even by many persons in an extended feudal domain—as well as the routinely shabby condition of the manuscripts, perhaps the inevitable result of extended "public" use. These hypotheses about reading in textual communities also give credence to the social messages I read in the manuscripts, messages encompassing groups of individuals that run the gamut of the aristocratic social hierarchy, not highly personal readings aimed at one individual patron.

Rather than treat individual manuscripts as discrete, disparate readings of these crises, this book isolates different social groups whose shifting status is reread through the lens of single or paired illuminated manuscripts. In five chapters it examines the changing situation of the knightly class, consecutively as clerics, youths, seigneurs, soldiers, and king. Each chapter focuses mainly on one romance of Chrétien: chapters 1, 3, and 5 discuss *Le Conte del Graal (Perceval)* and its continuations as portraits of the knight as cleric, as seigneur, and as king; chapter 2 discusses *Le Chevalier au lion (Yvain)* and to a limited extent *Le Chevalier de la charrette (Lancelot)* as representations of the knight as youth; and chapter 4 discusses *Erec et Enide* as a construction of the knight as soldier. In each chapter the illuminated romances of Chrétien form part of a larger inquiry that takes into account the nature of the manuscript anthology, that is, the other texts and their miniatures with which Chrétien's romances are bound.

The book deliberately does not follow a strict chronology, because I believe the manuscripts together offer a surprisingly homogeneous view of feudal society and reveal related notions about reading. Since I follow neither the order in which Chrétien wrote the texts nor the order of production of the manuscripts, the chapters can easily be read independently. There is nevertheless some sense of historical flux. The two manuscripts studied in the last chapter, of *Le Conte del Graal* (Paris, Bibliothèque Nationale, MSS fr. 1453 and 12577), are the latest extant copies among Chrétien's illuminated manuscripts, dating about 1315 to 1325. They are, besides, the only Parisian copies. The book thus culminates with two unique readings of Chrétien's *Le Conte del Graal* and its continuations, readings that no longer have relevance for the northern nobility, since they are restructured for readers in the capital, for whom Perceval is recast in the model of a king. In this last chapter, my analysis of the reading process reveals a model in which the tension between oral and literate, between spoken and silent, is most evident as verse also begins to give way to prose.

The title of the book, *Sealed in Parchment,* is meant to evoke a milieu, essentially alien to us, where oral and literate modes of comprehension commingle, where the boundaries between literature and life are blurred—in short, the milieu in which I believe the illuminated manuscripts of Chrétien were written and used. Coming from the last verse of Manessier's text, the fourth and last continuation of Chrétien's *Le Conte del Graal,* the phrase "sealed in parchment" signals at once the authority of the fictional "sourcebook" for the Arthurian legend, whose testimony Manessier claims to have followed. It also inevitably calls forth a preliterate oral transaction, the act of applying a seal—a personalized symbol, a sort of charm—to a notarial document in order to authenticate the conveyance it records.[23] But when in the imaginative rhymed couplet Manessier invites the reader to travel the road (*par le chemin*) to visit and "see" the book (*parchemin*), he inventively transforms the analogy of the transaction of sealing into one that instead describes the act of reading. In bridging the gap between oral and literate activities, the language of Manessier thus ratifies the process of cultural change so distinctly apparent in the illuminated manuscripts of Chrétien de Troyes.

CHAPTER ONE

THE KNIGHT *Li Clerc*

> He cherished and honored him deeply, and gave him fine instruction in letters; and Perceval devoted such care and effort and attention to them . . . that the hermit made him a cleric and an acolyte, and subdeacon and deacon after that.
>
> Manessier's Continuation to *Le Conte del Graal*[1]

MORE THAN ANY OF CHRÉTIEN'S OTHER STORIES, THE TEXT OF *LE CONTE DEL GRAAL (PERCEVAL)*, ESPECIALLY CONSIDERED ALONG WITH ITS FOUR CONTINUATIONS, HAS AN OVERTLY RELIGIOUS theme (Frappier 1972). In *Le Conte del Graal* Perceval, the rough, unschooled Welsh youth, comes across five knights, whom he so greatly admires that he too seeks a career as a knight, rushing off to Arthur's court and leaving his mother behind to die in the forest. For Chrétien, Perceval's development as a knight includes both military and religious training. Early in the tale Perceval learns martial skills from his mentor, Gornemant of Gohort, but these do not equip him to penetrate the secrets of the Grail and the lance when he visits the castle of the Fisher King. Spending five years as an accomplished warrior, Perceval vanquishes some sixty knights. But he subsequently learns—rather late in the original story during a visit to a hermit uncle (verses 6217 ff.)—that he has yet to master the spiritual side of knighthood, since he sinned when he caused the death of his mother, a sin he never repented. Only after he has performed penance for this sin will he be judged worthy to learn the secrets of the Grail castle. After his encounter with the hermit uncle, Perceval drops out of the story, which switches to the adventures of Gawain. Since Chrétien left off in mid-sentence after fewer than 10,000 verses, critics can only speculate on how he would have accomplished Perceval's spiritual preparation had he ended the story himself.

Focusing increasingly on the Christian side of the Grail story, Chrétien's four continuators sought different ways of bringing the poem to completion.[2] The First Continuation extends the story of Gawain, who becomes, like Perceval, a sort of Grail quester (*Continuations* 1949–83, vols. 1–3).

Gawain arrives at the Grail castle, meets the Fisher King, but falls asleep before he can learn the mysteries of the Grail and the lance. Three versions of this continuation of varied lengths (Short Redaction, Mixed Redaction, and Long Redaction, between 10,000 and 15,000 verses) and probably by different authors, who all remain anonymous, were written from as early as 1194 and to as late as 1227. Then about 1220 the second continuator, who may be someone known as Wauchier de Denain, writing under the protection of the counts of Flanders, added approximately 13,000 verses to the poem, resuming the quest of Perceval, who finds his way a second time to the Grail castle (on the author's identity, see Vial 1978). This time, just when he is about to learn the Grail's secrets, he is denied the knowledge because he has not perfectly welded the two parts of his broken sword.[3]

Probably both written between 1220 and 1230 but entirely independently of each other, the Third and Fourth Continuations, by Gerbert and by Manessier, recount in considerable detail Perceval's final triumph as a Christian knight.[4] Naming himself three times in his text, Gerbert is thought to be identical with the cleric Gerbert de Montreuil, author of the *Roman de la Violette.* His lengthy continuation of 17,000 verses most consistently explores the religious theme (see the study by Stanton 1939). He has the hermit explain to Perceval that "a knight's sword has two edges," which stand for Holy Church and earthly justice. Eventually Gerbert has Perceval mend the notch in his sword, and the Fisher King bequeaths him "everything I have."

Writing for Johanna, countess of Flanders (d. 1244) and great-niece of Philip of Flanders, for whom Chrétien's own poem was initially begun, Manessier appends a different conclusion in another 10,000 verses. He introduces a tale of vengeance whereby Perceval must slay Partinal, the knight who killed the Fisher King's brother, in order to cure the Fisher King. After accomplishing this feat, Perceval learns the secrets of the Grail, succeeds the Grail king, and rules peaceably for seven years. But he then bequeaths his lands to the husband of the daughter of the Fisher King and retires from the material world to a hermitage, where he becomes first a cleric, then an acolyte, subdeacon, and deacon, and finally a priest.

Particularly during the first third of the thirteenth century and roughly contemporary with the continuations of Gerbert and Manessier, prose writers were similarly preoccupied with the Grail's secrets and, inspired by Chrétien's story, wrote lengthy versions of the Perceval legend, such as the so-called Vulgate cycle (Bruce 1928). For them, even more than for the continuators, the Grail became a sacred relic symbolic of Christ's suffering and death and Perceval a chaste virgin hero, a thoroughly Christian knight.

My analysis in this chapter focuses on the only illuminated manuscript that fully develops the religious dimension of Chrétien's story and its continuations (Paris, Bibliothèque Nationale, MS fr. 12576).[5] Among the earliest and most complete copies of the text, the Paris manuscript is also one of just two that include, along with the other three continuations that appear in most of the manuscripts, Gerbert's Continuation, which offers the most distinctly religious perspective.[6] The Paris manuscript also includes two didactic religious poems by a monk from the Abbey of Saint-Fuscien, called the Rencluse of Molliens, the *Roman de Carité* and the *Miserere,* as well as an otherwise unknown and anonymous poem on the death of a local count and some intriguing contemporary notes.[7] In all, this manuscript has thirty miniatures or historiated initials, twenty-eight for *Le Conte del Graal* and its continuations and two for the poems by the Rencluse of Molliens. Although the original owner is not known, the copy can nevertheless be relatively securely localized in Picardy based on dialect and provenance, and it must date from the latter half of the thirteenth century, perhaps about 1275.

I believe the distinctive features of text and illustration in the Paris manuscript offer a unique interpretation of *Le Conte del Graal* and its continuations, an interpretation that responds to regional sociohistorical concerns. The manuscript presents a glimpse of the interrelated feudal and clerical systems in provincial France at a time when both were in crisis, and it argues not so much for the sacred qualities of the Grail relics as for the social viability of the clerical life. At the same time, the organization of its text and illustrations, as well as some of their unusual features, displays evidence of both oral performance and silent reading that situates the manuscript on the threshold between oral and written cultures.

THE FRONTISPIECE TO *LE CONTE DEL GRAAL* IN THE PARIS MANUSCRIPT SETS THE STAGE FOR THE RELIGIOUS THEME OF THE MANUSCRIPT AS I HAVE OUTLINED IT (FRONTISPIECE AND FIG. 1).[8] ON two registers, it depicts three events. In the upper register, spread over two frames, five knights on horseback approach Perceval, who wears a blue tunic over a pink shirt and has red boots, while his three javelins stand upright in the ground next to him (verses 100, 121, 202–3). Before a small turreted dwelling, his mother's house in the forest, Perceval kneels in front of the knights, his hands clasped in prayer (105). Two swaying trees adorn the otherwise sparse landscape (105–6). Many of the rich details of the miniature closely correspond with verses in the text. More interesting, however, is the illustrator's emphasis on a very specific moment, one that shows Perceval's essential lack of religious education, even if he is devout. Perceval, the well-meaning but thoroughly naive youth, mistakes these knights for angels, whom he therefore worships: "Sir God, be merciful to me, for here are angels that I see . . . the fairest beings that exist. . . . My mother said herself the Lord, above all else, should be adored: so I will pray to him foremost and then to all the angel host. That very moment, with one bound, he flung himself upon the ground. And recited the Creed through, and every prayer he knew" (137–38, 144, 151–58).[9] As the miniature illustrates, it is in part Perceval's very lack of proper religious training that not only leads to his absurdly mistaking the knights for angels but attracts him to knighthood in the first place.

That this miniature sets out to articulate the spiritual and earthly callings—both underdeveloped in the character of the young Perceval as he first appears to the viewer—is further apparent when it is compared with other frontispieces. Closely related is a more elaborate frontispiece is another manuscript in Paris (Bibliothèque Nationale, MS fr. 12577), which also emphasizes Perceval's dual calling. Like our miniature, it includes the scene of Perceval praying before the five knights, which now shares the space on a single register with an image of Perceval's mother falling dead before her door, which occurs at a somewhat later moment in the story (fig. 96). The repetition of Perceval's mother in the lower register gives her added emphasis and reminds us that this is the episode to which Chrétien and the continuators return when they emphasize Perceval's unworthiness for the Grail. Other manuscripts of *Le Conte del Graal,* such as the version in Mons, begin pictorially in different, unrelated ways (fig. 42).

In the lower register of our manuscript Perceval achieves his vocation as a knight. On the left the Welsh youth, readily recognizable because he wears the same costume and carries his three javelins, rides to the court of Arthur, who is seated at the head of the table while another figure standing behind him addresses Perceval. This is probably Yvonet, interrupted while he is carving meat, of whom Perceval bluntly demands, "Show me the king" (919). On the right Perceval fights the Red Knight, putting his javelin through the knight's eye before he strips him of his armor. By virtue of possessing the material attributes of knighthood, Perceval has now become a knight and, pending his education by Gornemant—a scene that is not illustrated—is ready to embark on his secular career.

The abridged sequence of illuminations accompanying *Le Conte del Graal* develops the theme introduced in the frontispiece. It begins (one miniature, the introductory historiated initial, is irretrievably defaced) with a miniature of Perceval's defeat of Clamadeu (2785), the wicked knight who has besieged the castle of Beaurepaire where the fair Blancheflor, Perceval's ladylove, is mistress (fig. 2). "Clamadeu was forced at last to beg for mercy" (2682–83) from the "new-created knight." The second miniature illustrates Perceval lost in thought as he contemplates three drops of blood in the snow, which remind him of his lover's face, while Gawain, explaining that Arthur is eager for news of him, attempts to shake him out of his reverie (fig. 3). Appearing next to the verse that describes Perceval as having "lost his memory . . . so he remembered God no more" (6217–19), the third miniature depicts him before the hermit at the door of the hermitage, where he confesses that "for five years, I have not known where I was, and did not believe in God or love God" (6364–65; fig. 4). There Perceval laments his failure to learn the secrets of the Grail. The hermit explains that Perceval must now do penance for the sin he committed when he caused the death of his mother. He recommends that Perceval worship at every chapel along the way: "You must stay until he's [the priest] ceased to chant and pray" (6453–55). A single historiated initial of Gawain on horseback, illustrating his subsequent adventures, marks the point in the story where "the book relates no more of Perceval" (6515) (fig. 5).

Taken together, the miniatures in this truncated cycle provide a neat introduction to the Paris manuscript by elaborating on the unresolved conflict between the earthly and religious dimensions of Perceval's mission. Significantly, as though for added emphasis, the two central miniatures depart from the customary format of historiated initials used throughout the first part of this manuscript, and they are accompanied by burnished gold ground initials, *G* and *P* (perhaps for Gawain and Perceval, whose behavior will be contrasted throughout the manuscript). The first of these two miniatures, by referring to Perceval's love for Blancheflor, illustrates the reason he did not ask about the Grail. The second, depicting his encounter with the hermit, gives center stage to the crucial encounter that reveals Perceval's sin, the topic the continuations will attempt to resolve. What is at issue here is Perceval's religious training, which he has not yet accomplished even though he has demonstrated his prowess as a knight.

The First Continuation focuses almost entirely on the earthly dimensions of knighthood, from which Perceval will eventually turn away. A group of miniatures illustrates a romantic interlude, the story of Ysave and Carados (3083–8734; figs. 6–8). King Arthur marries his niece Ysave to King Caradeus of Nantes, but she is in love with a knight named Eliavret, who is also a sorcerer. So as to spend each night with Ysave, her lover replaces her with an animal—a dog, a sow, and a horse, which Caradeus unwittingly beds—while the lover takes her for himself. They thus conceive a child, whom they name Carados; but one day the boy learns that Eliavret, not Caradeus, is his father. Distraught, he tells Caradeus of his mother's infidelity, and so Caradeus imprisons his unfaithful wife in a tower, which does nothing to prevent Eliavret from visiting her. As punishment for the disgrace brought upon the family, Eliavret is made to sleep with a dog, a sow, and a horse, from which he sires three animals. Then Ysave demands revenge against her son, and Eliavret causes a serpent to attach itself to Carados's arm, where it will stay for two and a half years, after which Carados will die. Finally, through a clever ruse in which Carados and Guiner, the lady he eventually marries, are placed respectively in vats of vinegar and of milk, the serpent leaps out of the vat of vinegar into the vat of milk, and Carados is cured. In consecutive historiated initials, the manuscript illustrates three scenes from the story: the marriage of Ysave and Caradeus (fig. 6), Eliavret's visit to Ysave in the tower (fig. 7), and Carados and the serpent (fig. 8). With its carnal intrigue and occult events, this subplot, as illustrated in the pictures, stands in stark contrast to the chaste and spiritual affair between Perceval and Blancheflor.

Like those in the First Continuation, miniatures in the Second Continuation focus primarily on characters other than Perceval, such as Bagomedes and Gawain, whose lives in the secular world are in a sense antitypes for that of Perceval. The Second Continuation concludes, however, not with Perceval's visit to the Fisher King, which ends all but one other manuscript, but with a miniature of the episode of the Tree Child, which provides an effective transition to the increasing focus on the spiritual in the rest of the manuscript (fig. 9). While seeking the Grail castle, Perceval comes across a child in a tree, "sitting so high that he could not have been reached even with a lance" (33767–69).[10] Perceval asks directions from the child, who "would tell him nothing," and then, before Perceval's eyes, the child climbs from branch to branch to the top of the tree and disappears. The miniature illustrates the conversation between Perceval and the Tree Child.

Later, at the Grail castle, the Fisher King explains this episode to Perceval (34781–840). The child in the tree was actually a divine being who so hated Perceval for his many sins that he climbed toward heaven to teach Perceval a lesson. Perceval, who has been "enmeshed in folly for a long time," should contemplate God so that "He may be sure to receive your soul and place it in His Paradise" (34824–27). Coming just before the continuation of Gerbert de Montreuil, which opens with Perceval brashly knocking in vain at the gate of paradise, so that he breaks his sword in two and thus lengthens by seven and a half years the period of required penance (135 ff.), this miniature calls attention to the remaining imperfections in Perceval's behavior while it simultaneously alludes, when read with the subsequent text, to the idea that Perceval has been chosen for a divinely orchestrated destiny for which he will eventually qualify through continuing instruction.

To show Perceval's increasing comprehension of the spiritual path, Perceval and Gawain are overtly contrasted in Gerbert de Montreuil's Continuation, which opens with a miniature that depicts the two mounted knights facing each other (fig. 10). This miniature illustrates the moment in the narrative when, coming to a chapel at a crossroads, Gawain declares that he will go to Montesclaire, where there is a girl he desires, while Perceval chooses the other road, which leads to the Grail. Through the metaphor of the crossroads, the miniature symbolically sets up the divergent behavior of the two knights, which becomes one of the themes of the illustrations in this continuation. Before arriving at the Grail castle, Perceval returns to the castle of Beaurepaire, where he finally marries Blancheflor, agreeing to live with her chastely. The marriage, however, is never illustrated. In its place appears a miniature where Perceval bids farewell to Blancheflor, which effectively illustrates his renunciation of her instead of their reunion (fig. 11). The next miniature shows Perceval before a hermit (fig. 12). This picture refers to the episode where Perceval, after leaving Blancheflor, comes across a chapel in which a man lies on a bed covered with a silken cloth while a priest performs the mass, offering the host to the wounded man, whose crown he lays on the altar. The hermit explains to Perceval that the man is King Mordrain. Joseph of Arimathea himself had shown him the Grail in an attempt to cure him, but an angel with a fiery sword descended to declare that only a true knight who is free of sin and loved by Jesus Christ will be able to do so. The promise is clear: Perceval can become the true knight free of sin capable of curing not only King Mordrain but the Fisher King.

1: Frontispiece, *Le Conte del Graal*
Paris, Bibliothèque Nationale, MS fr. 12576, fol. 1

2: Perceval defeats Clamadeu, *Le Conte del Graal*
Paris, Bibliothèque Nationale, MS fr. 12576, fol. 11v

3: Perceval contemplates the three drops of blood, *Le Conte del Graal*
Paris, Bibliothèque Nationale, MS fr. 12576, fol. 19

4: Perceval at the door of the hermitage, *Le Conte del Graal*
Paris, Bibliothèque Nationale, MS fr. 12576, fol. 25

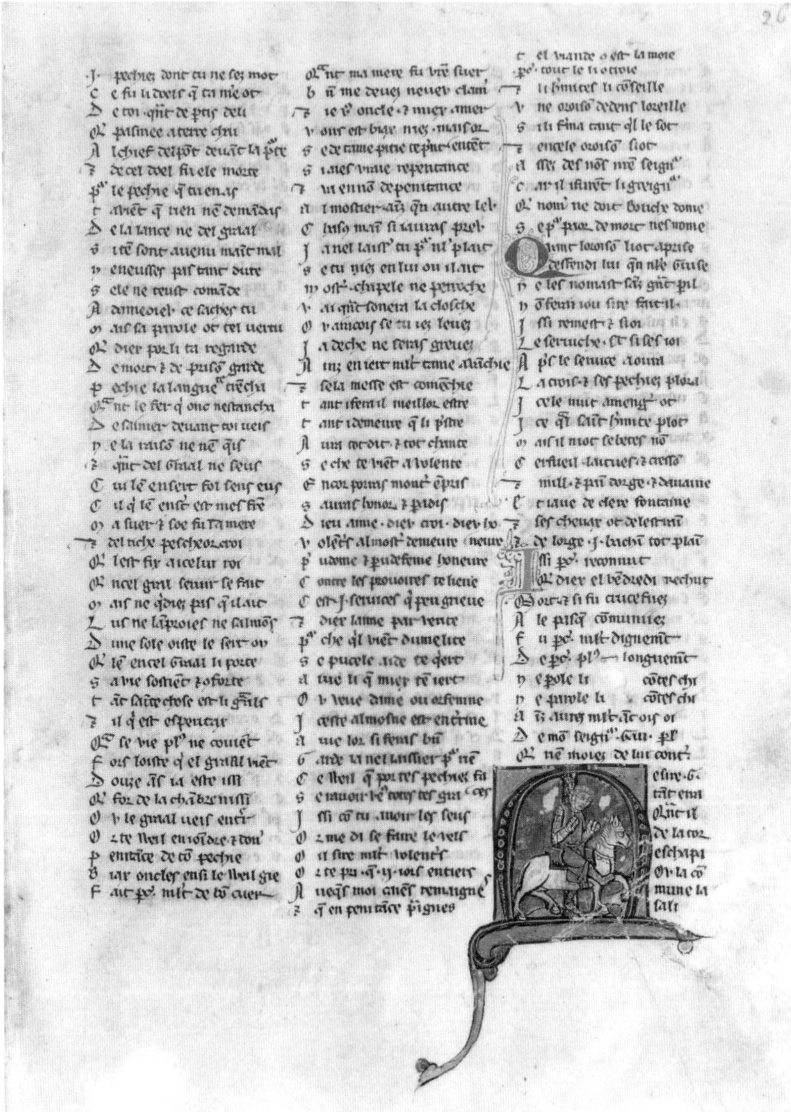

5: Gawain on horseback, *Le Conte del Graal*
Paris, Bibliothèque Nationale, MS fr. 12576, fol. 26

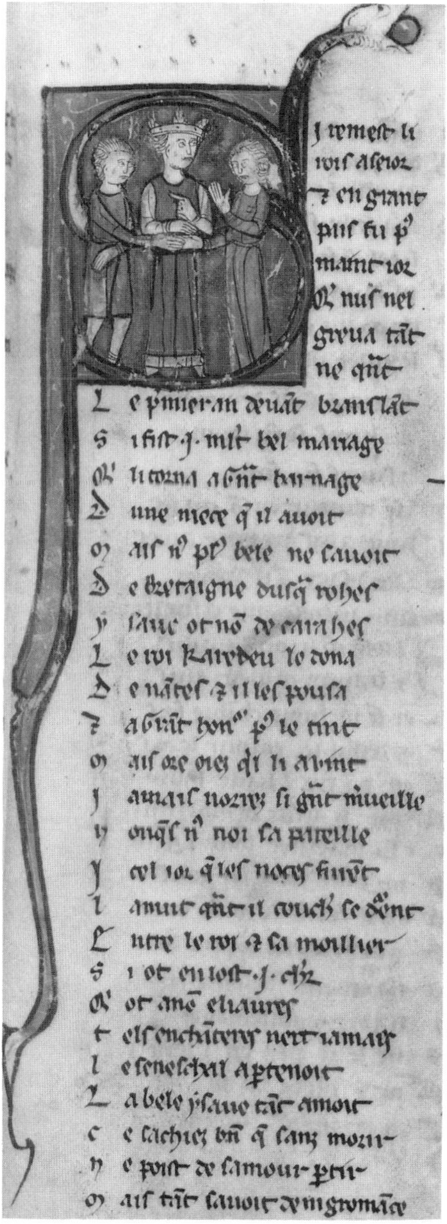

6: Marriage of Ysave and Caradeus, First Continuation
Paris, Bibliothèque Nationale, MS fr. 12576, fol. 49

7: Eliavret's visit to Ysave in the tower, First Continuation
Paris, Bibliothèque Nationale, MS fr. 12576, fol. 60

8: Carados and the serpent, First Continuation
Paris, Bibliothèque Nationale, MS fr. 12576, fol. 68

9: Perceval and the Tree Child, Second Continuation
Paris, Bibliothèque Nationale, MS fr. 12576, fol. 148

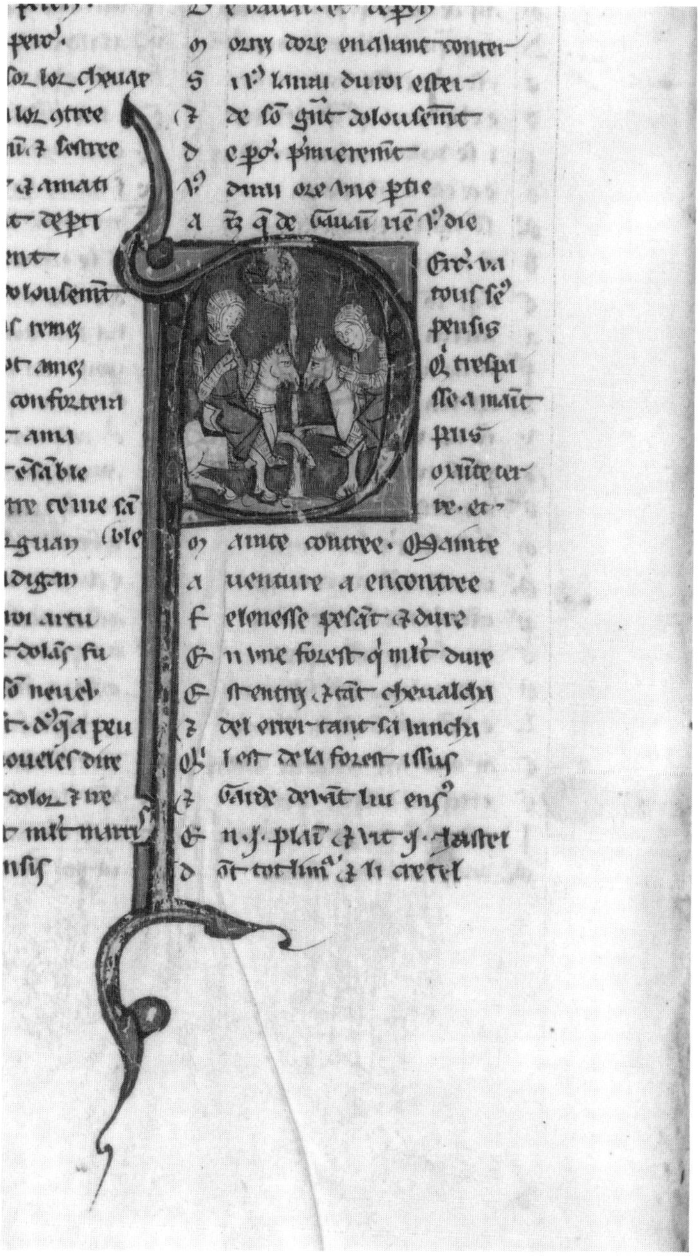

10: Perceval and Gawain, Gerbert de Montreuil's Continuation
Paris, Bibliothèque Nationale, MS fr. 12576, fol. 171v

11: Perceval bids farewell to Blancheflor, Gerbert de Montreuil's Continuation
Paris, Bibliothèque Nationale, MS fr. 12576, fol. 180

12: Perceval before a hermit, Gerbert de Montreuil's Continuation
Paris, Bibliothèque Nationale, MS fr. 12576, fol. 193

13: Gawain in bed in a pavilion, Gerbert de Montreuil's Continuation
Paris, Bibliothèque Nationale, MS fr. 12576, fol. 201v

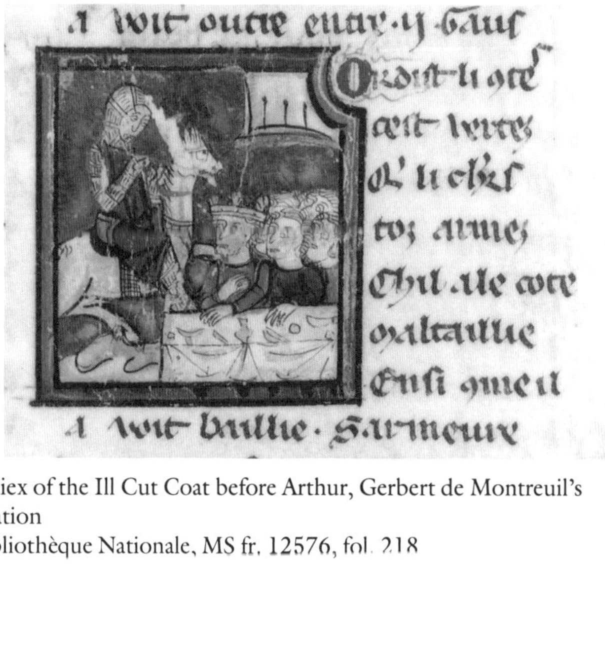

14: Madiex of the Ill Cut Coat before Arthur, Gerbert de Montreuil's Continuation
Paris, Bibliothèque Nationale, MS fr. 12576, fol. 218

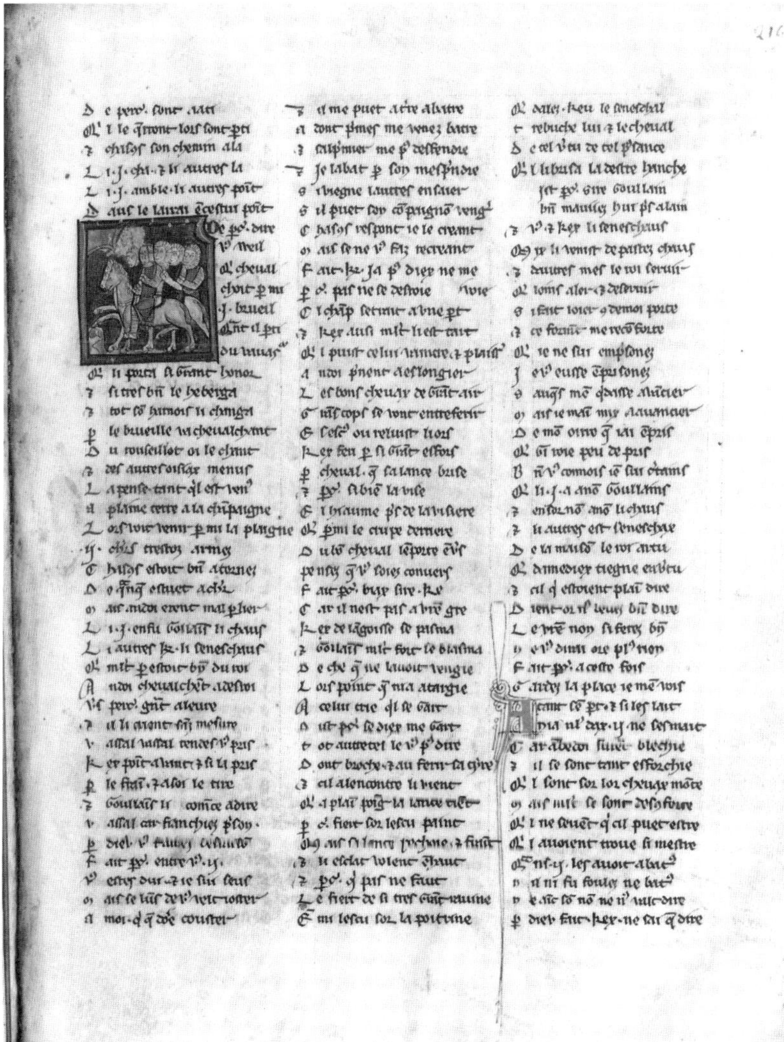

15: Knights in search of Perceval, Gerbert de Montreuil's Continuation
Paris, Bibliothèque Nationale, MS fr. 12576, fol. 219

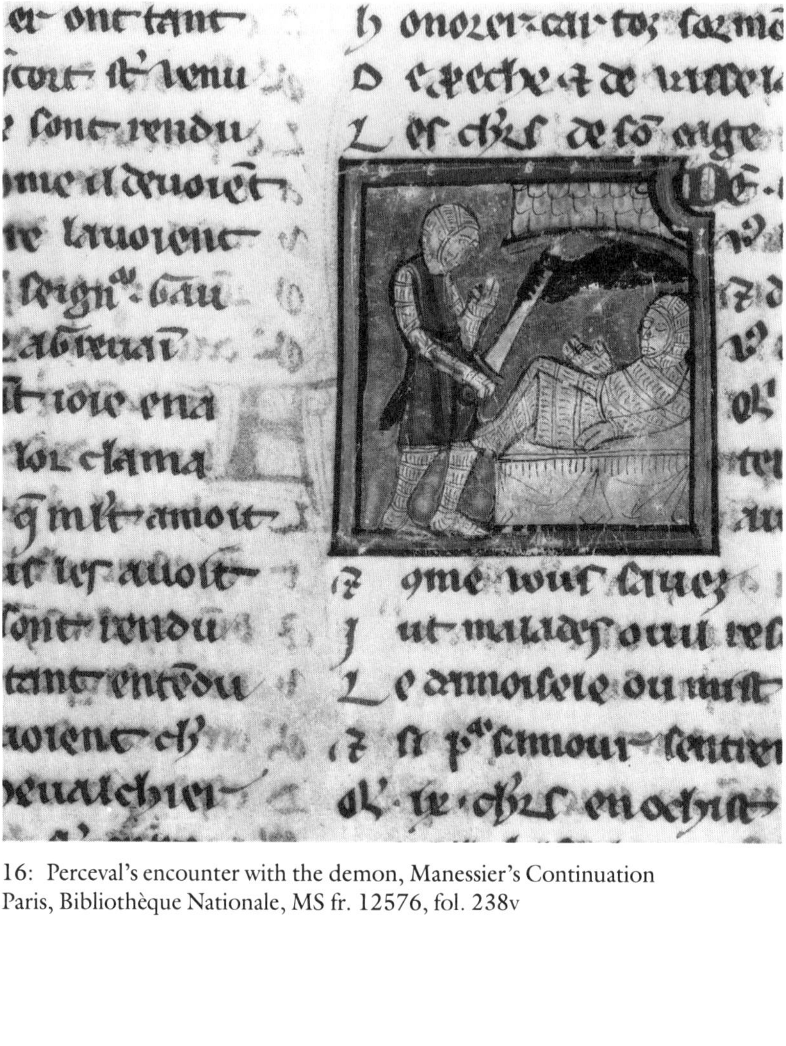

16: Perceval's encounter with the demon, Manessier's Continuation
Paris, Bibliothèque Nationale, MS fr. 12576, fol. 238v

17: Perceval and the Grail, Manessier's Continuation
Paris, Bibliothèque Nationale, MS fr. 12576, fol. 261

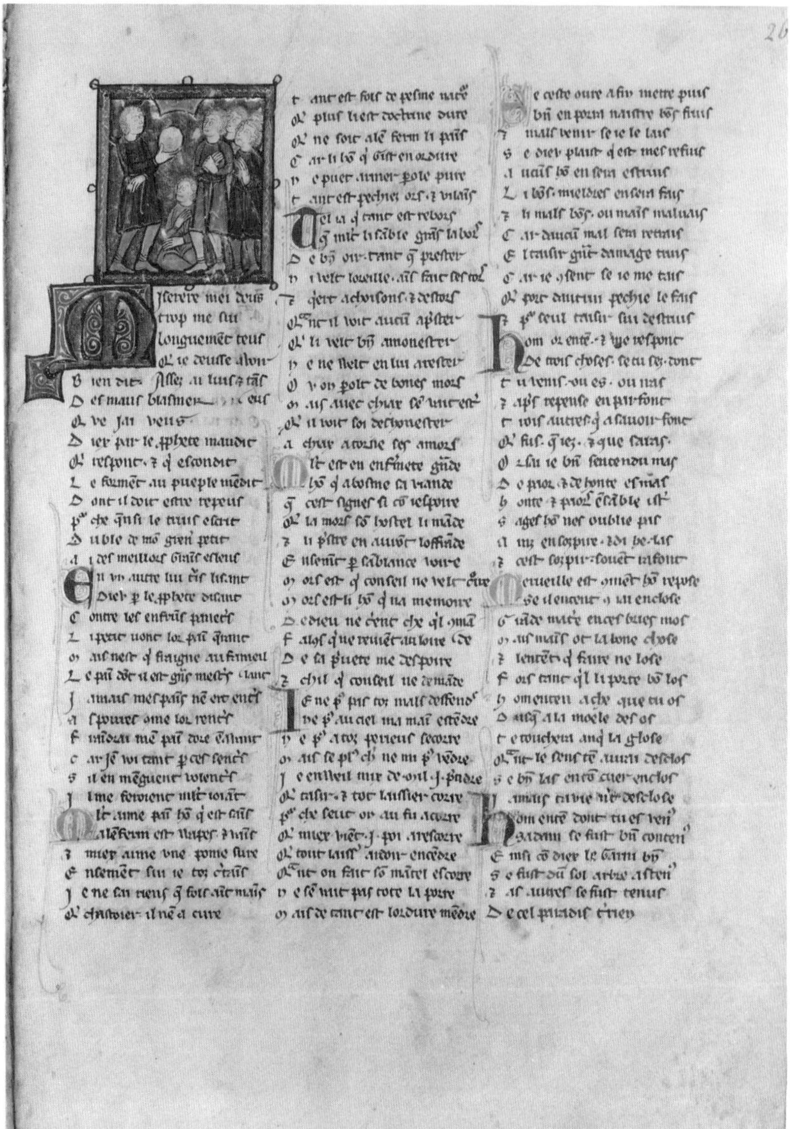

18: Distribution of bread to the poor, Rencluse of Molliens, *Miserere*
Paris, Bibliothèque Nationale, MS fr. 12576, fol. 263

19: Last Judgment, Rencluse of Molliens, *Roman de Carité*
Paris, Bibliothèque Nationale, MS fr. 12576, fol. 275v

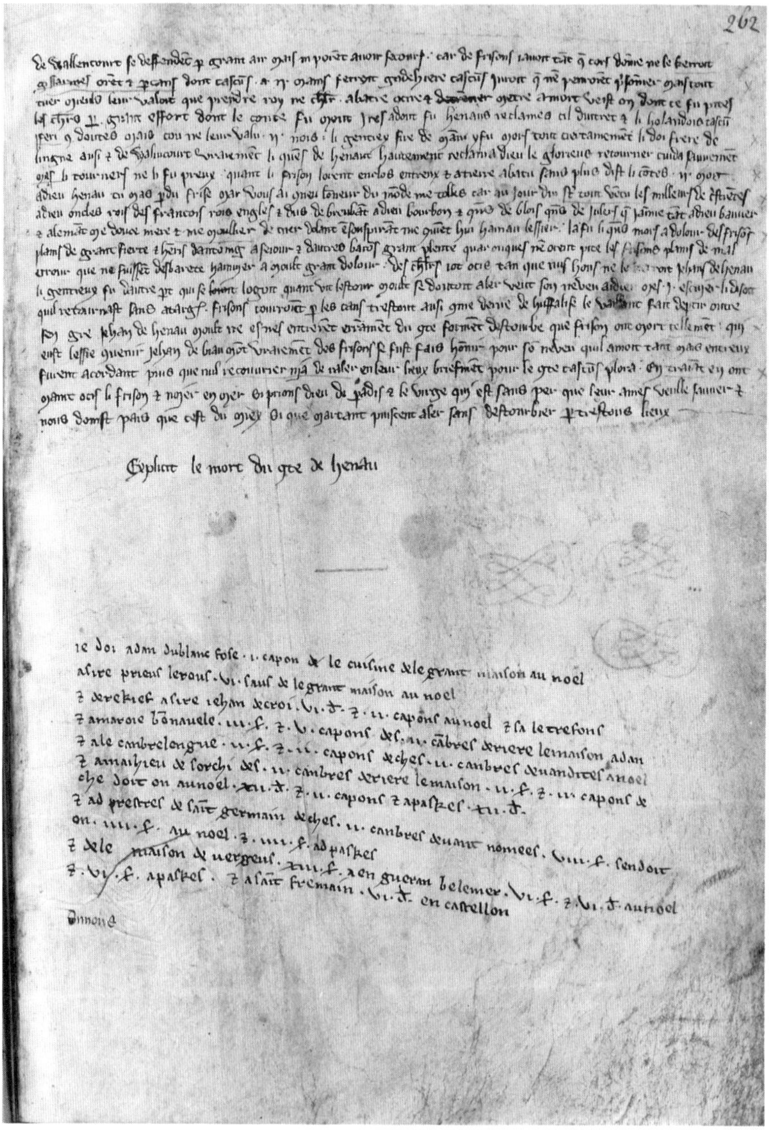

20: Record of obligations
Paris, Bibliothèque Nationale, MS fr. 12576, fol. 262

By turning away from Perceval at this point and focusing instead on action in the material world, the pictures delay the fulfillment of that promise. The next miniatures show Gawain, first, riding to a pavilion where he finds the girl he desires and, second, in bed with the girl, who tries to kill him with a knife (fig. 13). Gawain wrestles the knife away from her and rapes her. His behavior contrasts markedly with that of Perceval, who remains chaste, renouncing Blancheflor even in marriage. Next the miniature of Madiex of the Ill Cut Coat, who surrenders at the court of Arthur after combat with Perceval, reminds us that Perceval is still unable to resist a challenge to fight (fig. 14). Finally, a miniature in which the knights of Arthur's court, fearing that Perceval is lost, set out to find him concludes the continuation by putting off the visit to the Grail castle (fig. 15). In a sense this miniature deflects the quest for the Grail to a quest for Perceval.

Manessier's Continuation concludes the story with Perceval's ultimate rejection of the material world. One miniature illustrates Perceval's final deed, his encounter with the demon, whom he defeats before he sprinkles holy water throughout the chapel and prays to God, as he was instructed first in *Le Conte del Graal* and then in the continuations, particularly that of Gerbert (fig. 16).

Finally, in a large extratextual picture that serves almost as a visual epilogue, Perceval, dressed in clerical garb, kneels before a woman symbolizing the church, who holds the Grail, draped in cloth, which she receives from an angel, while another angel waves a censer above her (fig. 17). This image undoubtedly illustrates the passage at the end of the continuation that describes Perceval as a cleric, serving "God faithfully for fully ten years" in prayer and in worship before the Holy Grail, "which he saw and which served him night and day" (42584–89). Dressed in a different short garment, Perceval appears a second time on the far right, holding the burning lance as though he were walking out of the picture. This more puzzling image probably depicts Perceval as he "painlessly left this world and ended his life" when the "Holy Grail and the lance and the beautiful silver trencher went with him" (42617–20). The privileged status of this miniature, which is much larger than most of the others and comes after the explicit, where it is set off from the text on the blank parchment, contributes to its importance as offering a concluding statement (for a discussion of this image see also Stones 1991, 23–24).

Reread with the opening miniature, as well as with the intervening text and pictures, the last miniature assures the reader of Perceval's ultimate triumph as a Christian knight. In fact the frontispiece and the concluding miniature are mirror images of each other as they provide striking contrasts of the secular and spiritual domains between which Perceval forever vacillates. At the beginning of the manuscript, Perceval kneels in prayer in front of the knights before he impetuously rushes off to the earthly court of the king, whereas at the end of the continuations he kneels in prayer in front of the Grail before he confidently departs for the heavenly court of paradise. In the intervening miniatures, by dutifully following the hermit's wise advice, by listening attentively to the instructions of the Tree Child, by resolutely leading a penitent life that is different from that of Gawain or Caradeus and even entails renouncing Blancheflor, and finally by triumphantly conquering the demon in the chapel, he has rightly earned his final reward.

Directly following the continuations in the Paris manuscript, two illustrated texts by the thirteenth-century Picard moralist the Rencluse of Molliens underscore the merit of Perceval's final choice to seek a spiritual existence. In a general sense, the Rencluse deplores the uncharitable, sinful ways of aristocratic society (see Van Hamel, ed. [1885]; Langlois 1925, 113–52). However, unique among manuscripts of the Perceval cycle, including also those that are not illustrated, the texts by the Rencluse with their pictures function in more specific ways to gloss the Perceval story.

In the first work, the *Miserere,* the text recounts how, coming from paradise, man has descended into a valley of tears. Whether he opts for heaven or hell, his destiny depends entirely on him. Like Perceval, each individual is exhorted to choose between service to God and to the world, although the Rencluse hastens to add that both clerics and knights can accomplish good works if they conscientiously perform the duties of their vocations. He appends an exhortation to penitence, with a list of sinners who have been pardoned and a prayer to the Virgin. The miniature that prefaces the *Miserere* depicts a group of people distributing bread to the poor (fig. 18). It provides a literal illustration of the introduction to the poem, in which a merchant offers bread to the poor, who benefit from its restorative properties, and bread then recurs as a metaphor for the productive life throughout the text of the poem. This miniature can also be understood as an allusion to Perceval's penitence, however, for it symbolically illustrates Christian charity, the ultimate act of penance.

The second text by the Rencluse, the *Roman de Carité,* is introduced by a miniature of the Last Judgment (fig. 19). The text despairs over the number of evil individuals in the world compared with good ones. After the author visits in turn all the countries, where he laments the absence of charity, he addresses the seigneurs of France and instructs them not to lose sight of the symbolism of their sword, which is "justice, by which the clerics guard the church." Then he addresses the priests in forty-seven verses, each beginning with an admonition. Finally, however, the Rencluse regrets that he finds charity nowhere except in the "city on the mountain" (paradise), where it is assured a place. Even more than as an illustration to the *Roman de Carité,* we can read the accompanying miniature as a final gloss on the Perceval story: having fully understood the value of the spiritual life and having served his penance, Perceval can rest assured that the gate of paradise will open to him. The miniature visually fulfills the end of Manessier's Continuation, which describes Perceval as "in the joy of Paradise at His right hand where the good long to be" (42612–14).

The choice of the poems by the Rencluse for the Paris volume is exceptional. These poems are typically compiled with other didactic texts, such as the *Miracles de la Vierge,* the *Testament de Jehan de Meung,* and the *Voie d'enfer et de paradis;* in only one other instance among the more than thirty-five manuscripts is either one compiled with a romance.[11] No less exceptional are the miniatures illustrating the poems. Although there is some variation in the nature of the illustrations, the poems are usually illustrated differently than they appear here—the *Miserere* with a sort of author portrait of an aged recluse writing in his cell or invoking God, and the *Roman de Carité* with an image of charity, the distribution of bread to the poor, not unlike the miniature for the *Miserere* in the Paris manuscript.[12] No other manuscript includes an image of the Last Judgment. In the Paris manuscript the very inclusion of these texts, coupled with the unique features of their illustrations, which apparently were specially tailored to go with the Perceval romance, thus helps to provide not only a smooth continuation but an expressive conclusion to the Perceval story, which is read as a moral allegory on the spiritual life.

THE UNIQUE PROGRAM OF TEXT AND ILLUSTRATION IN THE PARIS MANUSCRIPT IN RELATION TO OTHER ILLUMINATED MANUSCRIPTS OF THE PERCEVAL STORY REFLECTS, IN A GENERAL SENSE, THE strong presence of the church in Picardy. Fossier has noted that although Picardy was characterized by a relative lack of religious fanaticism (it produced neither heretics nor saints), the region was nonetheless populated with an unusually large number of monasteries and convents, many of considerable importance (see especially the discussion in Fossier 1988,

154–59). Unlike areas in central or southern France, where the Cistercians and the minor orders successfully established themselves, Picardy was known as the "land of canons" because of the proliferation there of episcopal sees (Amiens, Arras, Beauvais, Cambrai, Laon, Noyon, Senlis, and Soissons) and collegiate churches, both of which supported communities of canons or clerics. This development was apparently a response to a special political situation: local nobles founded collegiate churches partly to assert their own identities and to curb the growing power of the strong bishoprics. Whatever the cause, however, organized religion in Picardy was consequently characterized largely by the rule of the common life, subscribed to by the canons, and by an interest in letters and education in the numerous cathedral and collegiate schools, run by the clerics. Understood against this background, it can hardly be an accident that the Perceval in the Paris manuscript is modeled on his Picard contemporaries when he ends his days as a cleric, then a priest, having received "fine instruction in letters."

In attempting to understand the ways the Paris version of the Perceval story was read, we may well wonder whether, at the time the manuscript was composed, organized religion in Picardy was floundering or thriving. Or to put it another way, Did Perceval choose to enter an economically sound social system or a threatened one? This question is easily answered, for from at least the eleventh century through the thirteenth, the Picard church was exceptionally wealthy. Its wealth is reflected not only in the extensive rebuilding programs—many, such as those at Beauvais, Amiens, Noyon, Senlis, and Soissons, resumed in the thirteenth century—but in the relationship of the religious foundations to the landed economy (Fossier 1988, esp. 157). As the charters repeatedly show, Picard monasteries, cooperating with urban and rural establishments, busily set up mills, opened ateliers, and exploited the woods and streams (Fossier 1988, 509, 513, 523, 536). About 1250 the monks of Mont-Saint-Quentin, a modest establishment, bought or recuperated two tithes, the output of seven parish churches, two bakehouses, three forests, and one hundred hectares of land in three villages. About the same time the nuns of the Paraclete possessed seven thousand hectares of land, of which a major portion was farmed (see Fossier 1988, 158, and 1983, 55–56, on the use of woods). The life Perceval opted for was thus economically comfortable.

Certain crises in the feudal system, however, helped to promote the increasing prosperity of the Picard church and may also be reflected in the

Paris manuscript. As the custom of primogeniture faltered and noble families began to divide their patrimony, consigning a portion of it to the younger sons (and daughters), those offspring who chose to enter the church brought with them part of the family wealth, either land or money.[13] The foundation of collegiate churches was also tied to the crisis of the nobility. Intent on perpetuating their lineage and distinguishing themselves from the peasants and the rising bourgeoisie, who were usually buried in parish churchyards, the upper nobility endowed collegiate foundations in part to serve as necropolises where family members could be interred, not unlike the prestigious royal necropolis of Saint-Denis in Paris.[14] Less wealthy families gave gifts to other religious communities to secure the right to be buried there with the monks. The ancient nobility's desire to distinguish itself and preserve its differences in the face of the newer nobility, not to mention the townspeople, is evident in these practices, from which the church clearly benefited.

Whereas seigneurial domains of noble families faced economic hardship in the thirteenth century at the same time that the church throve difficulties did exist in the church, but they took a different form. In fact there is no evidence of lagging recruitment in monasteries and nunneries, nor is there much evidence of the selling off of lands, goods, and rights that characterizes seigneurial domains. Not a single Picard monastery shut down during the thirteenth century (Fossier 1988, 159). It is therefore unlikely that the Perceval story in our manuscript is meant to serve primarily as a recruitment tool for troubled religious foundations, although an additional son (or daughter) or two would always be welcome to augment conventual resources. But there is considerable evidence of internal troubles, particularly in the realm of misconduct, of which the Rencluse of Molliens, writing in Picardy at the beginning of the thirteenth century, is one outspoken witness. The clergyman who brazenly frequents taverns, the chaplain who solicits paid masses, and the canon who lives openly with his mistress are common enough stories in the thirteenth-century Picard fabliaux. It is these problems that the manuscript addresses. Young Perceval is made into an example of a knight from a noble family who sheds his ignorance as he learns to lead a proper religious life, which is the antithesis of that recounted in the fabliaux and criticized by the Rencluse. Indeed, our Perceval is as much a figure of the communities of canons in thirteenth-century Picardy as he is a knight from an aristocratic household.

CLERICAL CULTURE, TO WHICH PERCEVAL ASPIRES, WAS OF COURSE LITERATE LATIN CULTURE, WHEREAS KNIGHTLY CULTURE WAS FOR THE MOST PART ILLITERATE, ORAL, OR VERNACULAR. However blurred these distinctions remain—especially when applied to vernacular texts, since orality persists within literacy—for our purposes they can most usefully be taken to define two poles, which I will call performative and nonperformative cultures instead of literate and illiterate (Clanchy 1979; Ong 1982; Stock 1983). Performative culture, which is essentially based on orality, could include both those who read aloud to a group and those who could not themselves read but who listened. Nonperformative culture, like literate Latin culture, included those who read to themselves, whether silently or aloud, in Latin or the vernacular (Saenger 1982). In relation to these two cultures, written verse occupies a paradoxical status as a form that may recall the jongleur's performance even if not itself performed (Godzich and Kittay 1987, 15–16). What is fascinating in the Paris manuscript is how these two cultures appear to coexist in the text, the miniatures, and even the layout of the manuscript.

In fact, one way of rereading the text of the entire Perceval cycle (especially as it is presented in the Paris manuscript, where it includes Gerbert's Continuation) is to understand it as a story about Perceval's mastery of literate Latin culture, which goes hand in hand with his becoming a cleric. He progressively assimilates increasingly complex signifying practices and eventually written language itself, undergoing a transformation in several stages. In *Le Conte del Graal* Perceval emerges as an unlettered knight who learns the rudiments of military chivalry but has considerable difficulty with language because he cannot fix the identities of things with words. In Gerbert's Continuation, Perceval's spiritual development complements his mastery of arms, but his cognitive development remains inferior even though he can now recognize certain signs. Finally, at the conclusion of Manessier's Continuation Perceval, the cleric, has learned to read, and the whole Perceval story is preserved according to the testimony of the written word. We can follow this transformation more closely in the different units of the text.

In Chrétien's *Le Conte del Graal,* Perceval repeatedly demonstrates his cognitive inepititude. He mistakes the five knights for angels, the maiden's tent for the house of God, the three drops of blood in the snow for his ladylove's cheeks. And in our final encounter with Perceval, who is on his way to the hermit, he has completely lost his memory, "for he remembered

God no more." Some scholars have even understood Perceval's deficiency in Chrétien's story to be not so much his innocence about chivalry as his lack of memory, for of course in the crucial event he even forgets to pose the all-important questions about the Grail and the lance at the castle of the Fisher King (Gallais 1972, 144; Bozoky 1985).

One of the recurring motifs in Gerbert's Continuation, where Perceval's spiritual development is most at issue, is the importance of the written word, although Perceval's competence in this area is left ambiguous. After Perceval has knocked with his sword on the gates of paradise at the beginning of the continuation, a "worthy man" gives him a letter (*brief*) said to have the power to help defeat any man (284–94). We learn that although the letter looked like it could easily be read, it could not, even in a year. Perceval wears the small, neat round letter around his neck like an amulet, and in a subsequent episode he employs it like a magic talisman to revive two knights, Sagremor and Engrevain (1007–12). In a sense the letter and the use Perceval puts it to acknowledge or even create his illiteracy, which affects our understanding of subsequent episodes where inscription also figures prominently.

After marrying Blancheflor, when Perceval leaves Beaurepaire to seek the Grail castle he comes to a fork in the road where there is fastened a sheet of parchment that distinguishes between the broad, safe road, where the knight is instructed to turn, and the "adventurous road" (8248 ff.). Perceval chooses the latter, but we cannot be sure whether he does so because of his bravery or because he has not read the sign well. In one of the crucial events of this continuation, the episode with the red cross shield, the relation between Perceval's bravery and his cognition is again left vague. Carried by a girl, this shield has a holy relic embedded in it, but it bears an inscription "for the benefit of all who saw the shield and were able to read," warning that anyone but the bravest man will be destroyed if he removes the shield (8467–8517). "Without delay" (before reading the inscription?) Perceval rushes to take the shield from the lady, thus proving that he is the knight who can find the Grail and the lance. In yet another episode, when Perceval and two knights open a tomb, a letter held by the dead knight interred within (the Red Knight) identifies Perceval as his killer, and the others—the relatives—read the letter and fall upon him (12022 ff.). Finally, toward the end of the continuation, just as Perceval is about to find the Grail castle, he approaches another crossroads, where the paths split into three, and a cross in the middle with a wooden hand points "the way he should go." Perceval sees the hand and has "great faith in [it]"

(16910–17). In Gerbert's Continuation, Perceval has gradually acquired the ability to comprehend some signifying systems, such as the hand on the sign, but he still cannot read words.

Perceval's formation is complete only at the end of Manessier's Continuation when, after he finds the Grail and the lance, he receives instruction in letters and becomes a cleric. In this respect a reading of the text of the Paris manuscript is crucial, for it differs from others such as the Mons manuscript, which seems to privilege oral communication. The Paris manuscript ends with a topos about the book (a passage absent from the Mons manuscript). After Manessier asserts that he followed the written authority found in a book, he concludes, "All those who travel the road [*par le chemin*] can still see the story there, sealed in parchment [*parchemin*]." In short, once Perceval has learned to read, the entire Perceval cycle is recast from a *conte,* or tale, that we hear to a *livre,* or book, that we see. The weighty authority of the *livre* implies reliance on a written Latin source, quite different from a *conte,* the word most frequently used by Chrétien and his continuators to refer to the orally transmitted stories of romance. When Chrétien does use the word *livre,* as in *Erec et Enide,* he means Macrobius, a learned Latin source, as opposed to a *conte* (6680).[15] By claiming the testimony of a *livre,* Manessier also echoes Gerbert's insistence on written testimony as commemorative record; for example, when Gerbert informs us that Perceval is the knight who accomplishes the adventures no one else can perform, "as we find in written testimony" (7004–9). Given this reading of the Perceval story, it is striking that among all the versions, the Paris manuscript is the only copy that includes another variant, the word *clerc* in the passage cited at the beginning of the chapter.[16] In the end, in the Paris manuscript—where Perceval is presented in the pictures and the text as an untutored knight who becomes a model cleric—language achieves a social instrumentality, and the book acquires a privileged status as a repository of memory.

Features of the illustrations in the Paris manuscript, which includes both historiated initials and independent miniatures, suggest that the audience, like Perceval, spanned two cultures—one where books were read aloud to groups and one where they were mostly read privately in silence. Many of the historiated initials include drastically condensed narratives, in which a knight on horseback (sometimes two) dominates, giving visual form to Perceval's name, *par cheval:* Gawain riding toward the wounded knight, Gawain riding in worried thought, Gawain approaching a hermitage, Perceval before the Tree Child, Perceval and Gawain at the crossroads, Bagomedes before a vavasor, and so forth. Although each of these pictures refers to a precise moment in the narrative, they also function as nonnarrative markers, as visual cues that at a glance guide the reader or listener through the story. Embedded in the first letter of each word, these historiated initials become mimetically fused with the opening words, which they often illustrate: three times an initial *M* of Gawain on horseback introduces Messire Gawain, an initial *P* of Perceval on horseback stands for Perceval, an initial *B* of Bagomedes on horseback stands for Bagomedes, and so forth. In still other instances the initial, representing a key character or episode, introduces a phrase that in a sense personifies or animates the story itself: *L* for "Le contes dist," *O* for "Or dist li contes," *L* for "Lestoire dist." In short these images, even if read silently, readily recall performance.

However, the ubiquitous historiated initial of the knight on horseback also gives visual form to nonperformative reading in the interesting way it relates to the language of Manessier's conclusion, discussed above. The language in which this topos is couched, with the play on the words ***par chemin*** and ***parchemin***, refers at once to the visual image of the mounted knight, in some ways a figure that belongs to the oral world of mimetic learning, and to the physical object of the book, whose materiality is seen, held, and touched as in the literate world of contemplative reading. Read in this way, the mounted knight becomes a metaphor for the reader whose travel (***par le chemin***) is equated with the act of reading on the surface of the page (***parchemin***), a metaphor that belongs with literacy but emerges out of orality.

There is a self-consciousness about the act of reading evident in the Paris manuscript itself that lends support to my argument about this manuscript's position, at a crossroads in communication. An examination of its writing and decoration reveals an uneasiness about the form of the historiated initial, for about three-quarters of the way through it is abandoned and replaced by small rectangular miniatures that occupy the same space within a column of text. This switch in the format of the pictures does not seem to have been planned from the start, because the smaller, rectangular miniatures are irregularly framed to leave a notched space in the upper right corner for the first letter of the opening word. There the rubricator has awkwardly inserted the letter. The effect of this change in format is that henceforth in the manuscript the reader can assimilate the text in an uninterrupted fashion without referring to the pictures. Can it be accidental that this bifurcation of word and image occurs in Gerbert's Continuation, where there is such emphasis on inscription, and just after Perceval's visit to the hermit, the event that foreshadows his mastery of spiritual (clerical) learning?

Another striking feature of the Paris manuscript reinforces the separation of text and pictures and has an impact on reading. Needle holes that appear above each miniature reveal that all the pictures once had cloth flaps, probably silk, sewn over them. At the same time protecting the precious pigments and rich gold of the miniatures and enhancing the luxury of the manuscript, such flaps undeniably also altered the reading process. Although they do not interfere with the continuous reading of the text (quite the contrary, they reinforce it by blocking out the pictures), they do change the way the pictures are viewed, for to see them the reader must pause to raise the piece of material covering each miniature. Viewing has become practically a contemplative act. Coupled with the switch from historiated initial to rectangular miniature, this physical detail conveys a different attitude toward the book as a repository of two distinct forms of communication. The Paris manuscript has moved, ever so slightly, away from a model of reading that recalls the jongleur's performance, where the spoken word and what it refers to exist outside the book in collective memory, to a model of reading derived from literate Latin culture, where the word strings and painted tableaux provoke an individual contemplative exchange.

Studies of the reception of a particular manuscript nearly always raise the same difficult question: Who really read the manuscript? For this reason the Paris manuscript of Perceval is of special interest, because it evokes the seigneurial milieu in which it must have been written and used. On the first folio a note reads: "This book belongs to the Sire of Hargerie, who lends it to Madame de Contay, who promises to return it to him."[17] These individuals can be identified as François de Rasse (d. 1557), chevalier and seigneur of La Hargerie, and Françoise de Contay (married 1507), wife of Jean, seigneur of Humières.[18] Although these individuals are later owners of the manuscript, the note—as well as the proximity of the two domains, Bersee and Le Forest, in the Artois—suggests that romances were passed around the seigneury, undoubtedly accounting for their sometimes shabby condition. The note also calls attention to noblewomen as readers of romance (Krueger 1988, 1993).

Other notes included in the Paris copy help to broaden our view of its reception and use within the seigneury. Preserved between the continuations of *Le Conte del Graal* and the *Roman de Carité* is a carefully written record of obligations (fig. 20): "I owe Adam Du Blanc Fose one capon from the kitchen of the great house at Noel.[19] To Sire . . . Lerous six falcons from the great house at Noel. . . . To Sire Jean de Croi six livres and two capons. . . . And to Maroie Bonnavele three livres and five capons . . . behind the house of Adam. . . . And to the priests of Saint-Germain five falcons at Noel and four at Easter. . . . And from the house of Nergeul thirteen livres to Engueran Belemer . . . six livres at Noel and six livres at Easter and on the feast of Saint Firmin." Written perhaps by the lord himself, or more likely by the head of his household staff, this list conjures up a vivid picture of a feudal domain, the names of the people, the locations of their houses, including the proximity of the sires and the clerics, and their daily needs. It also suggests that the romance was a book left lying about the house, read and used by more than one reader, instead of hidden away on the shelves of a library. The mention of the feast of Saint Firmin, specially venerated in the north of France, where his relics were kept in the cathedral of Amiens, reinforces the regional character of the manuscript.[20]

The unique situation of the manuscript on the threshold between orality and literacy and the particular sociohistorical conditions of thirteenth-century northern France and Flanders, where a troubled feudal system attempted to come to terms with the hegemony of the Capetian government, come together in another feature of the Paris manuscript. Between the continuations of Perceval and the list of debts, one additional text was compiled in the fourteenth century, an otherwise unique copy of *La Mort du Conte de Henau* (The death of the count of Hainaut) (Potvin 1863). Although composed in verse, the poem is written out in long lines as if it were prose, so as to squeeze it into the limited space that remained on two blank folios. In the form of a popular chant, it recounts the death of Guillaume II, along with many of the seigneurs who fought and died with him, in 1345 at the battle of Friesland, a province the count was attempting to bring under control. Although we cannot know what led to the inclusion of this poem in the Paris manuscript—perhaps the copy was then owned by one of the seigneurs who perished in Friesland with Guillaume—its inclusion suggests that as late as the middle of the fourteenth century there was a fundamental compatibility between the popular chant concerning the regional impact of the death of a local count, whose fate was mingled with that of French Flanders, and the romance of Perceval, read as an allegory of provincial feudal society.

For the medieval audience that used the Paris compendium there was nothing anachronistic about the unusual anthology of literature, piety, and history that took the form of verse romances, didactic poems, and local chants. A study of the manuscript—copiously illustrated with expensive pictures yet scribbled on with everyday memoranda and clumsily modified to include a new poem, then collectively used by men and women in a feudal domain—lets us come surprisingly close to retrieving a complex and shifting experience of reading in the thirteenth century.

CHAPTER TWO

THE KNIGHT *Li Bacheler*

The whole court found the king's plan excellent and sound, and every baron, youth, and knight thought of the journey with delight.

Chrétien de Troyes, *Le Chevalier au lion*[1]

AT THE BEGINNING OF *LE CHEVALIER AU LION (YVAIN)*, THE KNIGHTS OF THE ROUND TABLE ARE GATHERED TO CELEBRATE THE FEAST OF PENTECOST AT KING ARTHUR'S COURT, AND AFTER DINner they amuse themselves by spinning tales of adventure. Calogrenant, a cousin of Yvain, tells how once upon a time, "seven years past," in the forest of Broceliande he visited a magical storm-producing fountain that was defended by a mighty knight who, outraged at the destruction Calogrenant wrought in his domain, handily vanquished him. After listening to Guinevere repeat Calogrenant's tale "word for word," Arthur himself earnestly vows to make a journey to the fountain within two weeks, and he generously invites his guests to join him. "With delight" the assembled knights (*li baron et li bacheler*) look forward to the promised journey.

These verses mark the end of what could be considered an extended prologue to Chrétien's romance. The substance of the romance then begins with the adventures of its hero Yvain, whose journey to the fountain is the first of a series of quests he undertakes as one of the youths or *bachelers* of Arthur's court. Challenged by his cousin's account of the fountain and eager to make a name for himself at court, Yvain secretly sets out alone to slay the defender of the fountain, Esclados the Red. He mortally wounds Esclados, then pursues him to his castle. Trapped in the castle, Yvain is befriended and concealed by a lady-in-waiting, Lunette, and thanks to her matchmaking he marries Esclados's grieving widow, Laudine, in a lavish ceremony. After the celebration of the marriage, Yvain requests permission from his new wife to go off to tournaments, and she acquiesces on condition that he return in a year. But Yvain forgets himself; a year passes, and Lunette comes to reclaim her lady's ring and inform him that he has lost his love. Grief-stricken, insane, and amnesiac, Yvain loses himself in the forest and recovers only thanks to the ministrations of a hermit and a lady. Upon recovery, he courageously saves a lion from an attacking serpent, assumes a new identity as "the knight with the lion," and sets off with the beast on a series of quests, rescuing ladies in need. He slays the giant Harpin of the Mountain, rescues falsely accused Lunette from being burned alive, and in the so-called Pesmes or "evil" adventure frees three hundred maidens destined for a lifetime of servitude weaving golden textiles. Returning to the court of Arthur he fights with Gawain, and his true identity is at last revealed. Only then, after another visit to the storm-producing fountain and through the further intervention of the matchmaker Lunette, is he reconciled with his wife, Laudine, and he lives happily ever after.

My rereading of *Le Chevalier au lion* understands Yvain as an example of a youth or *bacheler* (called *juvenis* in the Latin literature of the period), a term that in the twelfth and thirteenth centuries connoted a knight who had left the family home but had not yet become head of a household.[2] I will consider the two extant illuminated manuscripts of *Le Chevalier au lion,* which both date about 1300 and are localized in Picardy based on the dialect of their texts and the style of their miniatures (Paris, Bibliothèque Nationale, MS fr. 1433, and Princeton University Library, Garrett MS 125).[3] The Paris manuscript was perhaps made in Tournai, although the exact locality remains uncertain. The Princeton manuscript was probably made in the region of Amiens or Arras.

While featuring knights as youths or bachelors, the illustrated manuscripts of *Le Chevalier au lion* also respond to certain changes in feudal society in northern France in the second half of the thirteenth century, specifically with regard to the institution of marriage as it affected the youths. At the same time, features of their layout, as well as their miniatures, situate these manuscripts in an oral aristocratic culture. In fictional terms this oral milieu offers a culture of domesticity that may, in fact, coincide with the realities of the day, in which errant, illiterate youths return to court to recount their adventures and subsequently settle down with courteous, literate ladies who read aloud to them stories of romances.

The Paris manuscript includes eleven miniatures for *Le Chevalier au lion* and five for the *L'Atre périlleux* (The perilous cemetery), the anonymous Arthurian manuscript with which it is bound. In a sequence of well-placed miniatures that break the text at the corresponding junctures in the narrative, we can follow the main events of *Le Chevalier au lion:* Calogrenant's battle with Esclados at the fountain (fig. 26); in a three-part miniature, Yvain's battle with Esclados and his entry into the castle, Lunette's conspiracy with him, and the funeral of Esclados (fig. 28); in a two-part miniature, the tournaments after the marriage (fig. 30); in a four-part miniature, Lunette's return of the ring, Yvain's madness, his cure, and his rescue of the lion (fig. 31); in two four-part miniatures, the various quests, Harpin, Lunette, the Pesme adventure, and the revelation of Yvain's identity at Arthur's court (figs. 32 and 33). A final sequence of four scenes in one miniature depicts the reconciliation (fig. 34). These miniatures are rich in narrative details drawn directly from the text.

Before focusing on a few crucial miniatures that lead us to reinterpret the text in significant ways, I shall pause here to point out that all the miniatures have in common a resplendent display of the more public aspects of chivalry: costume and ceremony. The knights are elaborately outfitted in the contemporary gear of knighthood (Pakula 1972, 192ff.). They wear up-to-date suits of chain mail, conical metal helmets, and cloth tunics called coats of arms or surcoats, which bear their arms. They carry triangular shields, on which their identifying insignia also appear. In Yvain's case a gold lion rampant on an azure ground befits the "knight with the lion" (Brault 1972, 48–50; Pastoreau 1983). Their arms are also emblazoned on metal shoulder guards, or ailettes, and on the blankets worn by their horses. Lavishly dressed in this manner they wander through the countryside and forest, where they sometimes battle other knights and engage in jousts and tournaments.

Costume and accessories thus clearly identify the knights as belonging to a certain social group for whom heraldry served not just as a means of recognition but as authentication. Through his coat of arms a knight could be readily recognized in combat, as in the text of Chrétien's *Le Chevalier de la charrette (Lancelot),* where certain captured knights, in conversation with Queen Guinevere and her ladies-in-waiting during a tournament, explain to them how to distinguish between other knights by their armorial bearings. In the twelfth century, bearing arms was specifically associated with the ceremony of dubbing, of becoming a knight, and it connoted valor. But by the time the earliest rolls of arms were written in the middle of the thirteenth century, precisely the time when our manuscripts were transcribed and illustrated, description of arms recorded descent by blood or marriage and thus expressed lineage (Keen 1984, 90, 127–28). At the same time, many knights no longer bothered with the expense of dubbing: breeding was enough. In the sequence of miniatures in *Le Chevalier au lion,* then, there can be no mistaking that Yvain, with his emblazoned shield, is an aristocrat, accomplished in combat but distinguished by birth.

One of the most striking features of the Paris manuscript is how certain of its miniatures bring about a rereading of the story, particularly with regard to the marriage of Yvain and Laudine. These miniatures depict the funeral of Esclados and the reconciliation of Yvain and Laudine (figs. 28, 29, and 34). It is surprising to find the funeral of Esclados represented twice, first in one miniature, where it is combined with the conspiracy between Lunette and Yvain, and then in a second directly following, where it occupies the entire space of a large miniature instead of sharing its space with another episode on an adjoining register. The prominence of the funeral is all the more noteworthy because the marriage of Yvain and Laudine, which immediately follows the funeral in the text, is not illustrated at all. Instead the pictures skip directly to Yvain's participation in the tournaments at Arthur's court (fig. 30). Between the funeral(s) and the tournaments the marriage is, we might say, suppressed. In fact, contrary to the text, in the miniatures in the first part of the manuscript Laudine never meets Yvain. She appears only at the very end of the manuscript in the reconciliation scene, which serves, I will argue, as a kind of marriage miniature. The implication is clear: only after Yvain completes a series of quests is he united in marriage with his ladylove, as part of a domestic household. In a sense Yvain thus remains a bachelor until the end of the tale.

Text and illustration in *L'Atre périlleux,* which prefaces *Le Chevalier au lion* in the Paris manuscript, reinforce the rereading I have just suggested (Woledge 1930; *L'Atre périlleux,* 1936). Written about 1250, *L'Atre périlleux* opens, like *Le Chevalier au lion,* with the celebration of the feast of Pentecost at King Arthur's court, where the knights of the Round Table are gathered at dinner. The wicked knight Escanor of the Mountain rudely intrudes and abruptly kidnaps Arthur's cupbearer. The hero of the romance, Gawain, seeks to avenge the kidnapping and sets off on a series of quests that, like those of Yvain, revolve around doing good deeds, especially rescuing ladies in distress. Soon after Gawain sets out he meets three maidens who inform him that they have just seen Gawain killed, and so he hides his identity, becoming "the knight without a name" until he finds and defeats, toward the end of the romance, his supposed murderers. In the perilous cemetery from which the romance takes its title, he successfully vanquishes a devil who holds a young lady captive. He retrieves from a tree a sparrow belonging to another lady's lover. Then he rescues the wife of the king of the Red City from perpetual immersion in a fountain. Finally, joined by two bachelors, he eventually succeeds in rescuing the cupbearer and in identifying and defeating his supposed murderers, Gomeret Le Desmesure and Orgueilleux Fée. Revealing his true identity, he returns with his bachelor companions to Arthur's court, and they all marry women they have met during their adventures.

Obvious thematic similarities, such as the concealed identities of Gawain and Yvain, the episodes at the fountains, and the marriages, must have initially prompted the compilation of *Le Chevalier au lion* and *L'Atre périlleux* in one manuscript. The interpolation of the fountain incident in the Paris manuscript of *L'Atre périlleux,* the only copy that contains this episode, which is also illustrated in the double frontispiece, can surely also be explained by the importance of the fountain for Yvain's adventures and by the desire to forge closer links between the two stories for the reader of the manuscript.

It is the miniatures illustrating *L'Atre périlleux,* however, that most successfully reinforce the appearance of the entire manuscript as a unified, coherent romance. A lavish double frontispiece, although it prefaces *L'Atre périlleux,* can be read as introducing both romances (figs. 21 and 22). In this frontispiece Gawain wears the same costume and bears the same arms that distinguish Yvain later in the manuscript, even though Gawain's distinctive charge, a double-headed eagle, was firmly fixed by this time and appears in many other Arthurian romances, including a miniature of Gawain in the Princeton manuscript of *Le Chevalier au lion* (Brault 1972, 40–42; Pastoureau 1980, 1983, no. 3, 69–70). The identities of Gawain and Yvain are thus pictorially merged. In this way Gawain's quests in the first romance become precursors to Yvain's quests in the second. The repetition at the start of each romance of a historiated initial portraying a knight on horseback further underscores the similarity of the two protagonists (figs. 23 and 25).

Just as *Le Chevalier au lion* concludes with a miniature that focuses our attention on the marriage of the hero, so *L'Atre périlleux* concludes with an imposing miniature of the triple wedding that illustrates the last hundred verses of the text (fig. 24). That in *L'Atre périlleux* between the opening double frontispiece, which begins with the arrival of the cupbearer at Arthur's court and ends prematurely with the triumphant return of Gawain, and the conclusion of the romance there is only one generalized miniature, a battle scene, heightens the impact of the wedding miniature. With considerable pomp and circumstance, the marriages of Gawain's bachelor companions, Cadres, Espinogre, and Raguidel, and their girlfriends take place. According to the text, before they marry Gawain dubs them, to repay their assistance; he then gives them lands and castles, and finally they go together to a monastery, where the bishop of Chester presides over the ceremony before all the court, highborn and lowborn alike (*le grant et li menor*). In close harmony with the text, the miniature situates the scene in a monastery, where the bishop, the musicians, the three happy couples, the king, and the guests (including *li menor,* a peasant holding a shovel or rake) appear. Thus, as in *Le Chevalier au lion,* after a series of quests the bachelors are integrated into a stable domestic order when they finally marry and settle down.

The opening miniatures of both romances, each depicting a knight on horseback (figs. 23 and 25), reinforce my reading of Gawain and Yvain as itinerant bachelor knights. Similar miniatures, often as historiated initials, preface many other Arthurian romances, for example, the *Chevalier des deux épées,* which suggests that this subject told its readers the genre of the text (fig. 40). In an obvious sense the representation refers to the knight on horseback, *par cheval,* which even gives the prototypical knight Perceval his name. Yet the presence of these miniatures, particularly as introductory initials, still seems puzzling when other solutions to opening the romances were so clearly possible and must have been rejected. For example, in earlier manuscripts of the chansons de geste or in contemporary copies of the *Fables* of Marie de France, a singing jongleur or a writing scribe—both types of author portraits—open the text (fig. 41). But no Arthurian verse romance adopts the convention of the author portrait. Nor is the type of opening used in the "Guiot" manuscript of *Le Chevalier de la charrette* ever repeated: Marie de Champagne tells the story of Lancelot to Chrétien, giving visual form to a literary topos that is frequent in verse romance, the poet taking inspiration from a lady (fig. 41). Even when such a pictorial convention is appropriate, as in *L'Atre périlleux* in the Paris manuscript, where the opening lines evoke the same topos of a lady who "ordered and begged me to recount the story" (*L'Atre périlleux,* 1936, 1), the image of a knight on horseback recurs instead. Still other solutions might have been used: for example, two knights in combat, a tournament, a knight and his lady, or so forth. The bachelor knight, as a model well-behaved youth who roams the countryside in search of adventure, is most likely the figure pictured in these opening initials.

There is one additional miniature in the Paris manuscript, Yvain's visit to the vavasor, that seems out of place except when read with the entire picture cycle as an illustration of the requisite behavior for a bachelor youth. Coming right after the miniature of Calogrenant's visit to the fountain (fig. 26) and introducing Yvain for the first time in the sequence of illustrations, this miniature shows Yvain with a vavasor and his beautiful daughter at the moment when Yvain, on his way to challenge Esclados the Red, asks the man for lodging (fig. 27). We know from medieval literature, including other romances by Chrétien, that the vavasor is a vassal who is usually aged and of the lesser nobility; a good host, he is always ready to welcome and lodge the wandering knight.[4] The event, taking up only sixteen lines of verse in *Le Chevalier au lion,* permits Chrétien to pause and comment on "the sum of all the qualities you find in men and women good and kind."[5] In contrast to the text—which appears to gloss over the episode, though this has drawn little notice among critics of the romance—the miniature, presenting a single episode on one register instead of several subjects divided into compartments and separated in registers, assigns the subject an unusual importance. So too does the fact that Yvain's astonishing success at the storm-producing fountain is not illustrated at all. Instead it is this miniature of Yvain and the vavasor, paired with the preceding miniature of Calogrenant and the fountain—apart from the small opening miniature of the knight on horseback—that introduces the hero to the reader.

In fact this miniature presents an agenda for the youths that is in line with the times, including not only instruction in courtesy but promises of domestic rewards. To fully understand the function of this critical miniature, as well as the introductory miniatures of the knight on horseback, it is necessary to retrace the history of the youth or bachelor during this period. The exclusive legacy of a family's possessions to the firstborn male under primogeniture, which became the approved pattern of inheritance for the aristocracy by about 1100, helped create the social category known as youths or bachelors.[6] An obvious problem with primogeniture was how to take care of younger sons. Since it was not desirable to fragment the family's wealth by cutting off even small pieces of the patrimony, the younger sons, even though they qualified as knights, had nothing to offer in a marriage. So they frequently remained bachelors and became wandering knights, participating in tournaments, going on crusades, or seeking their living as they roamed aimlessly about the countryside. During their adventures they might hope to meet an eligible woman, either a widow with her own lands and money or a vavasor's daughter, wealthy though not herself an aristocrat. Especially in the twelfth century but also in the thirteenth, these youths constituted a violent fringe group within society, a group that robbed, raped, and plundered.

21: Frontispiece, *L'Atre périlleux*
Paris, Bibliothèque Nationale, MS fr. 1433, fol. Av

22: Frontispiece, *L'Atre périlleux*
Paris, Bibliothèque Nationale, MS fr. 1433, fol. Br

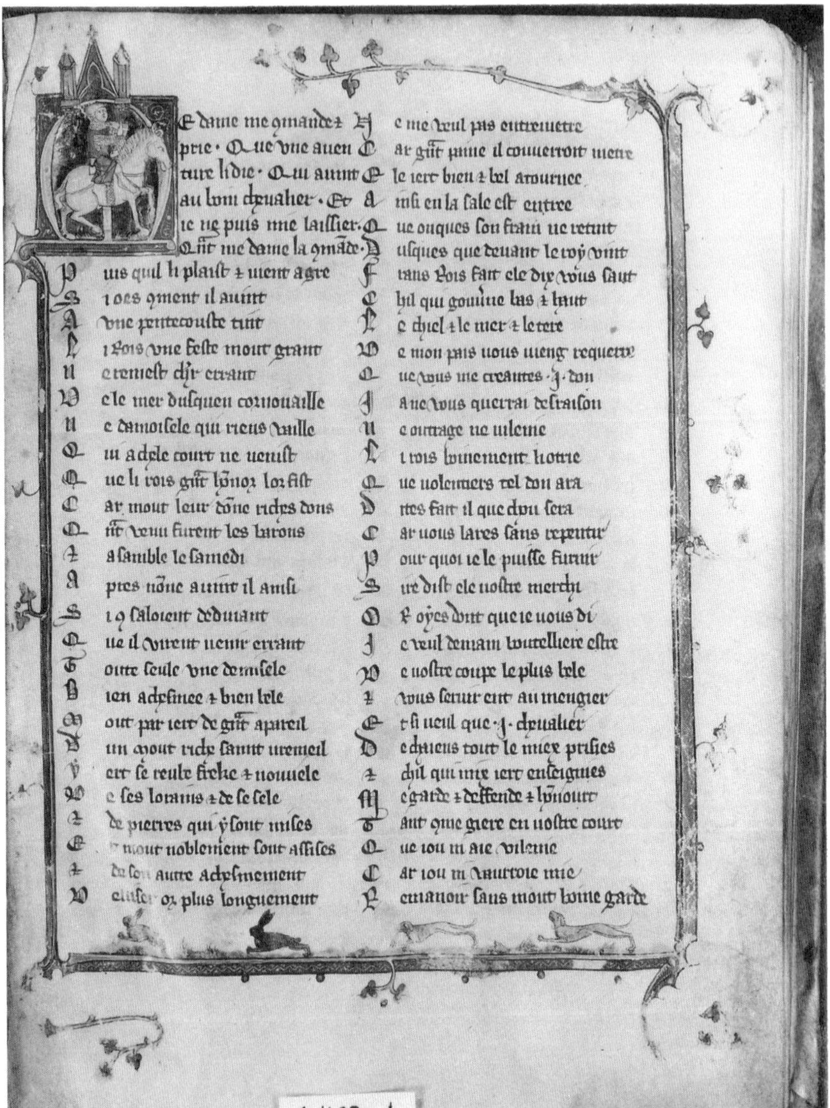

23: Knight on horseback, *L'Atre périlleux*
Paris, Bibliothèque Nationale, MS fr. 1433, fol. 1

24: Marriage of Cadrés, Espinogre, and Ragidel, *L'Atre périlleux*
Paris, Bibliothèque Nationale, MS fr. 1433, fol. 60

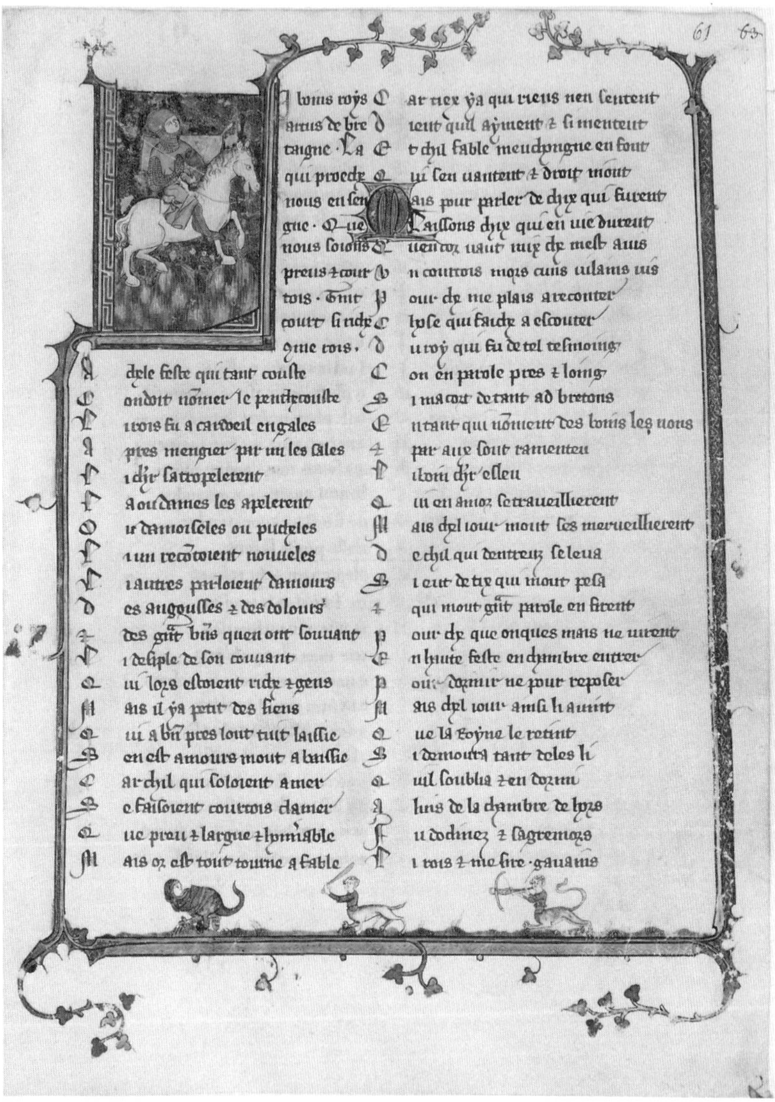

25: Knight on horseback, *Le Chevalier au lion*
Paris, Bibliothèque Nationale, MS fr. 1433, fol. 61

26: Calogrenant at the fountain, *Le Chevalier au lion*
Paris, Bibliothèque Nationale, MS fr. 1433, fol. 65

27: Yvain and the vavasor, *Le Chevalier au lion*
Paris, Bibliothèque Nationale, MS fr. 1433, fol. 67v

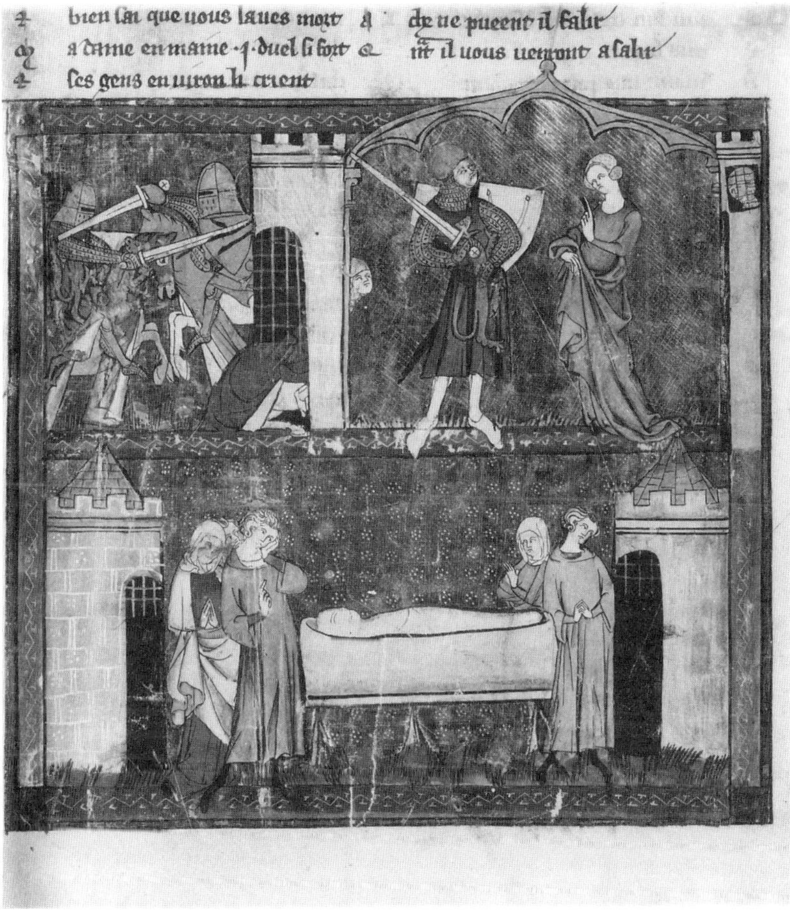

28: Yvain kills Esclados; Yvain and Lunette; and funeral of Esclados,
Le Chevalier au lion
Paris, Bibliothèque Nationale, MS fr. 1433, fol. 69v

29: Funeral of Esclados, *Le Chevalier au lion*
Paris, Bibliothèque Nationale, MS fr. 1433, fol. 72v

30: Tournaments at Arthur's court, *Le Chevalier au lion*
Paris, Bibliothèque Nationale, MS fr. 1433, fol. 80v

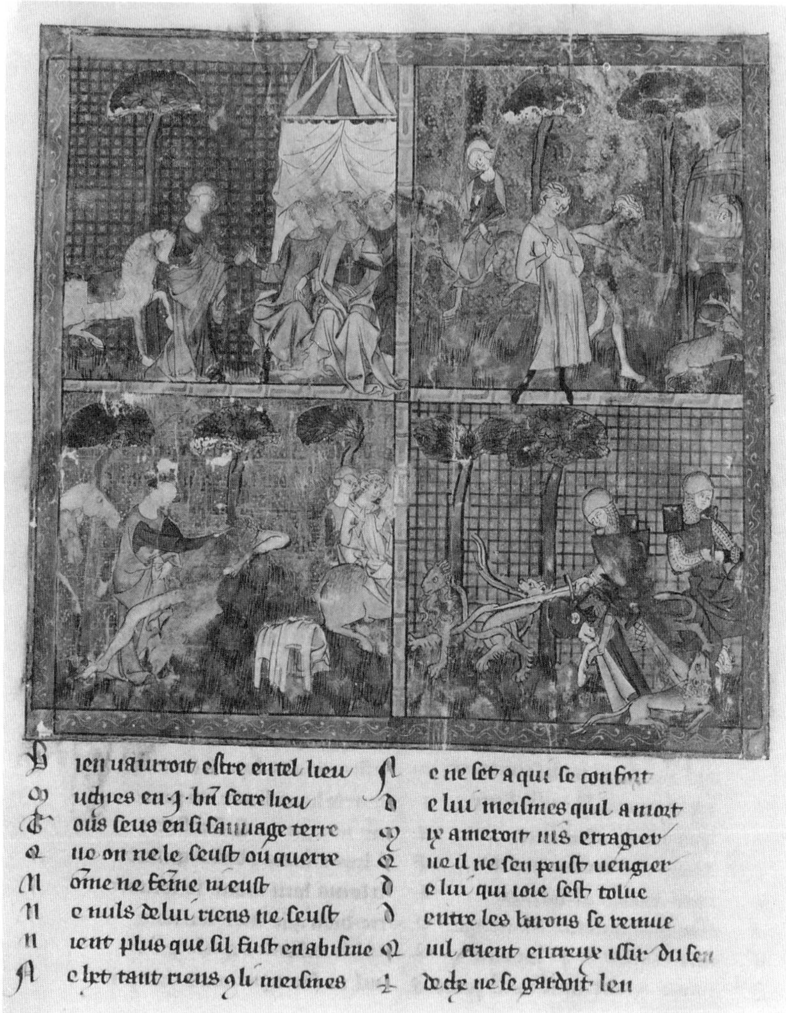

31: Lunette and Yvain; Yvain in the wilderness; Yvain's cure; and Yvain and the lion, *Le Chevalier au lion*
Paris, Bibliothèque Nationale, MS fr. 1433, fol. 85r

32: Yvain rescues Lunette; Yvain and Harpin of the Mountain; and Yvain battles the seneschal, *Le Chevalier au lion*
Paris, Bibliothèque Nationale, MS fr. 1433, fol. 90

33: Pesme adventure; Yvain battles sons of the devil; and Gawain and Yvain fight (Yvain's identity is revealed), *Le Chevalier au lion*
Paris, Bibliothèque Nationale, MS fr. 1433, fol. 104

34: Reconciliation of Yvain and Laudine, *Le Chevalier au lion*
Paris, Bibliothèque Nationale, MS fr. 1433, fol. 118

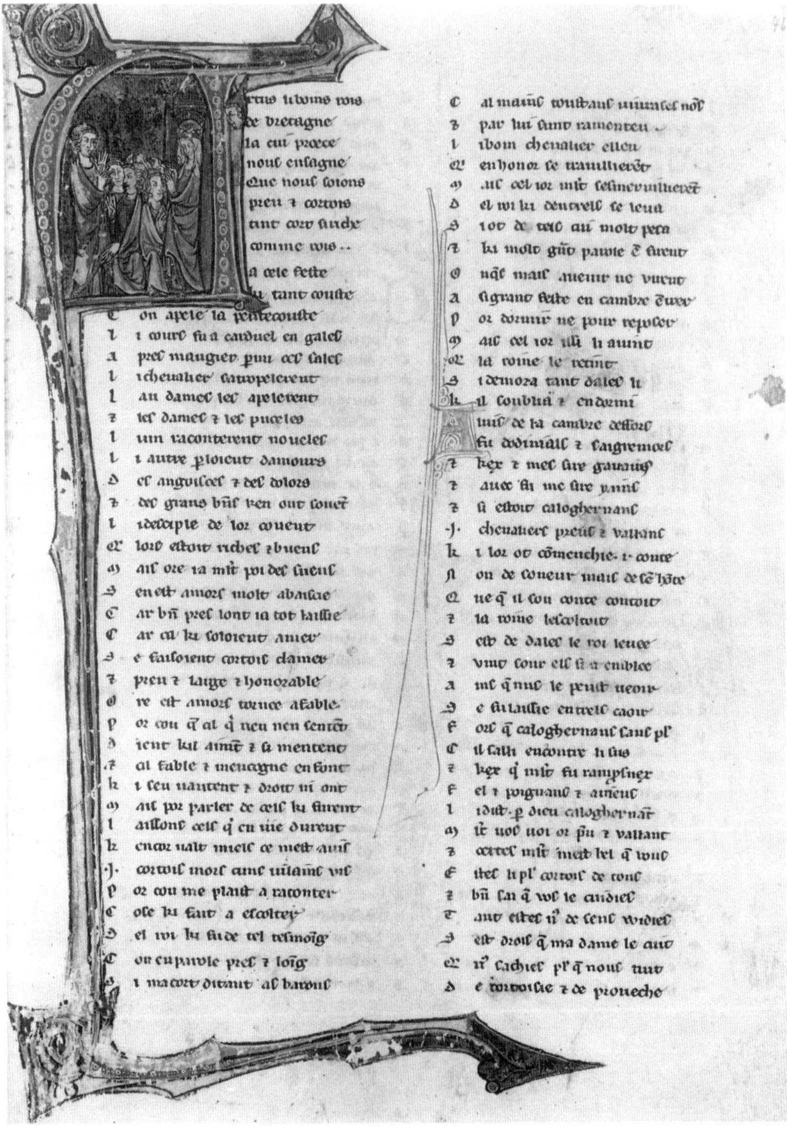

35: Calogrenant and Guinevere, *Le Chevalier au lion*
Princeton University Library, Garrett MS 125, fol. 40

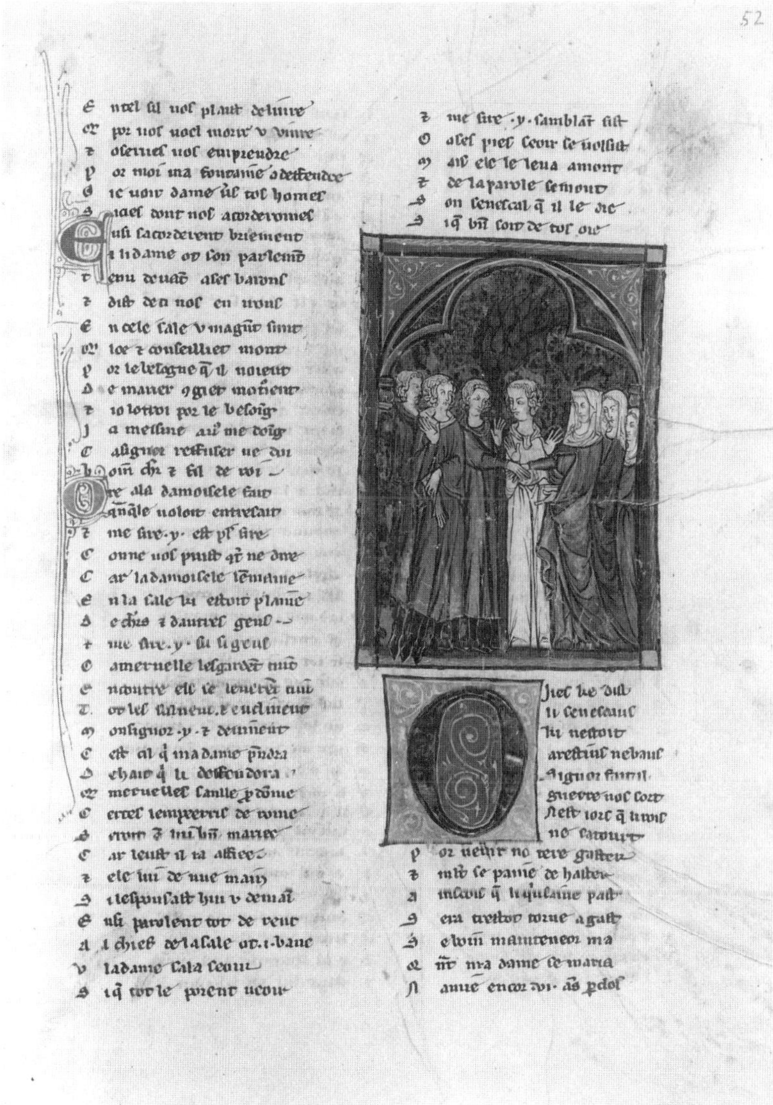

36: Marriage of Yvain and Laudine, *Le Chevalier au lion*
Princeton University Library, Garrett MS 125, fol. 52

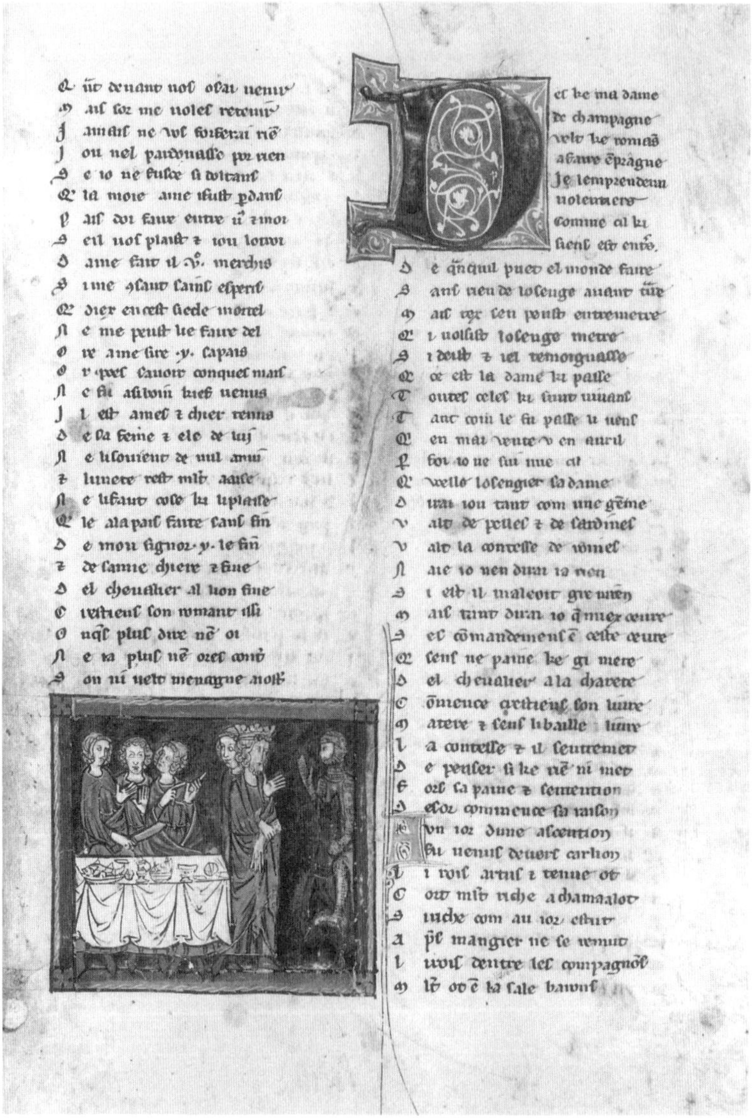

37: Meleagant's challenge at Arthur's court, *Le Chevalier de la charrette*
Princeton University Library, Garrett MS 125, fol. 34

38: Lancelot and the vavasor, *Le Chevalier de la charrette*
Princeton University Library, Garrett MS 125, fol. 22

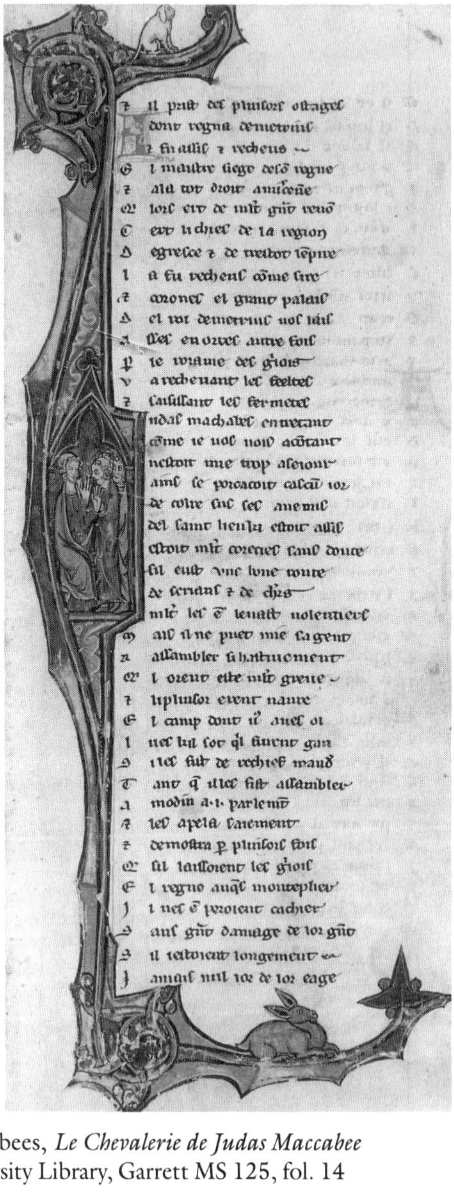

39: Judas Maccabees, *Le Chevalerie de Judas Maccabee*
Princeton University Library, Garrett MS 125, fol. 14

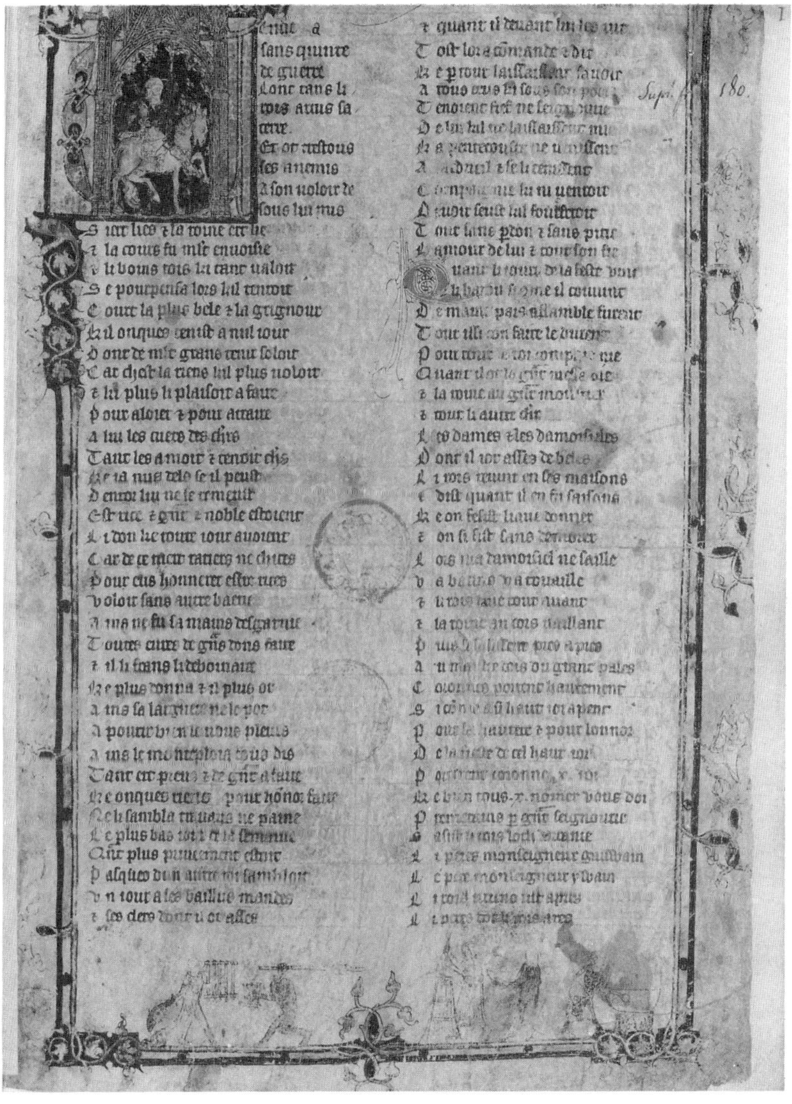

40: Knight on horseback, *Le Chevalier des deux épées*, Paris, Bibliothèque Nationale, MS fr. 12603, fol. 1

41: Marie de Champagne, *Le Chevalier de la charrette*
Paris, Bibliothèque Nationale, MS fr. 794, fol. 27

The texts of Arthurian romances can be construed as a response to the problem of these youths (Payen 1981, esp. 225). Wandering about the countryside engaged in adventures, Yvain, as well as other knights of the Round Table such as Gawain and his companions in *L'Atre périlleux*, is a bachelor or youth. Like Calogrenant, when Yvain encounters the vavasor, he might hope for the hand of his beautiful, wealthy daughter. Erec in *Erec et Enide* does marry a vavasor's daughter, even though she is not wealthy. By marrying a widow with a landed fortune, Yvain in fact fulfills one of the fantasies of all youths. In *L'Atre périlleux* the youths Cadres, Espinogre, and Ragidel are similarly rewarded. Although, unlike Yvain, they do not marry above their station, Gawain's generosity in granting them lands and castles ensures their economic prosperity as prospective heads of households.

In line with the texts, the protagonists of the romances are illustrated as belonging to the social category of the youths, for whom the pictures thus present a dual program implying that the quest, if the knight behaves himself, will lead to his betrothal. It is evident, however, that the pictures in *Le Chevalier au lion* in the Paris manuscript also rewrite the romance to forestall the marriage, giving it the same place and importance in Chrétien's story that it has in *L'Atre périlleux*.

Although the fragmentary condition of the Princeton manuscript makes a thorough analysis of its picture cycle difficult, certain features suggest that it presents a similar reading of the knight as a bachelor or youth. As it is now bound, the manuscript constitutes an anthology of three romances. Gautier de Belleperche's romance *La Chevalerie de Judas Maccabee*, precedes the texts of *Le Chevalier au lion* and *Le Chevalier de la charrette* as a kind of introduction. Writing in Picardy about the middle of the thirteenth century, Gautier had altered the biblical account of the Maccabees, the story of the heroic struggle of the Jews for political freedom and independence, by putting it into verse and couching it in the language of contemporary knighthood.[7] In exactly the same way that Gawain in *L'Atre périlleux* serves as a type for Yvain in *Le Chevalier au lion* in the Paris manuscript, the celebrated biblical hero-turned-knight Judas Maccabees thus serves as a type for the intrepid courage of Yvain and Lancelot in the Princeton manuscript (McGrath 1963b). His presence can only have elevated their stature, for already by the twelfth century in medieval literature and art, Judas had become one of the Nine Worthies, an exemplary model of knightly valor like Roland and Charlemagne, which was even to assure him a place in Dante's paradise.[8]

The full extent to which the illustrations emphasized textual links between *La Chevalerie de Judas Maccabee* and *Le Chevalier au lion* and *Le Chevalier de la charrette* remains unknown. Although the Princeton manuscript lacks its first folio, which undoubtedly was decorated with a miniature that introduced *Judas Maccabee,* several other extant manuscripts of the same text and executed about the same time in the same Picard milieu do begin either with a historiated initial virtually identical to those of our knight on horseback or, in the case of one manuscript, with a frontispiece in which each of a group of roundels depicts a knight on horseback. Such a frontispiece, identifying the main protagonists as itinerant knights and defining the genre of literature, would have been a fitting introduction to the compilation of three romances in the Princeton manuscript. In the rest of the miniatures of *Judas Maccabee* in the Princeton manuscript, Judas and his companions are portrayed rather like Yvain and Lancelot, that is, with the many contemporary trappings of knighthood—chain mail, helmets, shields, war-horses—and engaged in combat against powerful human adversaries as well as against lions, tigers, and mythical beasts.

At least two miniatures in the cycle of illustrations accompanying *Le Chevalier au lion* and *Le Chevalier de la charrette* in the Princeton manuscript confirm that it elaborated a program for the youths comparable to that in the Paris manuscript. In the Princeton manuscript, Lancelot's visit to a vavasor—again a minor episode in the romance, which leads up to his voyage to the sword bridge—is likewise illustrated, focusing as in the Paris manuscript on the greeting between the knight and the host (fig. 38). Without knowing what prominence this miniature had in the group of illustrations, it is difficult to form clear conclusions, except that since the incident has acquired no special importance in critical readings of the tale, it may be explained by a desire to portray the errant, though courteous, knight.

As in the Paris copy of *Le Chevalier au lion,* the theme of marriage is also stressed in the illustrations of the Princeton manuscript. Of the seven extant miniatures devoted to this text all but one, the marriage episode, routinely depict Yvain's quests. Instead of occurring at the end of the romance, the marriage miniature directly follows the introductory historiated initial as the first illustration of the unfolding narrative (fig. 36).[9] It interrupts the text more than seventy verses before the marriage itself, at the moment just after the funeral when the seneschal urges the barons to impress upon Laudine the need to remarry quickly because "if no brave knight will come within two weeks to fight, all this [the lands] will be destroyed."[10] Repeating the seneschal's arguments, the barons convince Laudine to marry, as she says, "the Lord Yvain, the lord of a nobler family than I am (Roques, ed. [1952–73], 65, v. 2132). The miniature refers to the barons' active role in promoting the arrangements by depicting them gesturing on the left. Laudine and Yvain clasp hands before her chaplain in the center, an act that alludes to Laudine's consent, which is also clearly shown in the text, for Chrétien says of Laudine that, although the barons approved the marriage, "that's what she'd have done anyway" (ibid., 66, vv. 2139–40). If the marriage miniature in the Princeton manuscript does not rewrite the story in the same way as the reconciliation miniature in the Paris manuscript, it nevertheless firmly underscores the idea of marriage as an important milestone in the life of the bachelor knight.

EMPHASIZED BY MINIATURES IN BOTH ROMANCES IN THE PARIS MANUSCRIPT, THEN, THE GLORIFICATION OF MARRIAGE FOR THE BACHELOR HEROES, WHICH HARMONIOUSLY BRINGS TO AN end a phase of restless wandering, is somewhat at odds with most readings of Chrétien's text of *Le Chevalier au lion*. Marriage does emerge as a central theme in criticism on the romance. Many critics, in fact, understand the original marriage episode as a setup for the ensuing problematic relationship between Yvain and Laudine, which Yvain strives to resolve as he makes himself worthy through the quests he undertakes in the second part of the text. For these critics the final reconciliation, not wholly unlike Erec's reconciliation with Enide, becomes the reward for Yvain's progress in love.[11] Several critics, calling attention to Laudine's virtual silence in the romance, nonetheless emphasize the inequality of the marriage in which the woman becomes an object of exchange (Vance 1986, 111–51). Read in this way and considered in light of the historical situation in the twelfth century when Chrétien wrote, the treatment of marriage in the text of *Le Chevalier au lion* reveals not only literary but also social nuances. The marriage can be understood as exemplifying the literary conventions of courtly love and, at the same time, as a paradigm of the diminished legal status and lower social position of women during this period. The shift in emphasis in our manuscripts, which cast marriage in a more favorable light, results in part, I believe, from changes in the status of the youths and in the institution of marriage in the thirteenth century.

Several changes documented from around 1200 profoundly altered the character of feudal society, in particular the status of the youths. From the end of the twelfth century to about 1240, the ranks of new knights increased sharply. The old distinction between the lord (*dominus*) and the knight (*miles*) blurred as the two groups came to form a single juridical *ordo* with common customs, including primogeniture (Fossier 1987, 2: 662–65). Simultaneously, the system of primogeniture began to falter (ibid., 2:582–85). The patrimony was thus more frequently split up and there was less land and money to go around, even though the number of offspring per household also coincidentally decreased (1:285). For many aristocratic families, diminished family wealth was coupled with an economic crunch brought about by crop failure and intensified by the rise of towns. Some families borrowed heavily (2:613–17). Others, to reduce their indebtedness, took to selling off their lands to the church and the rising bourgeoisie (2:617–21). Financial hardship also caused them to abandon some of the more prestigious but expensive features of knighthood, such as the ceremony of dubbing, which increasingly came to be reserved for the eldest son. During the latter half of the thirteenth century, contemporary charters commonly refer to undubbed younger sons from aristocratic families as *ecuyer* instead of *chevalier*, confirming their reduced status (2:661–62).

Whereas the decline of patrilineage brought with it a reduction in the status of youths or bachelors in the thirteenth century, it had the opposite effect on the status of women. Seeking brides outside their social milieu, many sons acquired title and property from the woman's line, contrary to the custom of primogeniture. Property also changed hands through remarriage. Widows were sometimes entitled to as much as one-third of their husband's property, which, when they remarried, passed to the new husband. Since older men frequently married younger women, widowhood was common. The average length of time before remarriage was nineteen and a half years, a statistic that makes Laudine's marriage almost immediately after the death of her husband stand out. Notarial documents confirm the improved social status of women as suggested by their enhanced ability to transfer title and property. From 1150 to 1300, female participation as either a donor or a witness to documents rose dramatically, from 21 percent before 1150 to 68 percent by 1300. Lower mortality rates for women after 1125 contribute to their greater presence—even a surplus—which the rise of beguinages and the proliferation of women's religious foundations also reflects (for these statistics see Hadju 1980, esp. 133; and Fossier 1987, 278–81).

The reduced status of bachelors and the increased rights of women came together in changes in the institution of marriage initiated in the twelfth century but observed more strictly in the thirteenth.[12] With Gratian (*Decretum,* ca. 1140) and Peter Lombard (*Sententiarum,* ca. 1150) in the twelfth century, consent between two parties was for the first time regarded as indispensable to a marriage contract. For Gratian clandestine marriage was valid provided the couple had affection for each other and consummated the marriage. Somewhat later the power of both parties to choose their mates without the intervention of anyone—family, friends, or feudal lord—was also endorsed by the church under Pope Alexander III (d. 1181), who simultaneously set the minimum age for marriage at fourteen for the bridegroom and twelve for the bride, although a seven-year-old was permitted to contract for a future marriage (Noonan 1973). Marriage between individuals related within seven degrees by blood, affinity, or baptism remained forbidden. When the Fourth Lateran Council convened in 1215, the forbidden degrees were reduced to four, and endowment of brides and public weddings were required, although clandestine marriages nonetheless continued. Along with the changing customs of the twelfth century, these additional transformations fostered an institution in which both man and woman enjoyed greater financial and psychological independence and the solidarity of the family unit increased (Fossier 1987, 2:70–72).

It is this "modern" thirteenth-century view of marriage that the Paris and Princeton manuscripts present. In the Paris manuscript our heroes, the bachelor knights Gawain and Yvain, strut across the double frontispiece and then through the sequence of miniatures in *Le Chevalier au lion* as eligible young adventurers. At the conclusion of *L'Atre périlleux,* they marry in a thirteenth-century public ceremony. Although King Arthur attends the wedding, at which he appears as a sort of benign patron standing behind the couples, he neither authorizes nor approves it. Here is a marriage by consent. So too the marriage miniature in the Princeton manuscript depicts an up-to-date marriage of mutual consent. At the conclusion of *Le Chevalier au lion* in the Paris manuscript, by contrast, Laudine and Yvain celebrate their reconciliation in the lower register of the last miniature first by clasping hands on the left and then by embracing in bed on the right. This is a pictorial version of a clandestine wedding, in which the ritual handclasp affirms the couple's mutual consent and the implied lovemaking "completes" the marriage according to the terms explicitly defined by Gratian. Through these various marriage ceremonies—public and private—the young bachelor knight has crossed the most significant threshold of adulthood. He has become the lord or seigneur, head of the household.

This relatively positive presentation of contemporary marriage in the Paris and Princeton manuscripts stands out in the light of the tensions of late thirteenth-century society as reflected both in literary topoi and in historical realities. For example, a group of literary works written at the end of the thirteenth century contemporary with the Paris and Princeton manuscripts are stridently antimarriage (Payen 1981). They include *La Chatelaine de Vergi, Joufroi de Poitiers, Le Jeu de la feuillee, Le Roman de la Rose*, and *Les Lamentations de Matheolus.* These vivid critiques of marriage have in common jealous and brutish husbands, nagging and loquacious wives, and also frequent reciprocal duplicity, which initially seem out of place in the new era of mutual consent. Complementary historical data, which reveal a sharp increase in physical abuse among married couples, for example, confirms the impact of a crisis of marriage at the end of the thirteenth century as reflected in contemporary literature.[13]

In the face of such a crisis, the view of marriage presented in our romances can be understood as a fanciful recasting of social experience, a displacement of the realities of contemporary society at a time when the status of knights and ladies was shifting dramatically. These illuminated manuscripts present for the culture of the knightly class a program that helps deflect and allay their anxieties. Certain related changes in twelfth- and thirteenth-century society, including the growing power of women to dispose of property, have been understood as providing the impetus for the development of courtly, or romantic, love as a strategy of disempowerment or debasement of women that replaces the misogyny of earlier times (Bloch 1991). Such an interpretation not only helps account for the discrepancy between the pictorial portrayals of harmonious marriage and its disquieting social realities, it also puts in better perspective the characterization in these manuscripts of the desirable bachelor knights, who are portrayed as the male paragons of an aristocratic culture that had in fact seen better days.

STORYTELLING ITSELF PLAYS AN IMPORTANT ROLE IN THE SOCIETY IN WHICH THE YOUTHS INITIALLY REBEL AND FINALLY SETTLE DOWN. YOUNG MEN FREQUENTLY EXPERIENCED SECONDHAND the prestige of literature (Duby 1982). The "typical" knight, William Marshall (d. 1219), who became an earl and regent of England, never learned to read (Duby 1985). In a vernacular chronicle of the Picard counts of Guines, the writer Lambert of Ardres suggests that literature had a dual function for the illiterate nobles of aristocratic culture. He describes how the younger count, the *bacheler,* delighted in war games and storytelling, specifically in tales of the Holy Land and fables of the matter of France or Brittany. The older count, the *seignor,* commissioned a Latin genealogy to enhance the prestige of his family.[14] In either case, like William Marshall, neither brother could read. Women, however, who had more leisure time, as well as merchants, who stood to gain more economically, were schooled in reading and writing (Parkes 1973). These distinctive roles—literate aristocratic ladies as readers and illiterate errant nobles as listeners and tellers—are reflected in the manuscripts, which evoke an oral culture where telling and reading were both performative acts.

I have already called attention to the idiosyncratic opening miniatures of the Paris manuscript, depicting knights on horseback, which I interpreted as representing images of the knights as youths. But these miniatures may at the same time be understood as showing the youths who return from battle or tournament to recount their adventures at Arthur's court, which is a literary topos common to many of the prose and verse Arthurian romances, as Burns (1985) has shown. Several of Chrétien's romances, including *Le Chevalier au lion,* begin with a scene of storytelling at court, and many incorporate episodes of storytelling at various junctures in the narrative. Referring to the oral deposition of the story by its teller, the fictional knight, at the same time as they represent him as the protagonist, these historiated initials effectively substitute for the author portraits that more customarily open a manuscript. They thus imaginatively put forward the fiction of the text's orality by coalescing the written voice of the author-storyteller and the spoken voice of the knight-storyteller in the prefatory picture.

Through their actual portrayal of the recounting of the story at Arthur's court, the opening miniatures in the Princeton manuscript make the oral milieu even more explicit. For example, *Le Chevalier au lion* opens with a historiated initial, *A[rtus],* which illustrates the beginning of the text when after dinner the queen, having heard Calogrenant begin his story while she takes a nap with Arthur, rises from bed and slips into the court, where she comes upon the knights engaged in storytelling (fig. 35). The miniature shows on the right the queen, who has just stealthily entered the room, and on the left Calogrenant, who jumps up quickly when he sees her. Seated in the midst of the group and scowling at Calogrenant is the quarrelsome seneschal Kay. Kay taunts Calogrenant for rising so courteously before the queen and dares him to resume his story in front of her. Calogrenant is about to decline because the story casts him in an unfavorable light, but the queen presses him to please her, and by the rules of courtesy that require him to honor his lady's request, he has no choice but to continue the tale. The miniature thus introduces the deposition of the tale at Arthur's court, which provides the background to Yvain's quest.

In a related sense, speech itself is the subject of the miniature. The raised hands of the queen, Calogrenant, and Kay, who all gesture as they speak, express the simultaneity of their discourse. The small head of a fool wearing a pointed red cap, embedded in the descender of the *A,* appears to be addressing the assembled group. (Is this another representation of Kay, whose speech forces Calogrenant to tell the story?) And though Arthur is conspicuously absent from the miniature (he remains asleep in bed), the locus of the deposition of the tale at his court is clearly implied by the large initial *A,* the opening letter of his name, that both inscribes and transcribes the event. Later in this manuscript another initial functions similarly: a large initial *I* interchangeable with *J*) in the *Chevalerie de Judas Maccabee* contains the gesticulating, speaking figure of Judas inscribed in the first initial of his name (fig. 39).

Like *Le Chevalier au lion,* the romance of *Le Chevalier de la charrette* in the Princeton manuscript begins with a miniature that, if it does not directly portray the recounting of the story at Arthur's court, at least suggests it. This miniature illustrates the moment when an unidentified knight, well equipped and fully armed, appears at Arthur's court on Ascension Day. He announces that he has taken prisoner knights, ladies, and damsels from Arthur's kingdom and will release them only on condition that Arthur entrust his queen to a knight who will escort her on a journey, defend her, and bring her back again to the court (fig. 37). On the right is the knight who addresses Arthur, while on the left are Kay and two other individuals "seated there at meat." In the center between the two groups appears Queen Guinevere, whose grimace suggests that she is already cognizant of her role in the events to come. The challenge of the unidentified knight at Arthur's court, the subject of the miniature, provides a setup for the subsequent series of quests in which Lancelot will star.

Oddly placed at the bottom of the left column at the end of the story of *Le Chevalier au lion* instead of before the actual beginning of *Le Chevalier de la charrette* in the right column, this miniature also reinforces the link between the two stories in the Princeton manuscript as a sequence of tales recounted at court. Since by its placement it simultaneously refers back to *Le Chevalier au lion* and forward to *Le Chevalier de la charrette,* it alludes to the telling of a tale after the successful conclusion of a quest. But it also recalls that the stories are textually linked, as stories in epic cycles are interwoven through the reappearance of their heroes: toward the end of *Le Chevalier au lion,* when the daughters of the Lord of the Black Thorn engage in a property dispute, there is an aside about Lancelot, who could not be present at court because he was being held captive in a tower as punishment for his (alleged) abduction of Guinevere. Several of Chrétien's other romances conclude with the telling of the story at court. This motif occurs in *Erec et Enide,* where at the end of his quest, before he is crowned king, Erec recounts his adventures to Arthur. And it occurs in Manessier's Continuation of *Le Conte del Graal* where, after finding the Grail, the knight dutifully returns to Arthur's court to relate his adventures to the king and his fellow knights.

The fiction of orality, which prevails in the text and pictures of the Paris and Princeton manuscripts, leads us to inquire whether they were actually used in a culture where performance predominated. Much evidence suggests that they were. The long-standing idea that Chrétien was a cleric has even been challenged in favor of the hypothesis that he was a minstrel, thus shifting his writings away from the written culture of the literati (Vitz 1990). The puzzling evidence from the manuscripts, which do not easily fit into families, is more readily explained by the supposition that they were generated in an oral tradition, where performance gave rise to multiple and idiosyncratic variants in the texts before they were written down and eventually became stable. The balance of the evidence for the twelfth century, including that from Chrétien's own works (like the passage in *Erec et Enide* where he asserts that his is the best version of the story, or the passage in *Le Chevalier au lion* where Yvain comes upon a young girl reading a romance aloud to her parents in an orchard) now prompts us to consider his writings—and perhaps the whole genre of octosyllabic romance itself—as witnesses to an oral culture of the courts.[15]

There is some corroborating literary evidence for the persistence of oral performance of courtly romance through the thirteenth century (Duggan 1989a, b; Vitz 1986). In an octosyllabic exchange between three minstrels titled *De deux bordeors ribaus,* each bard recites the names of works in his repertory, including various *romans d'aventure* such as those of Perceval and Partenopeu and fables such as Renart (*Mimes français* 1910, 93–111). The often-quoted passage in *Le Chevalier au lion,* mentioned above, in which a young girl reads a romance aloud in an orchard finds its counterpart in an Arthurian verse romance of the third quarter of the thirteenth century, *Hunbaut*.[16] In this romance the lady of Gaut Destroit is having a romance read when Kay and Sagremor arrive at her castle. The anonymous poet specifies that the audience comprises sixteen people, including more men than women (ten knights, *chevaliers*, and six young ladies, *pucelles*). These passages, like those about the recounting of the story at Arthur's court, suggest that one of the principal pastimes of courtly life was storytelling.

But the topos of storytelling also inscribes different roles for the knights and ladies in the actions of listening and reading that bear directly on the function of our manuscripts. The bachelor knight, spent from his wanderings, typically happens across a tranquil scene, a woman reading aloud from a romance. He stops and listens. These encounters usually disclose a love angle. In *Le Chevalier au lion* the father of the girl in the orchard announces that she wants to marry the errant knight. In *Hunbaut* the lady of Gaut Destroit interrupts her reading to reveal longingly to the intruding knights that in his absence she keeps a statue of her beloved Gawain in her bedroom. By implication the very confrontation between the knight and the lady—the listener and the reader—leads to the domestication of the illiterate youth by the literate lady, who turns him into a husband.

While the lady attempts to shape the knight as she reads aloud to him, offering role models for his behavior out of romances, the bachelor knight creates his own public image in the stories he recites at court. Successful love and marriage can take place only once the youth's persona, as reflected in his storytelling at court, matches that prescribed by the lady in the stories she reads to him. Of course it is within the romance itself that these two images of approved male behavior—the one self-generated, the other prescribed—actually do merge. In *Le Chevalier au lion*, as in other romances, knights brag at court about their escapades; Yvain wins Laudine through one such successful adventure, his conquest at the fountain. *Le Chevalier au lion* unfolds, however, to narrate the quests through which the errant knight with the lion also comes to deserve his bride. Just as the romances put forward suitable models of behavior for the knight turned husband, they also offer role models that prescribe wifely virtues: Laudine's patience and forgiveness, Enide's devotion and understanding, Blancheflor's chastity and fidelity, all in marked contrast to Guinevere's impatience, deception, and adultery. Seated outdoors in the orchard with her parents and reading aloud, the young girl in *Le Chevalier au lion* holds out the promise of domestic tranquillity through her virtuous demeanor.

For the youth in aristocratic court culture, the acts of listening and reading are thus inextricably linked to the business of love and marriage. Read aloud by ladies to knights, the Paris and Princeton manuscripts, combining romances by Chrétien de Troyes with other Arthurian and biblical tales, in this way participated in the social adaptation of the bachelors during the changing times of the thirteenth century.

CHAPTER THREE

THE KNIGHT *Li Seignor*

For well two years longer, during which time they could have no children, . . . until God had provided for it, such that the lady became pregnant, and all around were very joyous, who loved their lord in every way.

Bliocadran (prologue to *Le Conte del Graal*)[1]

IN CHRÉTIEN'S *LE CONTE DEL GRAAL (PERCEVAL)* and its FOUR CONTINUATIONS, PERCEVAL'S FAMILY BACKGROUND REMAINS OBSCURE. THE STORY OPENS WITH PERCEVAL GROWING UP WITH his mother deep in the Welsh forest, in ignorance of chivalry. One day the rough young lad, while out casting javelins, encounters five knights, whom he mistakes for angels, "the fairest beings that exist." Perceval rushes home to share this marvelous adventure with his mother, but his news deeply upsets her. She sadly recalls that he is "descended from the best knights of this land," including his father, who was "so revered, so greatly honored, and so feared," and that Perceval's two brothers became knights at his father's wish but "were slain in knightly combat" on their way to do service in the courts of kings. She tells how his father died of grief shortly thereafter, leaving behind two-year-old Perceval, the only surviving son, and the heartbroken widow. Whatever the further details of Perceval's origins might be, his mother's speech implies that, as the last surviving male of a great family, he is by virtue of his birth an aristocrat whose claims to knighthood are legitimate rather than foolish.

The rest of the story is, in a sense, about the making of a knight. Heedless of his mother's warnings, Perceval is driven by just one desire—to become a knight—and he obstinately rushes off to the court of King Arthur, "the king who makes the knights." Arthur is charmed by the simplicity of the impetuous youth, and Kay taunts him into doing combat with the villainous Red Knight. Perceval, using his crude Welsh javelins, quickly defeats him and helps himself to his armor. After his victory Perceval is befriended by an older knight, Gornemant of Gohort, a vavasor who teaches him the use of weapons as well as a few social niceties (such as

Don't talk too much). Naturally skilled in combat, Perceval quickly distinguishes himself defending the castle of Beaurepaire, where he falls in love with its mistress, Blancheflor. One day Perceval comes upon a nobleman fishing—the Fisher King—and is lavishly entertained at his castle. During dinner Perceval sees a young man carrying a bleeding white lance and a beautiful maiden bearing a bejeweled golden Grail; but remembering the advice of Gornemant (Don't talk too much), he fails to ask two crucial questions: Whom are they serving with the Grail? Why does the lance bleed? In one of the continuations he learns from a wise hermit that he did not ask these questions because he had sinned by causing the death of his mother. Perceval (alternating with Gawain in both *Le Conte del Graal* and its four continuations) goes on to become worthy of learning the secrets of the Grail and the lance. As the Fisher King's cousin, he eventually succeeds him, is crowned, and rules for seven years. In the end, however, he turns away from the material world, relinquishes his throne, and takes religious vows.

What little more we learn about Perceval's uncertain lineage in *Le Conte del Graal* and the continuations reinforces the inevitability of his succession to the throne of the Grail king (West 1971–72). Perceval has two uncles: one is a hermit, plainly childless, and the other is the father of the maimed and childless Fisher King, his only surviving child and Perceval's cousin. The Fisher King himself had a brother or sister whose line ends in a female, the niece who sends Perceval's sword to the Grail castle. Perceval's cousin-german, a lady who upbraids him in the forest after his failure at the Grail castle, also represents the end of a family line. His sister (an invention of the continuations), who takes him to visit the hermit uncle and tells him about his mother's death, evidently does not count.

Among the six illuminated manuscripts of *Le Conte del Graal,* I am concerned here with the copy in Mons (Bibliothèque de l'Université, MS 331/206), one of the earliest extant versions of the text.[2] The Mons manuscript includes, in addition to three of the four continuations (it lacks the continuation by Gerbert de Montreuil), two anonymous prologues: the so-called *Elucidation* and also the *Bliocadran,* which provides a fuller history of Perceval's family background. It is the only illuminated manuscript to include these two prologues, which in this copy substitute for Chrétien's own prologue to the poem. Copied and illustrated in the area of the counties of Flanders and Hainaut probably between 1275 and 1285, judging from the dialect and the decoration, the Mons manuscript also includes forty-one miniatures.[3]

The reading I propose of *Le Conte del Graal* understands Perceval as an example of a *seignor,* the male head of a household in feudal society. I will argue that unique to this manuscript among the illuminated manuscripts of *Le Conte del Graal* is a program of text and illustration that focuses on lineage or genealogy, stressed through the presentation of Perceval's status as a seigneur, and further, that this program had special social and political relevance for the aristocracy in the area where this manuscript was made and perhaps even for a specific aristocrat. I will also suggest that certain features of the illustrations, which appropriate the visual language of seals, inventively reinforce the theme of the seigneur while at the same time evoking a milieu where setting down something in writing with a seal was still essentially an oral act.

AT THE BEGINNING OF THE MONS MANUSCRIPT, THE *ELUCIDATION* OFFERS A CAPSULE HISTORY OF THE GRAIL QUEST. ITS OPENING PASSAGE RECOMMENDS THAT THE SECRET STORY OR STORIES be told only at the proper time by "the seven guards who have charge throughout the world of all the good stories that have been told." It continues with two brief narrative digressions about, first, the kidnapping of the maidens at the well and the theft of their golden cups by King Amangons and his followers and, second, the attempt by the rival knights of King Arthur's court to rescue the maidens and retrieve their cups. Next the Grail castle is introduced, and the story is told of how Gawain and Perceval both found the castle of the Fisher King. It concludes with a long passage on the seven guards, who are to be understood as both the seven quests for the Grail and the seven stories of those quests. The anonymous author of this prologue closes by adapting part of Chrétien's own prologue, which refers to how the count (Philip of Alsace) commissioned the poet to undertake the "rhyming of the best story . . . recounted at the royal court."[4]

A large rectangular miniature prefacing the *Elucidation* portrays, on the left, a knight on horseback and, on the right, eight figures seated beneath niches at a long table covered with a white cloth (fig. 42). There seems little doubt that the knight on horseback is Perceval, and the first seated figure, who is crowned, is probably Arthur. Who then are the seven other seated figures? Most likely they represent both the knights at Arthur's court and the seven guards mentioned in the *Elucidation*.[5]

Understood in this way the miniature presents two themes, which will recur throughout the manuscript: the telling of the story at Arthur's court and the making of a knight. The figure of Perceval refers to the knight who returns from tournament or battle to recount his adventures, a topos that is common in Arthurian romance (Burns 1985). The seven guards seated next to Arthur at the table are the seven other storytellers. The prologue's insistence on orality thus finds a visual counterpart in the miniature suggesting recitation. At the same time, the figure of Perceval appearing before Arthur and the assembled knights refers to the critical moment at the beginning of *Le Conte del Graal* when Perceval rashly bursts into the court to demand that Arthur make him a knight.

Immediately following the *Elucidation* and introduced as though it were the actual beginning of *Le Conte del Graal* (the introductory rubric reads, "Ci endroit comence li contes del saint greaul"),[6] the second prologue, the *Bliocadran*, supplies precise details about Perceval's lineage and thus sets the stage for his destiny. It begins by clarifying the identity and background of his father, Bliocadran. Along with his eleven brothers, all accomplished knights, Bliocadran descends from one of the richest and most powerful families in Wales. His brothers were killed, however, leaving Bliocadran as the last surviving knight of a renowned family. Although married, Bliocadran remained childless for a long time, but his wife is expecting a baby at the beginning of the poem, which makes "all around . . . very joyous, who loved their lord [*seignor*] in every way." Before his wife gives birth, however, Bliocadran is invited to participate in a celebrated tournament. Unable to resist the temptation to excel, he accepts, much to the dismay of his wife and his people. The inevitable tragedy occurs: Bliocadran is killed in a joust. These textual details reinforce the social status of Bliocadran's own illustrious ancestry and underscore the importance of Perceval's birth, since all other males on his father's side have died without male progeny.

Three days later Bliocadran's wife gives birth to a son, Perceval. When she learns shortly thereafter of her husband's death, she determines to protect her son by preventing him from becoming a knight, and she devises a plan whereby she will retire to the waste forest, letting her people believe she has gone on a pilgrimage. In a lengthy passage that has been entirely overlooked by critics but, I argue, is neither accidental nor insignificant, she conspires with her steward to assemble her subjects so that they may swear allegiance to her young son as their lord (*seignor*) and pledge to protect his lands until his return ("and in the interest of your son, as you wish, that he will be called *sire*, and that all will consider him as *seignor*").[7] Perceval and his mother depart, eventually settling in a suitably isolated spot, and fourteen years pass, during which the son learns the ways of the forest and, just in case he ever encounters knights, is warned against those men "covered with iron [who are] clearly devils." This prologue powerfully articulates what is only implied in the speech by Perceval's mother at the actual beginning of *Le Conte del Graal*—that Perceval's lineage fully legitimizes his status as a lord even if he is not yet a knight.

The historiated initial that introduces the *Bliocadran* portrays Perceval's father bidding farewell to Perceval's mother, presumably as he departs for the fateful joust (fig. 43). Fully outfitted as a knight with a helmet and a tunic worn over chain mail, Bliocadran, on horseback, raises his arm in this final parting from his wife, who stands in the window of a building on the right and raises her arm in response. Compared with the historiated initials that follow, this initial visually presents a model of filiation between the figures of the father and the son, who are similarly portrayed as knight-seigneur in the manuscript. Further, the initial pictorially situates the father at the head of an imaginary family tree that begins in the prologue *Bliocadran,* which appears in the Mons manuscript as integral with *Le Conte del Graal.* From this perspective the suppression of Chrétien's prologue, where the poet dwells at length on his dedication of the story to Philip of Alsace, count of Flanders, enhances the illusion of a genealogy that is uninterrupted from Bliocadran to Perceval at the very beginning of *Le Conte del Graal.*

What remains is for Perceval to become a knight, and not surprisingly, a sequence of miniatures near the beginning of *Le Conte del Graal* illustrates his knighthood. At first he is portrayed in marked contrast to Bliocadran. Dressed in a shapeless blue smock, he stands clumsily grasping his javelins as he points toward a knight on horseback (fig. 44). Presumably this historiated initial depicts Perceval's first encounter with the five anonymous knights whom he meets in the Welsh forest and naively queries, asking the names of a lance, a shield, and a helmet. Next Perceval is shown, similarly outfitted, though this time on horseback, at King Arthur's court (fig. 45). These two subjects occur in most of the manuscripts of *Le Conte del Graal,* where they are often condensed in a single frontispiece (see frontispiece, figs. 1 and 96).

Illustrating the ceremonial making of the knight, the next miniature appears in no other manuscript of *Le Conte del Graal.* It portrays the formula *gladio aut cingulo accictus* ("girded with the sword and the belt"), which by the end of the twelfth century came to signify the consecration of the knight, who was presented with the sword in its belt during the dubbing ceremony (fig. 46). The granting of arms, with the sword the principal emblem of power, had long been associated with the knightly function. In imitation of the royal coronation ritual, the dubbing ceremony evolved to include the knight's putting the belt on the altar and asking that the sword be blessed while he promised God to serve the sword before his altar. The secular component of this quasi-religious ceremony is depicted here. Gornemant, in front of a small group of onlookers, places the belt holding the sword around Perceval's waist. Perceval is outfitted head to toe in chain mail, over which he wears a tunic. Although the text refers to the moment when Gornemant fastens the sword in place in front of a group of squires, this action is only one in a sequence during which Perceval is fully costumed. By paying special attention to the delivery of the sword and belt, the miniature illustrates not so much an informal moment in the narrative as the ceremonial ritual of dubbing, which Perceval's hieratic frontal stance also reinforces.

Having become a knight, in the miniatures in the Mons manuscript Perceval goes on to engage in knightly acts, which—inexplicably, it seems at first—eclipse the "main" narrative events in the texts that recount the quest of the Grail. In *Le Conte del Graal,* for example, skipping over the story of Perceval's encounter with his sweetheart Blancheflor and their love for each other (as well as the prolonged battle at her domain, the castle of Beaurepaire), the next miniature illustrates instead the surrender of Clamadeu, the dreaded enemy of Blancheflor and her people at the court of King Arthur (fig. 47). The miniature thus affirms that Perceval has taken to heart the advice of Gornemant, that he should not slay knights—however villainous—but instead should show them mercy. The episode at Beaurepaire is directly followed in the text by Perceval's encounter with the Fisher King, his visit to the Grail castle, and his failure to ask the crucial questions upon seeing the lance and the Grail. The next miniature in the Mons manuscript instead depicts a later, relatively trivial incident, however, during which Perceval fights the Proud Knight of the Heath to avenge the maiden he has treated with contempt because he is suspicious of her immodest behavior with Perceval earlier in the story (fig. 48). This miniature gives Perceval a chance to demonstrate that he has mended his ways and corrected his earlier, crude behavior.

Among the ten miniatures illustrating *Le Conte del Graal* in the Mons manuscript, not a single one ever alludes to the quest of the Grail, which does provide a focal point in other manuscripts of the Perceval story. In fact the sequence of miniatures argues against any coherent linear reading of

Le Conte del Graal. Representing discontinuous episodes, these miniatures seem designed chiefly to show how well Perceval has learned the practical precepts of knighthood.

An overview of the miniatures included in the continuations in the Mons manuscript indicates a similar interest in Perceval's knightly prowess coupled with a relative lack of interest in the Grail quest. Not until the end of the First Continuation is the Grail quest pictured at all, when Gawain makes his second visit to the Grail castle, partially restoring the land by his question about the lance (fig. 51). Other miniatures in the First Continuation focus, like those in *Le Conte del Graal,* on knightly pastimes: for example, Gawain's combat with Guiromelant, then with Bran de Lis (fig. 50).

The Second Continuation opens and closes with miniatures of Perceval on horseback riding toward the Grail castle, as the rubrics specify, but between these two events there is little to remind us visually of his mission (figs. 52 and 55). Instead he visits the castle of Beaurepaire, where he again meets Blancheflor (fig. 53); he plays chess, a pastime well suited to knights and ladies, and he crosses the bridge of marvels on his way to the tournament at the Proud Castle (fols. 280 and 310). We never see him inside the Grail castle, and he never mends, however imperfectly, the broken sword, the act generally considered to be the climax of the Second Continuation.

Just as the Second Continuation is framed by miniatures of Perceval on horseback, Manessier's Continuation opens and closes with miniatures of Perceval telling his story to King Arthur at court (figs. 56 and 61). No other manuscript concludes with a representation of this episode, "where he recounts his adventures to King Arthur and also to the queen," as the rubric specifies. It occurs in the text before either Perceval's coronation or his religious calling, events generally considered important to the conclusion of the tale and illustrated in other manuscripts. Nor does any other manuscript begin Manessier's Continuation with such a miniature, which in fact offers a misreading—perhaps willful—of the text. Manessier's Continuation opens not with Perceval recounting his tale to King Arthur (as the extratextual rubric in our manuscript makes clear: "Ci raconte Pierchevaus au roi Artus dou graal"), but with Perceval in conversation with the Fisher King at the Grail castle. These idiosyncrasies further underscore the oral milieu of the Mons manuscript, for which additional evidence is provided by the textual redaction, which includes the so-called Short Redaction of the First Continuation, considered closer to performance than other longer, reworked versions (see *Continuations* 1947–83, I:xxxix; Torrini-Roblin 1989).

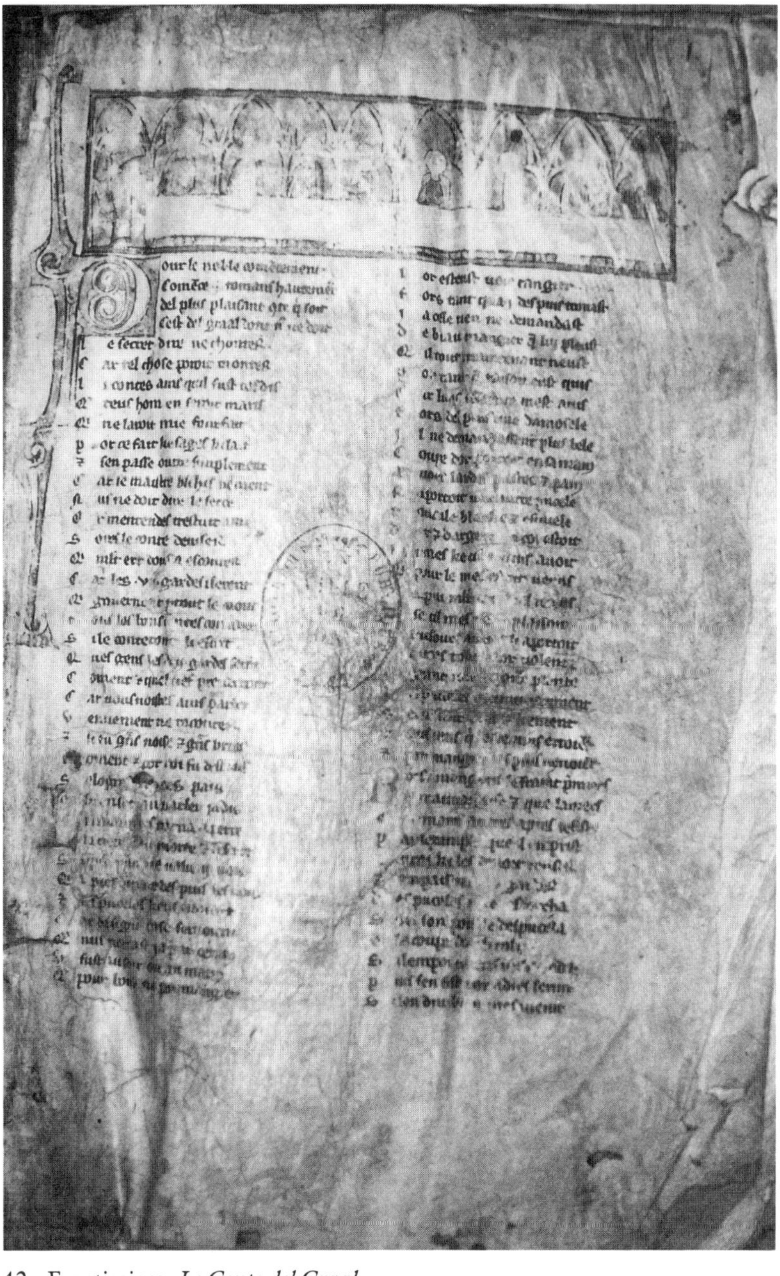

42: Frontispiece, *Le Conte del Graal*
Mons, Bibliothèque de l'Université, MS 331/206, fol. 1

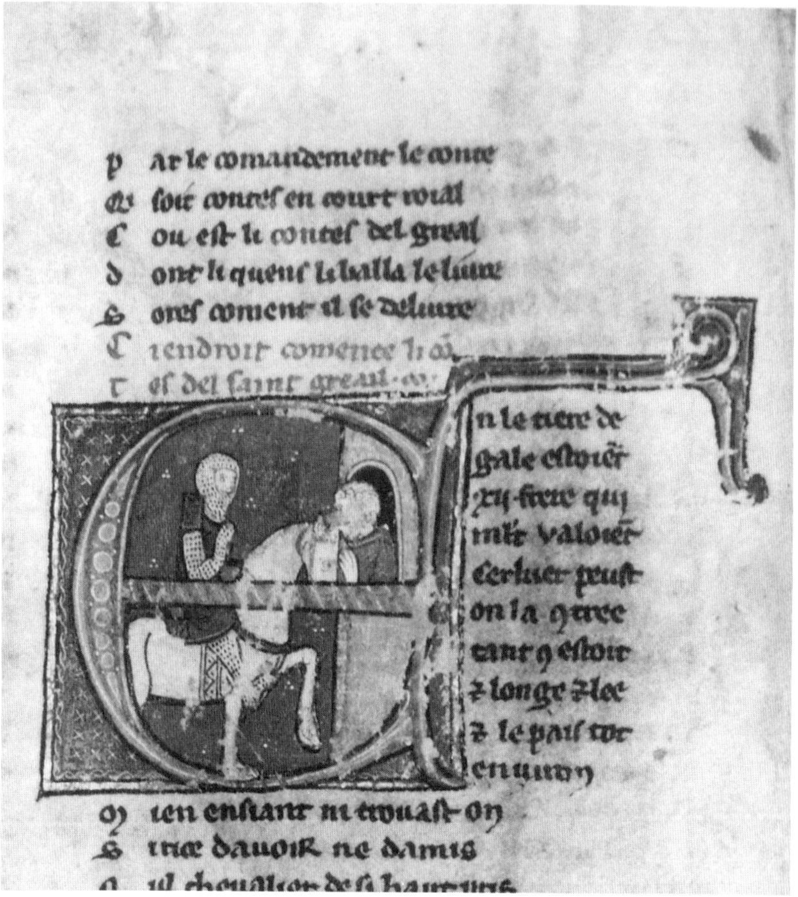

43: Bliocadran departs for a tournament, *Le Conte del Graal*
Mons, Bibliothèque de l'Université, MS 331/206, fol. 6

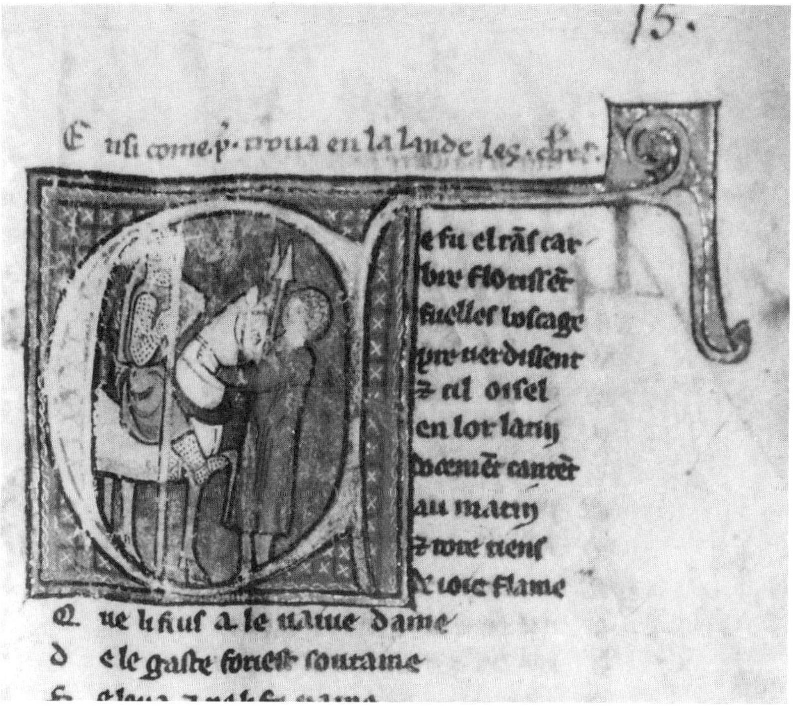

44: Perceval encounters the knights, *Le Conte del Graal*
Mons, Bibliothèque de l'Université, MS 331/206, fol. 15

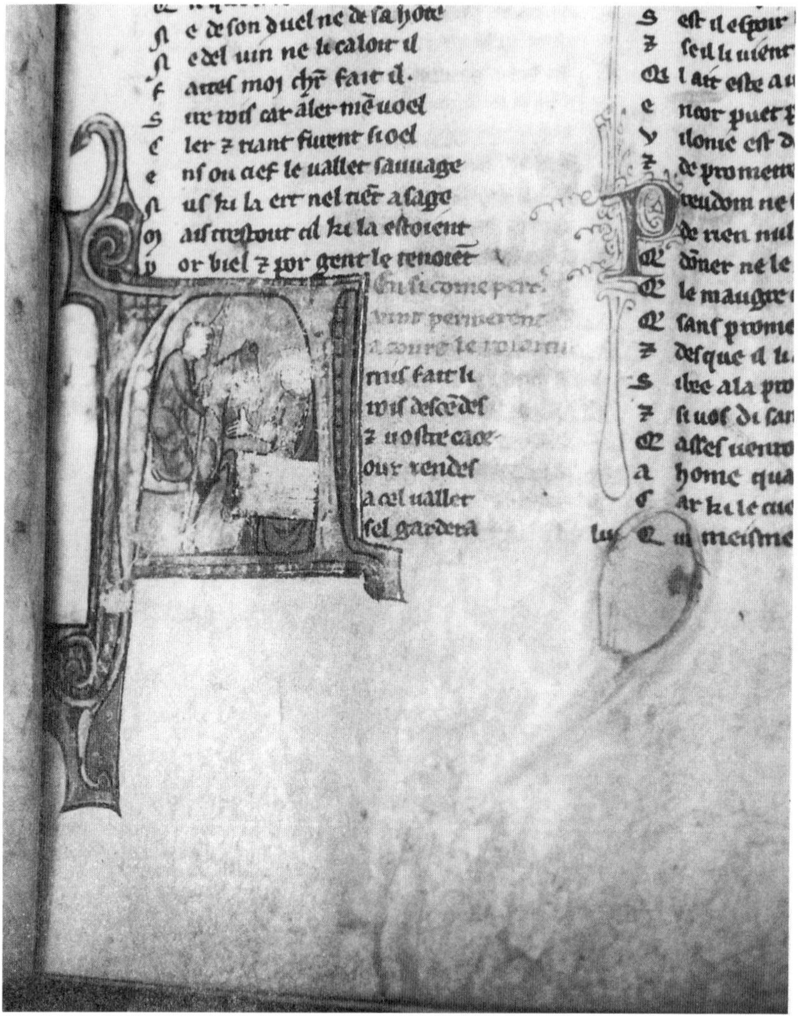

45: Perceval at King Arthur's court, *Le Conte del Graal*
Mons, Bibliothèque de l'Université, MS 331/206, fol. 25

46: Gornemant dubs Perceval, *Le Conte del Graal*
Mons, Bibliothèque de l'Université, MS 331/206, fol. 30v

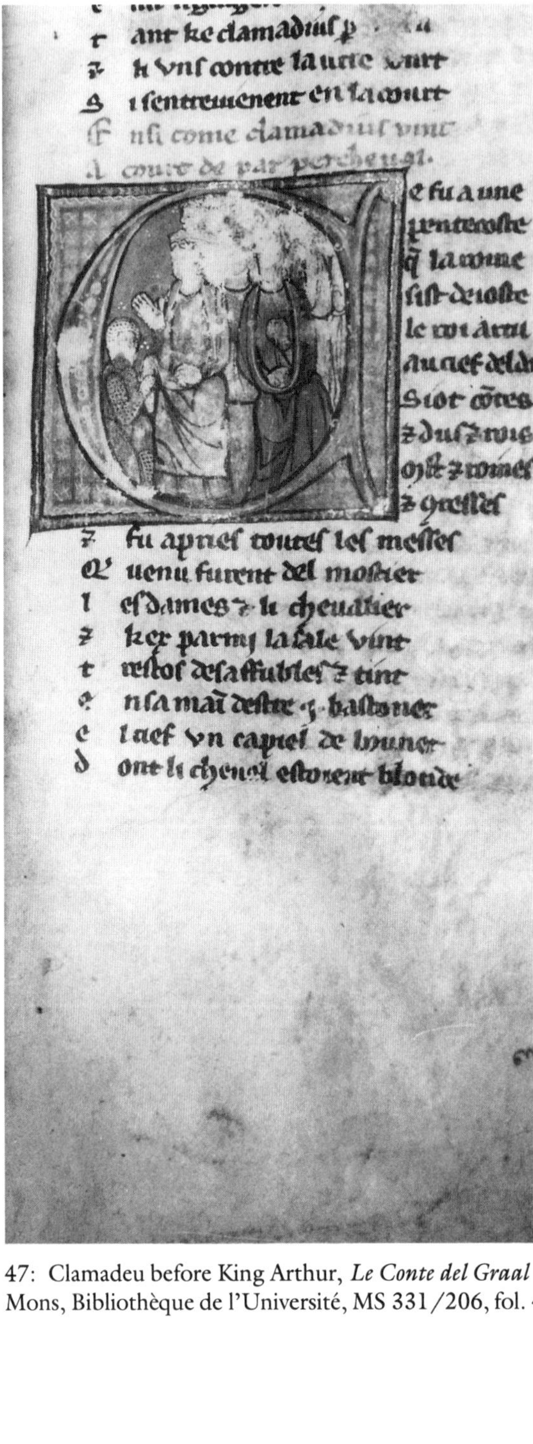

47: Clamadeu before King Arthur, *Le Conte del Graal*
Mons, Bibliothèque de l'Université, MS 331/206, fol. 45

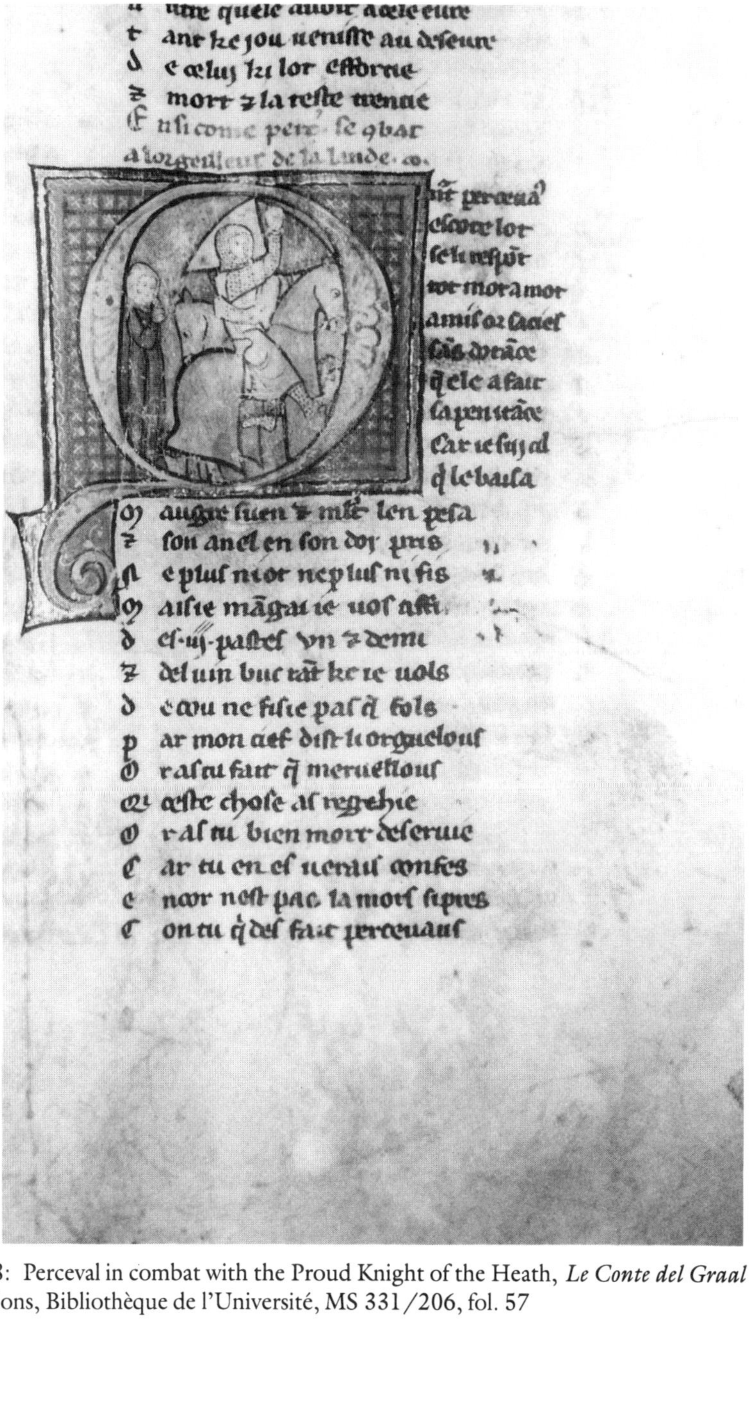

48: Perceval in combat with the Proud Knight of the Heath, *Le Conte del Graal*
Mons, Bibliothèque de l'Université, MS 331/206, fol. 57

49: Gawain and the perilous bed, *Le Conte del Graal*
Mons, Bibliothèque de l'Université, MS 331/206, fol. 103

50: Gawain battling Guiromelant, First Continuation
Mons, Bibliothèque de l'Université, MS 331/206, fol. 127

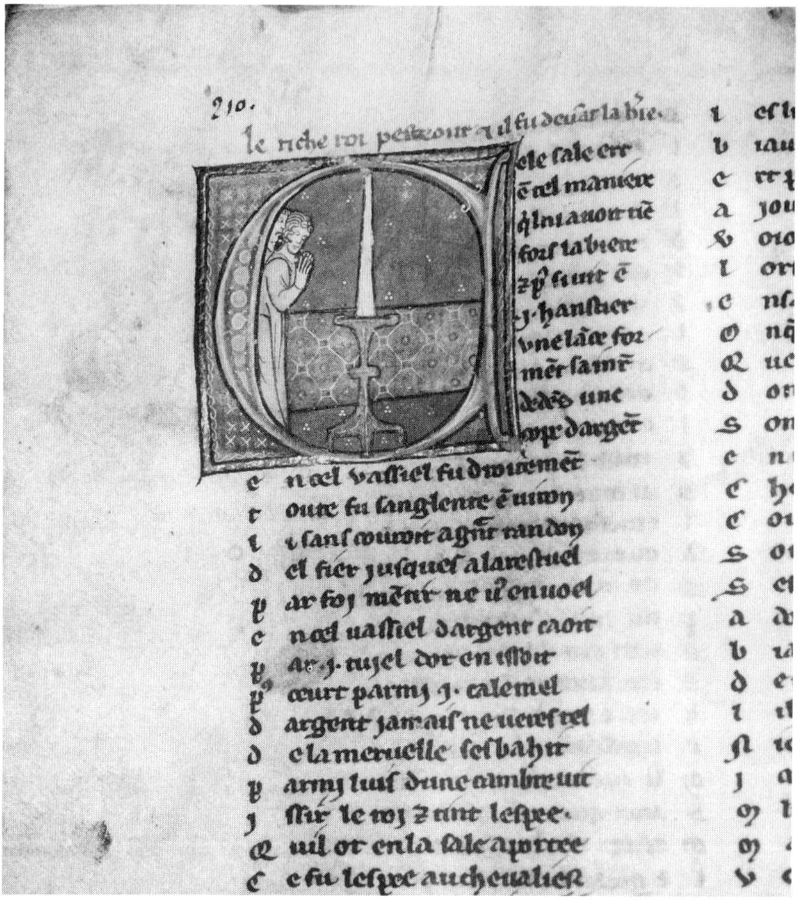

51: Gawain at the Grail castle, First Continuation
Mons, Bibliothèque de l'Université, MS 331/206, fol. 210

52: Perceval on horseback before the Grail castle, Second Continuation
Mons, Bibliothèque de l'Université, MS 311/206, fol. 229

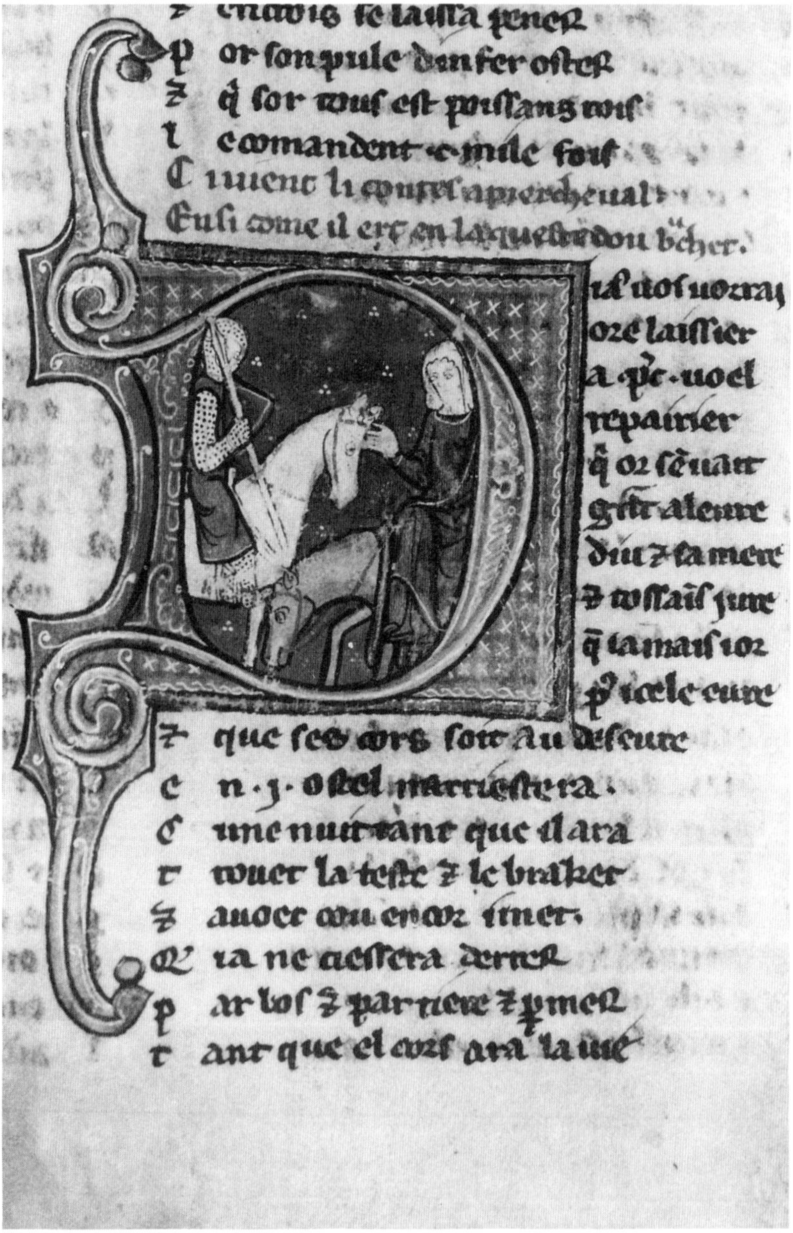

53: Perceval and Blancheflor, Second Continuation
Mons, Bibliothèque de l'Université, MS 331/206, fol. 267

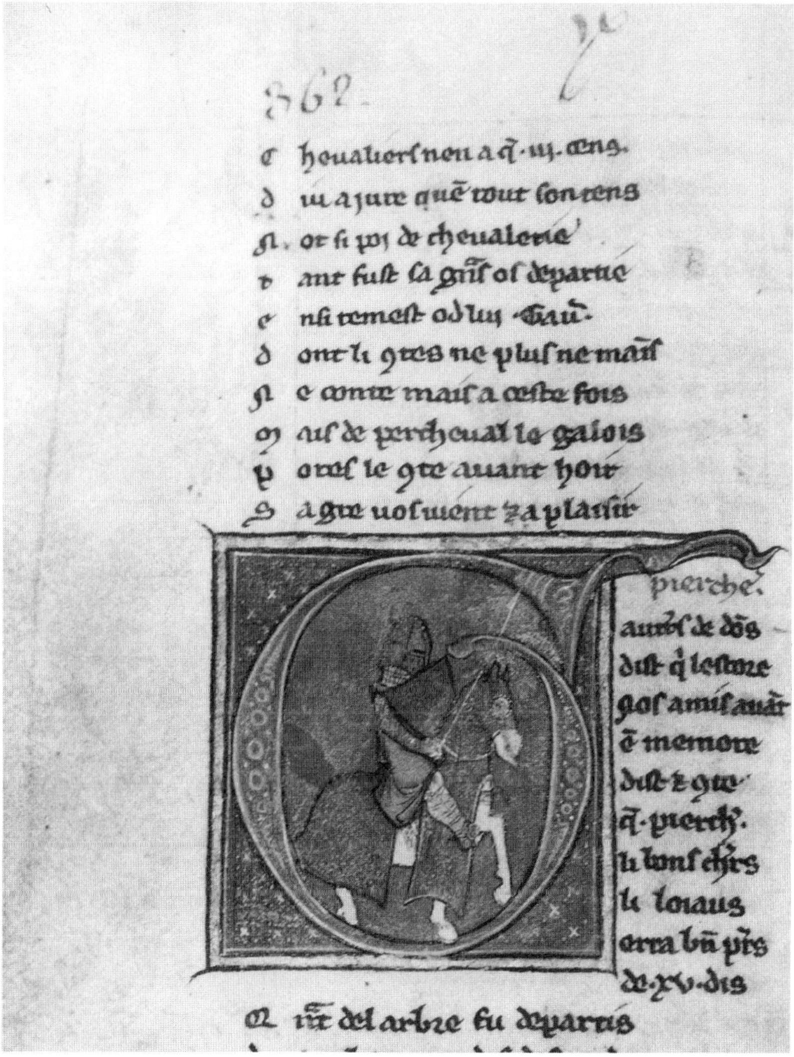

54: Perceval on horseback, Second Continuation
Mons, Bibliothèque de l'Université, MS 331/206, fol. 362

55: Perceval at the Grail castle, Second Continuation
Mons, Bibliothèque de l'Université, MS 331/206, fol. 371

56: Perceval recounts the Grail story to Arthur, Manessier's Continuation
Mons, Bibliothèque de l'Université, MS 331/206, fol. 378

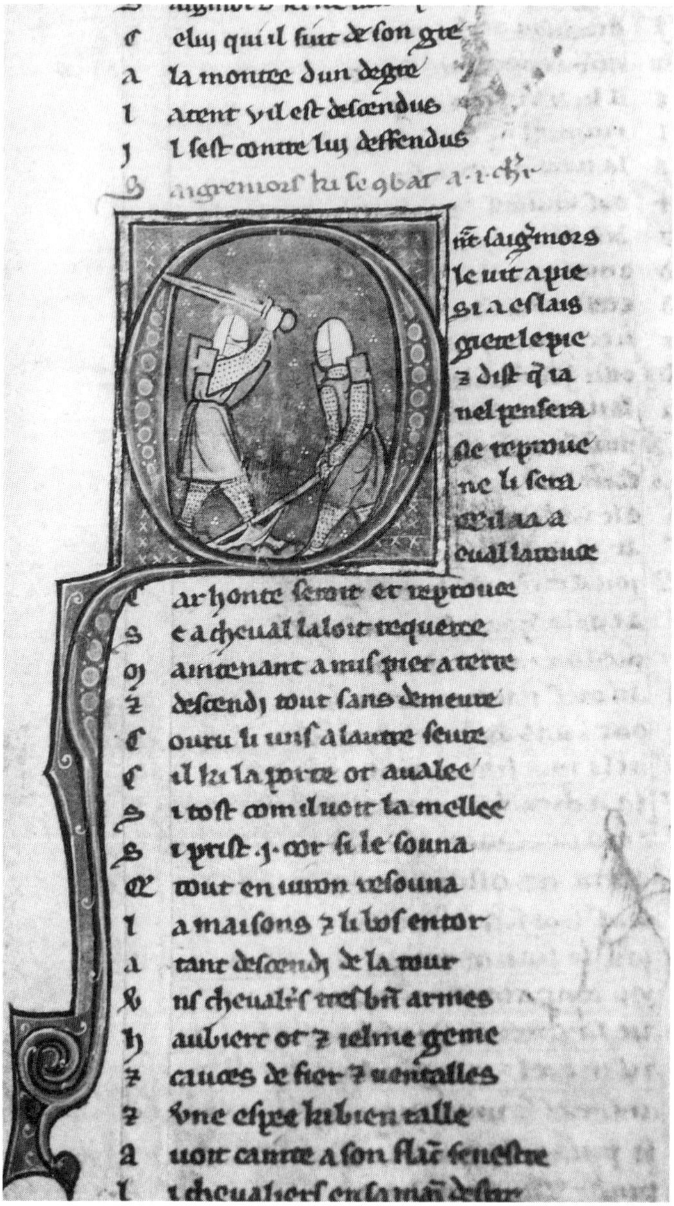

57: Saigremor combats the robber knight, Manessier's Continuation
Mons, Bibliothèque de l'Université, MS 331/206, fol. 389

58: Gawain on horseback, Manessier's Continuation
Mons, Bibliothèque de l'Université, MS 331/206, fol. 408

59: Arides brought before King Arthur, Manessier's Continuation
Mons, Bibliothèque de l'Université, MS 331/206, fol. 457

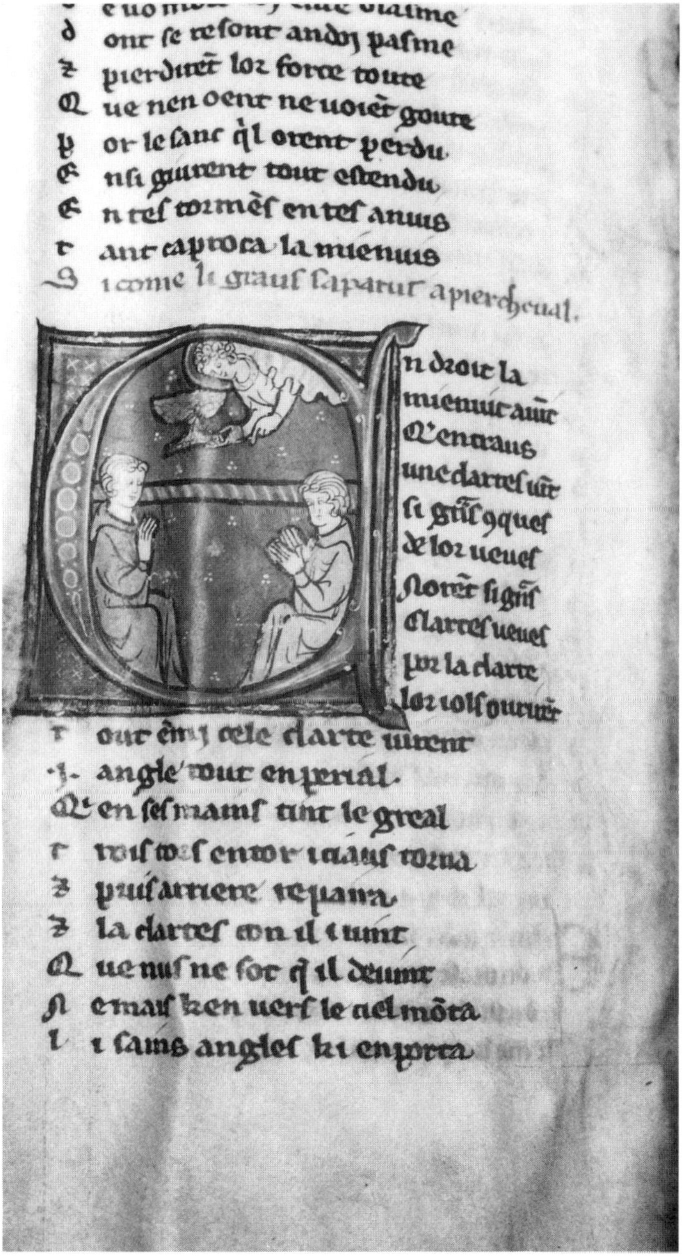

60: Perceval and Hector healed of their wounds by the Grail, Manessier's Continuation
Mons, Bibliothèque de l'Université, MS 331/206, fol. 474

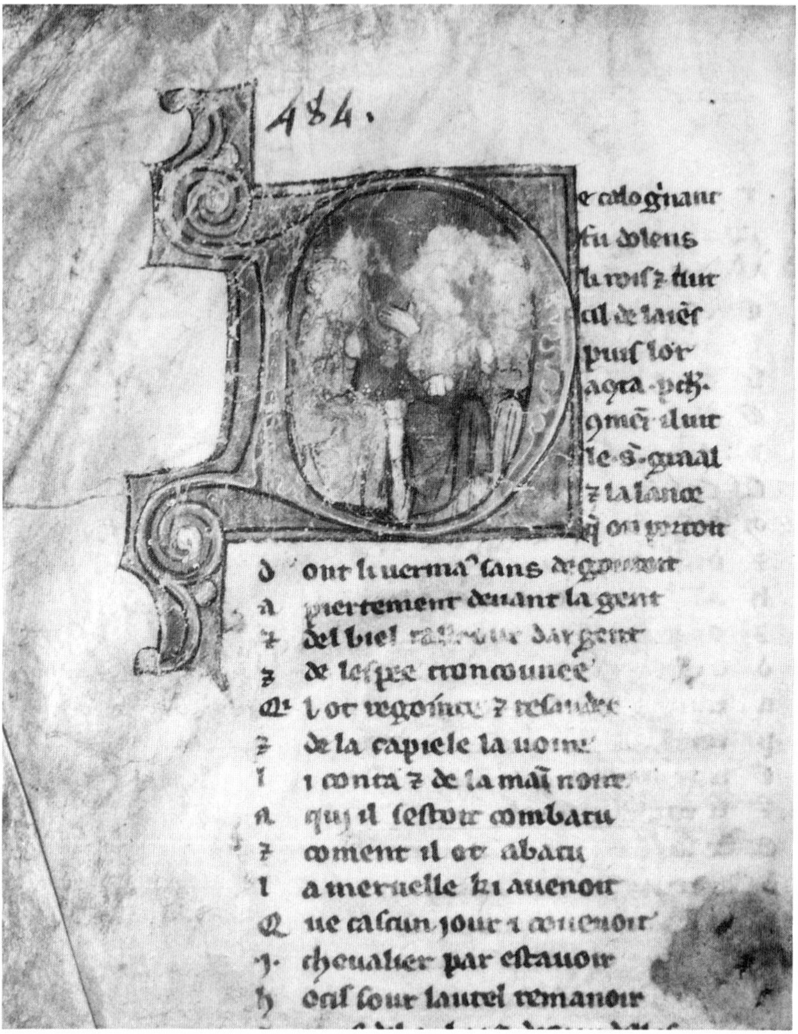

61: Perceval recounts his story to Arthur, Manessier's Continuation
Mons, Bibliothèque de l'Université, MS 331/206, fol. 484

62: Thierry of Alsace, count of Flanders, Cartulary of Marchiennes
Lille, Archives Départementales du Nord, 10 H 323, p. 118

63: Seal of Philip of Alsace, count of Flanders
Demay 1873, no. 138

64: Seal of Alix or Adelaide, widow of Henry III, duke of Lotharingia and Brabant
Demay 1873, no. 238

Between these illustrations of storytelling, little or no attention is paid to Perceval and the Grail. In one miniature near the end Perceval appears with the Grail, when his and Hector's wounds are healed by their vision of the holy vessel (fig. 60), but he never slays Partinel, the owner of the broken sword, or mends the sword, episodes in the text that enable him to cure the Fisher King, who then bequeaths his kingdom to Perceval. Instead the viewer is treated, for example, to scenes of Saigremor and the robber knight in battle (fig. 57) and of Arides, the attacker of Blancheflor's domain, defeated and brought before Arthur, as was Clamadeu in *Le Conte del Graal* (fig. 59). These miniatures continue to emphasize the theme of secular knighthood that runs through the manuscript.

Even the casual viewer of the Mons manuscript cannot help but be struck by the historiated initial of the knight on horseback, which recurs as the subject of at least one-quarter of the miniatures, including each time one of the heroes visits the Grail castle (e.g., figs. 52, 54, 55, 58). I have already discussed the possible multiple meanings of such an image, concluding that it might convey the status of the knight as a bachelor or youth and that it might also refer to the knight who returns from battle or tournament to recount his adventures at Arthur's court. It could even be argued that this stock hieratic image was adopted in many instances for the sake of simplicity, as a kind of artistic shortcut, where more complex portrayals of narrative events would have better suited the story. But I do not think this is so. I believe that the frequent depiction of the knight on horseback in the Mons manuscript was fully intentional and immediately meaningful to the viewer, who understood it in part as a painted version of a seal. As such, it served as a sign both of identification and of authority. The equestrian type in the thirteenth century refers even more specifically to a particular group of sealers, the feudal lords or seigneurs of the upper aristocracy.

That these miniature paintings are closely comparable to seals can be quickly demonstrated. In the Mons manuscript at the beginning of the Second Continuation, Perceval, portrayed as a mounted warrior, sits astride his war-horse, whose gait is captured in midstep (fig. 52). He wears spurs, metal armor, a gold tunic, and an oval helmet, and he carries a shield and lance. His horse is elaborately decked out with a caparison. This image corresponds exactly with the iconography of the equestrian seal, which, as Bedos Rezak (1982, 1986, 1988) and others have shown, began in the eleventh century with the mounted warrior holding the gonfanon, or flag lance, and by the end of the twelfth century evolved, with minor variations, to the present image of the mounted warrior bearing a shield and holding a lance. As if to affirm that the miniature, like a seal, functions as a symbol of identification, the nonnarrative rubric next to it, rare in this manuscript, reads simply "piercheval." It is also significant that no other manuscript begins the Second Continuation in this way; it typically starts with no break whatever—that is, without any illustration or decoration after the First Continuation—giving the impression of one long, continuous text.[8] Nor does any other manuscript illustrate the juncture where Wauchier, the presumed author of the Second Continuation, names himself with a nonnarrative miniature of the knight on horseback instead of a narrative scene such as Perceval and the Tree Child.

A cartulary from the Abbey of Marchiennes with historiated initials similar to those in the Mons manuscript confirms that our miniatures deliberately suggest the imprints of seals.[9] Made within the orbit of the counts of Flanders, the cartulary provides a record of documents from the founding of the monastery in the seventh century through the thirteenth century. In fact a cartulary is literally a copy of various charters; the originals would have each borne seals pertaining to the history and rights of an abbey. A twelfth-century section in this cartulary copies acts that are divided into three categories: those approved by kings and emperors, by ecclesiastics, and by feudal lords (mostly counts). Each of the acts sanctioned by lords is preceded by a historiated initial of a mounted warrior with a lance and shield, portrayed exactly as in the Mons manuscript and on seals of the period (fig. 62). One scholar (Loisne 1903, 476), struck by the similarities, even compared the miniatures of the cartulary to seals, wondering whether the latter might have served as models for them (fig. 63). Confirming that this resemblance is not accidental, the miniatures of kings and bishops in the cartulary, like those of the lords, bear similar relationships to their official emblems. As on their seals, each king or emperor and bishop is depicted in his official posture, invested with attributes of his function and authority, the scepter and the pastoral staff (for illustrations see Loisne 1903). What makes the cartulary so interesting and unusual is that its miniatures clearly authenticate the inscribed documents and offer legal guarantees of the acts they contain. For our purposes they also demonstrate that in our period the painted equestrian warrior readily recalled the wax impression of a seal.

Whereas the miniatures in the cartulary serve a quasi-legal function in what could be considered a juridical document, it is not so immediately apparent what function our miniatures, which also recall seals, serve in a courtly romance. I believe, however, that the answer lies in the conjunction of the meaning of the equestrian seal during the period and the interpretation of Perceval as seigneur presented in the manuscript. To understand the significance of the equestrian seal and the meaning it conveys in our miniatures, it is essential to trace some of the transformations in seal iconography among the aristocracy during the thirteenth century.

Before the middle of the thirteenth century, 95 percent of the extant seals represent the equestrian warrior, which was the preferred motif for seals of families of the upper aristocracy. Little by little the lesser aristocracy, the bourgeoisie, women, and civic corporations, among others, appropriated the practice of sealing, and the variety of motifs concurrently expanded to include, for example, heraldic shields, personal emblems, and edifices. For our purposes it is useful to examine the distinctions that came to exist in sealing among different groups of the aristocracy, specifically feudal lords, the "newer" nobility (such as some castellans), knights who were not lords, and squires. After about 1200 only the feudal lords seem to have willfully preserved the traditional image of the equestrian warrior. The "newer" nobility, knights, and squires normally adopted the more up-to-date image of the heraldic shield with the coat of arms of their family, thus acknowledging a dynastic lineage that the coat of arms signaled.

But paradoxically, the archaic motif of the knight on horseback endured as *the* sign of a more esteemed aristocratic family, whose senior inheritant used the equestrian figure on his seal to call attention to the historical basis of the family's importance, even if the younger brothers and sons adopted the coat of arms on their seals. At the same time, feudal ladies of the upper aristocracy, such as Countess Johanna of Flanders or Duchess Alix of Brabant, preserve the image of a horsewoman, sometimes holding a hawk, as a counterpart to the equestrian warrior (fig. 64; see Demay 1873, vol. 1, no. 145). These transformations suggest that the identity and authority of the upper aristocracy in the thirteenth century were undermined as members self-consciously sought to buttress their position in the social hierarchy.

So, to follow this line of reasoning, if our miniatures of Perceval are to be viewed partly as seals, the conclusion appears inescapable: they represent Perceval as the senior inheritant of an esteemed aristocratic family and thus set him apart from the lesser aristocracy of the period. Of course this is exactly the message I have already suggested is implied in the opening speech by Perceval's mother and made explicit in the *Bliocadran*. I suggest further that, in embedding the equestrian image in the initial *M* of Messire, the manuscript claims for the knight the term of address fitting for the upper aristocracy. Apparently in the thirteenth century the lesser nobility and even the bourgeoisie appropriated the earlier term of address *sire,* or "lord," while the upper aristocracy began, as a result, to adopt the term *messire,* or "my lord," to differentiate themselves (Foulet 1950–51, esp. 219). And in showing Blancheflor as a horsewoman in the only miniature where she appears (that is, in an image that recalls the seal of a feudal lady), the manuscript—ignoring altogether the love angle of the story—goes so far as to suggest that as an individual with the same distinguished lineage, she is well suited to Perceval (fig. 53).

CERTAIN CHARACTERISTICS OF THE SOCIOPOLITICAL SITUATION IN THIRTEENTH-CENTURY FLANDERS HELP EXPLAIN THE FEATURES I HAVE DESCRIBED IN THE MONS MANUSCRIPT. MUCH AS IN Picardy during the same period, Flanders witnessed widespread social and economic developments that threatened to undermine the status of the aristocracy (Warlop 1975–, esp. vol. 1). The growth of towns, especially those where the rich textile industry flourished, such as Ghent, Bruges, Douai, Lille, and Arras, fostered the establishment of new centers that had access to considerable money and resources. The simultaneous impoverishment of the heavily indebted aristocracy, causing many families to sell off their lands, diminished the traditional power of the seigneurial strongholds. Changes in the patterns of marriage and of knighthood contributed to the general social leveling. Many aristocrats married outside their class, sometimes sons and daughters of wealthy townsmen, which expanded the total number of nobles but diminished the "purity" of their lineage and altered the basis of their titles and wealth. Since dubbing was expensive, not all nobles continued to receive it, so many were no longer knights. And simultaneously, as knighthood came to be purchasable, like a commodity, many nonnobles became knights. By the end of the thirteenth century, then, the social lines were blurred between the classes of nobleman, knight, and bourgeois.

In these respects thirteenth-century Flanders was not much different from Picardy; but what distinguishes the two regions is the presence in Flanders of a strong class of feudal lords, the Flemish counts, who sought to turn the socioeconomic tide to their advantage (Genicot 1961). In contrast to the nobles, heirs and heiresses of this group almost never married outside their class, although members of the cadet and collateral branches did marry nobles, with the result that many noble families were related to the feudal lords, to whom they therefore owed family loyalty. The Flemish sovereigns, especially Countess Johanna (d. 1244) and then Countess Margaret (d. 1280), freed from feudal obligations large numbers of nobles and serfs during the period. This astute political gesture, in addition to fostering goodwill, enabled them to buy their lands, expanding the territorial basis of the county (Margaret even passed a law prohibiting the church from purchasing alienated fiefs). Creating at the same time a system of peers, analogous to the council that had existed under Charlemagne, the counts dispensed justice and ensured further loyalties, which were also guaranteed by their granting administrative offices for which favors were in turn owed. The overall result was, in somewhat simplified terms, that the Flemish lords effectively put in place a system of sovereignty that set them apart and, even in the face of socioeconomic conflict, preserved and increased their authority over their territories.

Efforts to establish a strong regional government in Flanders were perhaps stimulated by Flanders's more precarious relationship with the French monarchy. In the twelfth century the Flemish counts had enjoyed a privileged relationship with the French monarchs. Participating at the coronation of King Philip Augustus, Philip of Alsace even became the tutor of the young king, to whom he married his niece Isabel of Hainaut, heir to the county of Artois. The ambitious count of Flanders, however, set out to incorporate large chunks of land in northern France, advancing to within forty miles of Paris, when he was finally stopped in 1185 by the Treaty of Boves. But by the end of the century Philip Augustus had initiated an aggressive counterattack, claiming, through the rights of his marriage to Isabel, control of the county of Artois along with overlordship of the counties of Guines, Saint-Pol, and Boulogne. After a resounding victory by the French over the Flemish in the battle of Bouvines in 1214, Anonymous of Bethune declared in his *Chronique française des rois de France,* "After [Bouvines] there was no one who dared make war against the king" (1904, esp. 770).

Problems of succession then plagued Flanders for most of the thirteenth century, whereas the Capetian monarchy gained strength, especially during the reigns of Philip Augustus and Louis IX. Dying in 1190 without a male heir, Philip of Alsace was succeeded by his sister Margaret of Alsace, who died in 1195. Although she was succeeded by her eldest son, Baldwin, who was much loved in Flanders, he emigrated to Constantinople, where he disappeared in 1204 when he was captured in battle and presumed dead. Baldwin's only heirs were his two daughters, Johanna and Margaret, whose reigns were similarly beset by uncertainties over sovereign authority. Johanna's reign was threatened by the reappearance in Flanders of the so-called false Baldwin, claiming to be the rightful count, Baldwin of Constantinople, who was long thought dead. Categorically rejecting Baldwin's claims, Johanna finally had him hanged, an act that caused considerable public outrage because it was popularly believed to be patricide. Margaret fared little better. She caused a scandal by marrying at age twelve her tutor, Bouchard of Avesnes, who was also a priest and by whom she had two children, heirs to the county of Avesnes. The children were later declared illegitimate when the validity of her marriage was denied. She then married Guillaume of Dampierre, by whom she had two daughters and three sons; the eldest, Guy de Dampierre, became on her death the first male count of Flanders in nearly a century, although his succession was fiercely contested.

Given the dynastic instability of the counts of Flanders, it is no wonder they became obsessed with genealogy. Genealogical literature originates at the end of the eleventh century and flourishes primarily in the twelfth, especially in the Flemish territories of northern France.[10] In increasingly elaborate narrative and schematic grids, the great Flemish lords organized their family trees agnatically to legitimize their power and authority by justifying the hereditary basis of their titles and patrimony. Genealogical writings frequently trace the filiation of the family all the way back to the Carolingian era, thus establishing a model of kinship that links the count to the first French kings and connects his lands to a historically great regional principality. In this respect genealogical literature testifies to the acute awareness these Flemish lords had of the threat an increasingly centralized monarchy posed to regional power.

Like genealogical literature, vernacular prose historiography, inaugurated at the beginning of the thirteenth century in the same geographical milieu in Flanders, expressed a similar concern with dynastic legitimacy (see Spiegel 1983, 1986, and esp. 1993). Especially the *Pseudo-Turpin*, a chronicle with six independent versions dating between 1200 and 1230, all written for Flemish sponsors, shows a preoccupation with chivalric virtues, with the moral lessons of history, and above all with ancestral models. The use of—even insistence on—prose as the language of historical veracity has been seen as a strategy to enhance "the credibility of aristocratic ideology." In a certain sense this initiative is placed in direct opposition to verse romance, whose "failure" lies in its inability to articulate adequately the crisis of the aristocracy.

Based on the manuscript evidence, however, I would put the case of verse romance a bit differently. Judging from the large number of extant thirteenth-century manuscripts of verse romance, its continuing popularity evidently coincides closely with the initial composition and frequent transcription of prose historiography. Couldn't we therefore see the persistence of verse romance as evidence that, serving the same function, it met some of the same needs that gave rise to prose historiography, with which it was therefore compatible instead of at odds? The interpretation I have offered thus far of the Mons manuscript, directly engaged with the issue of dynastic lineage, supports this alternative point of view.

In at least one instance, in fact, there is a direct connection between Arthurian verse romance and prose genealogical literature that supports my argument. In a thirteenth-century manuscript *recueil* that contains thirty-four different works, mostly in verse, there appears a little-known genealogy of the counts of Boulogne, vassals of the counts of Flanders.[11] This genealogy, written in prose, bears all the stereotypical characteristics of such writings (Spiegel 1983): a repetitive litany of descent based primarily on agnatic consanguinity, the recovery of a glorious ancestor from the time of Charlemagne, and the filiation between the counts of Flanders and the great houses of Europe, including the ruling classes of England and Portugal. What is unique about this genealogy, however, is its inclusion at its head, as the base of the family tree, of "Arthur, king of Britain, [who] gave and ceded, freely and entirely, to the noble man, Legier, the county of Boulogne, Amiens, Terouanne, and Tournai."[12] Here the counts of Flanders and Arthur are explicitly linked, as Arthur becomes a kind of antitype for the king of France, to whom the counts of Flanders normally owe homage for their lands. In the actual manuscript the genealogy is neatly sandwiched between the antique romances, specifically the *Roman de Thebes,* the *Roman de Troie,* and the *Alexandre,* and romances by Chrétien de Troyes, specifically *Cligès* and *Erec et Enide.* Such anthologizing, coupled with the argument I have just framed, suggests that all these texts may share a stake in an antiroyal, anti-Capetian stance that in fact constitutes a search for regional origins (on the use of genealogy in compilations of Old French literature, see Huot 1987).

At first it does not seem at all surprising that the Mons manuscript expresses concerns generated in the milieu of the counts of Flanders, because *Le Conte del Graal* and its continuations were so inextricably bound up with the sponsorship of the Flemish sovereigns (Stanger 1957). Whatever its precise date, Chrétien's poem was written before 1190 expressly for

Philip of Alsace (d. 1191), the count of Flanders, whose virtues he extols in the dedication prologue. It may even be that the poem was intended as a tongue-in-cheek teaching manual for the young king, Philip Augustus, to whom Philip of Alsace became tutor between 1178 and 1181, before there was a falling-out between the count and the monarchy. Some have gone so far as to see in Perceval, the crude, unschooled knight, a veiled reference to the young Philip Augustus, while others have understood details of *Le Conte del Graal* as mirroring Philip of Alsace's own life (Frappier 1972, 51; Lejeune 1954; Adolf 1943). Then the Fourth Continuation was written about 1230 by an unknown poet who identifies himself simply as Manessier, for Countess Johanna of Flanders, whom the author extols as the "worthy and wealthy lady whom God has endowed with such wisdom, valor, goodness, courtesy and beauty, nobility, generosity and worth" (Roach, ed. [1949–83], 5:343, vv. 42643–48). Providing a kind of closure to the association of *Le Conte del Graal* and its continuations with the counts of Flanders, Manessier then goes on to remind Johanna that the story was begun "in the name of her ancestor [Philip]" but was left incomplete until "Manessier had labored to finish it."

With this background in mind, then, the suppression in the Mons manuscript of both Chrétien's dedication to Philip of Alsace and Manessier's epilogue to Johanna of Flanders seems curious, especially when the manuscript itself was produced in Flanders. At the same time, the conspicuous inclusion of a shield bearing the coat of arms of the counts of Flanders (a rampant lion, sable, on gold) is striking (fig. 49). In a miniature toward the end of *Le Conte del Graal,* Gawain, fully outfitted as a knight, stands hieratically facing the viewer, holding his shield in one hand and his sword in the other, in front of what must be the perilous bed. The unusual composition, including the imaginative depiction of a real lion standing on its hind feet (rampant) and pawing at the shield, focuses attention on the shield, whose design inexplicably deviates from Gawain's traditional heraldic charge, a double-headed eagle (Brault 1972, 40–42; Pastoureau 1980, 1983, no. 83). That this illustration is the only large-scale miniature in the Mons manuscript, which, as we have seen, is otherwise illustrated exclusively with historiated initials, further emphasizes the shield.

Just how unusual this miniature is becomes clear when it is compared with its counterparts illustrating the same subject in other illuminated versions of *Le Conte del Graal.* This miniature depicts a moment in the adventures of Gawain when, going in search of the haughty girl, he is instead ferried to a magnificent castle where the many noble inhabitants (we later learn that they include Gawain's grandmother, mother, and sister) are awaiting the perfect knight to free them from a magic spell. To rescue them the knight must withstand the perils he encounters in the room of marvels. He must first sit on the perilous bed which causes the windows to open and shoot more than seven hundred arrows into his shield. He must subsequently vanquish a mighty and ferocious lion, which rushes into the room. Needless to say, Gawain succeeds admirably, the magic spell is lifted, and he becomes lord of the castle.

This episode is illustrated, though very differently, in all but one of the illuminated manuscripts of *Le Conte del Graal.* In the Montpellier copy Gawain stands on the perilous bed, presumably awaiting the flying arrows, while two bystanders (including the ferryman who warns him about the bed?) stand behind the headboard. In a copy in Paris Gawain battles the lion, while another person holding a key locks (or unlocks?) the door on the left. In another version in Paris, in a miniature in two compartments Gawain appears twice, lying across the perilous bed, where he prepares to pull the arrows out of his shield, and again battling the lion (fig. 103). Whatever their differences, each of these versions, unlike the Mons miniature, portrays a clearly identified moment in the rich narrative.

Understood as part of a larger program of text and pictures, which I have already outlined for the Mons manuscript, what meaning does our miniature of Gawain convey? And how might it relate to the suppression of the references to Philip and Johanna in the prologue and epilogue? I shall put forward two possible interpretations, one general and one particular. In general terms the miniature offers yet another representation of a thoroughly secular hero, here clearly identified as an aristocrat—a feudal lord distinguished through his genealogy, which grants him inalienable rights to title and lands. He bears, after all, the charge of a count of Flanders. But he is not just the senior inheritant of an important territory over which he is sovereign, for he is also the perfect knight, decked out in the customary garb of knighthood and qualified by his superhuman accomplishments in the room of marvels. Coupled with the historiated initials of the knight on horseback, in which the sign of the family appears as on their seal, and with those showing the making of a knight, this miniature of Gawain (whose identity is merged with Perceval's) fulfills the promise of the mother's speech and of the *Bliocadran.* It could even be that in suppressing the prologue and epilogue the manuscript more readily embraces the entire group of feudal lords at the very top of the social hierarchy, who were so intent during this era on setting themselves apart, on appropriating power and asserting their authority individually and as a group.

A more particularized interpretation, an allusion to a specific count in Flanders, also seems likely, however. Because of the unique historical circumstances in Flanders during this period, to which I believe the manuscript makes explicit reference, there are two possibilities: to Guy de Dampierre, count of Flanders, or to Jean II d'Avesnes, count of Hainaut, who both bore the same shield, which signified their competing claims to the county of Flanders. I believe the shield is that of Jean II d'Avesnes, grandson of Countess Margaret of Flanders and heir to the county of Flanders through his father, Jean, the eldest son of Margaret of Flanders by her first marriage. To understand how the complex issues of succession in Flanders take visual form in the Mons manuscript, where they came to be pictured in heraldic terms, we must review the stormy history of succession during Margaret's reign.

During Margaret's lifetime (when she became countess in 1244, she was already widowed) sons from both marriages put forward claims to Flanders (see Vandermaeser 1980). Although one of the Margaret's first political moves was to go to Paris to render homage for Flanders to King Louis IX in favor of Guy de Dampierre, who was the eldest son from her second marriage, the illegitimate sons of her first marriage, especially Jean I d'Avesnes, nonetheless claimed all the lands of Flanders through fealty to the empire. Troops fighting under the banner of the countess engaged in battle against the emperor, who supported his brother-in-law, Jean I d'Avesnes, and in 1251 Margaret's sons Guy and Jean de Dampierre were taken captive. The conflict was only partially resolved in 1256, when under the terms of the Treaty of Péronne, signed by Louis IX, the county of Hainaut was alienated from Flanders and passed, on the death of Margaret, to the Avesnes branch, first to Jean I d'Avesnes, who died in 1257, and then to his eldest son, Jean II d'Avesnes, who died in 1304.

Neither Guy de Dampierre nor Jean d'Avesnes accepted the terms of the treaty, however; each claimed sovereignty over the entire lands of Flanders, so-called French Flanders and Imperial Flanders (Hainaut), a contest that intensified when Margaret died in 1280. From the time of the signing of the Treaty of Péronne, the arms of Hainaut had already, in fact, been altered from three chevrons to the rampant lion of Flanders to signify the claim of the Avesnes branch of the family. Then in 1280, in an act that singularly demonstrates the use of genealogy as a means of manipulating collective memory, Jean II d'Avesnes, to affirm his rights as count of Flanders, exhumed his father's corpse, which he paraded from town to town throughout the territories. He had a new funeral monument constructed, with sculpted figures of his father and mother, each displaying their armorial shields (a rampant lion, sable, on gold, for his father), which he set up in the middle of the choir of the Dominican church in Valenciennes. In 1279, when Margaret abdicated in favor of her son Guy—an act reminiscent of the *Bliocadran,* where Perceval's mother has the nobility pledge their loyalty to her son—Guy de Dampierre received homage from all the towns in Flanders. In 1289 an uneasy peace finally appears to have been concluded, and Jean II d'Avesnes went on to inherit the counties of Holland, Zeeland, and Luxembourg. When his title passed to his son in 1304, three lions, one for each of his new counties, joined the lion of Hainaut-Flanders on the shield.

If we understand Jean II d'Avesnes as the specific recipient of the Mons manuscript, then both the unusual focus on the heraldry of Flanders, to which he pretends through fealty to the empire, and the suppression of the references to other counts of Flanders, who owe their fealty to France, in the prologue and epilogue make more sense. As *the* senior inheritant of the illustrious counts of Flanders and as *the* perfect knight, Jean II d'Avesnes represents the renewed hopes of the counts of Flanders, weakened from within by vast socioeconomic change as well as by a contest over succession, and menaced from without by the strong French monarchy. Only a great lord who is a perfect knight—modeled after Perceval and Gawain—can save them. (The execution of the manuscript in a town neighboring Mons, proposed based on unusual linguistic features of the text [noted by Thompson in *Elucidation* 1931, 26–27], also points to a member of the Avesnes family, whose feudal domain was just south of Mons in Avesnes near Valenciennes.)

Consistent with the dynastic message of the manuscript, which puts forward Perceval's destiny as a great feudal lord as a kind of allegory for Jean's social mobility, the prevalence of imagery derived from seals acquires further significance. Descended on his father's side from the lesser nobility, in one sense Jean's adoption of the equestrian form of seal underscores his rise in rank. But in a more important sense the book, like a legal document, itself becomes a seal, a *signa*. Registering the legitimacy of Jean's claim by visual inscription while simultaneously echoing the oral act of conveyance, the manuscript functions as a symbolic object. In this context the insistence on orality in its historiated initials also reminds us that it was written and used in a transitional milieu where the discourses of speaking and writing were still in flux—recalling, in the words of John of Salisbury, that "letters are shapes indicating voices . . . they speak voicelessly the utterances of the absent."[13]

CHAPTER FOUR

THE KNIGHT
Li Combateor

For [Erec] saw a wondrous thing, which might arouse fear in the bravest warrior of all whom we know, be it Thiebaut the Esclavon, or Ospinel, or Fernagu.

Chrétien de Troyes, *Erec et Enide*[1]

CHRÉTIEN'S EARLIEST KNOWN ROMANCE, *EREC ET ENIDE*, CONSIDERED BY MANY TO BE THE "FIRST ARTHURIAN ROMANCE," TELLS OF THE LOVE MATCH BETWEEN EREC, A DISTINGUISHED KNIGHT at Arthur's court and heir to the kingdom of King Lac, and Enide, a vavasor's beautiful daughter. Most of the extended critical debate on the romance focuses on what the evolving relationship between Erec and Enide as a couple conveys about ideals of love in chivalric society.[2] For such critics the story moves from the winning of Enide and her introduction at Arthur's court in the first section to her testing in a series of adventures in the second, to the resolution of the newly defined relationship in the third section, which ends with the triumphal coronation of Erec and Enide. Simply put, the story mediates between a narcissistic view of love, what we could call romantic love, and a communal view in which love recognizes and serves the needs of society at large. I suggest, however, that *Erec et Enide* can be read quite differently. In this analysis I understand it as a story chiefly about the knight as an accomplished warrior or *combateor.*

My rereading of *Erec et Enide* as a story about the martial prowess of the knight grows out of my analysis of an illuminated manuscript of *Erec et Enide* (Paris, Bibliothèque Nationale, MS fr. 24403).[3] The Paris manuscript, which is the only extant illuminated manuscript of this romance,[4] includes *Erec et Enide* sandwiched between two epic poems or chansons de geste. The first chanson de geste is the anonymous *Garin de Monglane,* written in the beginning of the thirteenth century, and the second is the *Chevalerie d'Ogier le Danois,* written by the minstrel Raimbert de Paris about 1200. The dialect of the texts and the style of the illustrations place the Paris manuscript securely in Picardy, perhaps in the region of Arras, about 1300 or slightly earlier.[5] The manuscript is of special interest in part because it is so richly illustrated, including five miniatures for *Garin de Monglane,* three for *Erec et Enide,* and twelve for *Ogier le Danois.* Unfortunately, the identity of the original owner remains unknown.

I believe the particular combination of texts in the Paris manuscript, coupled with the special character of the picture cycle, is purposeful.[6] It is striking that, among the seven extant manuscripts of *Erec et Enide,* this is the only one that is joined with epics, especially since it is extremely rare to find any of Chretien's romances anthologized with chansons de geste.[7] These observations lead me to postulate that *Erec et Enide* was most likely read in thirteenth-century Picardy, at least in the Paris manuscript, as in some way compatible with the chansons de geste. I will argue that *Erec et Enide* became a vehicle for the very idealization of the knight's excellence at arms, like the valiant heroes of the chansons de geste, at a time when the role of knights as warriors was in considerable flux. Changes in the practices of warfare in Picardy, such as the appearance of mercenaries and the rise of the infantry, threatened the once privileged status of the equestrian warrior knight. I also suggest that, read with the epics, which narrate an uneasy, though idealized, relationship between hero and sovereign, *Erec et Enide* alludes to a precarious relationship between the Picard knights and the French kings just when the autonomy of provincial feudal society was being undermined by the strong Capetian monarchy. In the end such an analysis breaks down the common distinctions between the genres of epic and romance. In the Paris manuscript the two genres, generally considered to reflect the different needs of oral and literate cultures, harmoniously coexist in the transitional milieu I have already characterized.

THE RICHNESS OF THE NARRATIVE IN *EREC ET ENIDE* NATURALLY PRESENTED MYRIAD POSSIBILITIES TO THE ILLUMINATOR, WHO INCLUDED ONLY THREE MINIATURES FOR THIS STORY IN THE PARIS manuscript. Although it might be said that the cycle is too sparse to permit a probing analysis, my experience is that pictorial subjects were nearly always chosen carefully instead of randomly and that omissions count for as much as inclusions in reading the pictures with their texts in order to understand the message conveyed. It is instructive, therefore, to consider carefully what the miniaturist of the Paris manuscript did and did not illustrate.

Ignoring certain key episodes in the story, the cycle appears to privilege apparently minor episodes. At the opening of the text of *Erec et Enide,* a miniature of one episode from the first section of the romance is included, the hunt of the white stag, which takes place at King Arthur's court on Easter Day (fig. 65). According to ancient custom, the knight who kills the stag will kiss the fairest maiden of the court. The manuscript then skips over the other episodes from the first section of the romance, such as Erec's visit to the vavasor, where he first meets Enide; the sparrowhawk contest, where Erec challenges an evil knight and wins Enide; the introduction of Enide at Arthur's court; and Arthur's bestowal of the kiss on Enide, "the most charming and beautiful to be found." Nor are there any miniatures for the beginning of the second section of the romance. This section narrates the wedding, the period of marital bliss, and the critical confrontation between the lovers when Enide calls Erec's attention to the widespread gossip that her husband is so consumed by love and abandoned to its pleasures that he has neglected his military commitments, showing that he "no longer wish[es] to bear arms." Following the unhappy confrontation between the loving couple, two miniatures of episodes from the second section illustrate subsequent events during which Erec displays his skills as a combatant: his combat in the forest with three robbers and his battle there with two giants to free Cadoc de Cabruel (figs. 66 and 67). Although Erec and Enide are eventually reconciled as lovers after a series of such trials, there is no miniature showing their reconciliation. Nor are there any miniatures whatever of events in the third section of the romance, such as the Joy of the Court, where Erec fights a mighty knight named Mabonagrain, or the concluding coronation of Erec and Enide.

Read as putting forward an interpretation of the text, the cycle of miniatures in the Paris manuscript presents *Erec et Enide* as a swift adventure that takes place exclusively in the forest and features knights as warriors. This interpretation depends especially on the two miniatures illustrating the quest in the second section of the romance. In the first miniature, the full costume and surging posture of Erec, decked out as a knight on a caparisoned horse. convey well the sense of the text, which describes Erec as rushing at a robber, whom he "attacks . . . with a stout heart" and handily defeats. The second miniature likewise emphasizes Erec's success in combat. It vividly depicts the moment when he "strikes the foremost of them through the eye so deep into the brain that blood and brains spurt out at the back of his neck." Enide makes one cameo appearance; otherwise women are entirely absent. In the first of the two miniatures, clasping her breast to indicate that she "saw the robbers, and was seized with great fear"—the words next to the miniature of Erec battling three robbers—she appears just behind Erec.

But Enide plays a far more active role in the text of the quest, which concentrates not only on Erec's rehabilitation as a knight through his success at combat, but on a resolution of the couple's relationship. At the outset of the quest Erec, believing that Enide has dishonored him through her outspoken critique, orders her to remain silent whatever the consequences. Yet each time Erec comes upon a perilous situation, to which he appears oblivious—such as the encounters with the robbers and giants pictured in the miniatures—Enide, ignoring his command to silence, speaks out to alert him to the lurking danger. Still outraged, Erec berates her for breaking her silence and thinks nothing of leaving her in dangerous circumstances while he fights, an idea in the text that is implied in the miniatures by Enide's absence and by the depiction of her fear. But what is expressed nowhere in the miniatures is the idea that, in helping Erec to succeed at combat, Enide eventually also restores his confidence in her love for him. Entirely ignoring the love angle of the quest by their marginalization of Enide, these two miniatures thus rewrite the romance to focus exclusively on Erec's military achievements. Especially in the first miniature, where Enide stands behind Erec and watches, she becomes, like the reader, nothing more than a spectator who is impressed with Erec's prowess as a knight.

Depicting the hunt of the white stag, the opening miniature in *Erec et Enide* initially seemed to me somewhat at odds with the others in the cycle, for it does not focus on Erec's prowess (he does not even attend the hunt), nor does it adopt any of the subjects conventionally found in openings for Chrétien's romances. His other works begin with miniatures of the knight on horseback or of diversions at the court, both suggesting the theme of recounting the story. The images of the knight on horseback or the telling of the story at court would have been appropriate for *Erec et Enide,* since it opens, like *Le Chevalier au lion* and *Le Chevalier de la charrette,* with a gathering at court (the hunt does not begin until v. 67). However, I believe the miniature of the hunt of the white stag presents, along with the others just discussed, a consistent view of adventure, for it valorizes the forest where the subsequent combats during the quest also take place. In fact, pictorially all the action in *Erec et Enide* takes place in the forest—a locus for spontaneous or haphazard adventure (a characteristic of epic)—instead of at the court, where the ideals of chivalric society are preserved in courtly love and ritualized adventure (as in romance). Even the formal composition of the miniature launches the action of the story in the forest, in part through the momentum of the riders, the stag, and the dog. In subject and composition this miniature thus nicely sets up Erec's adventures in the second part of the romance. By situating the locus for adventure in the forest, it simultaneously offers a smooth transition from the military adventures of Garin de Montglane that precede those of Erec.

My rereading of the text and pictures in the Paris manuscript of *Erec et Enide* prompts a rereading of the text of the Joy of the Court episode at the end of the tale as it relates to the rest of the story. For the reader already familiar with the miniatures that precede it, this episode may be understood as less about the power of love than about excellence at arms (Sturm-Madox 1982; Niemeyer 1969). The Joy of the Court adventure involves Erec in combat, this time with a formidable knight named Mabonagrain. Coming upon a beautiful, abundant garden, Erec sees "a wondrous thing," a row of sharpened stakes on which are impaled the heads of knights wearing helmets, except for the last one, "where as yet there is nothing but a horn." When he learns that the last stake awaits his head, Erec, confident of his newly regained military skill, boasts that he is as brave a warrior as Thiebaut the Esclavon, Ospinel, and Fernagu, three heroes from epic. Needless to say, Erec defeats Mabonagrain, who subsequently reveals to him that he has been imprisoned in the garden because of a vow he made as a youth to his lover ("a maiden of comely body and lovely face").

Though their skills are closely matched, Erec and Mabonagrain stand in sharp contrast as warriors. Mabonagrain's military aptitude finds its expression only in ritualized combat, since he is confined with his lover to an enchanted garden. Erec's skill as a warrior, however, has been tried in a setting outside the court, in the forest fraught with unpredictable dangers, and unlike Mabonagrain he has demonstrated that his lover need not impede his military performance. In a curious turnabout, this episode casts Erec as a brave warrior from epic and Mabonagrain as a fickle hero from courtly romance. Erec even compares himself to historical heroes from chansons de geste, whereas Mabonagrain's lover is compared to Lavinia, the courtly heroine from the *Aeneid*. This reference to epic within the romance form cannot be accidental, for it is rare in Chrétien's works. It suggests that even for Chrétien there may be a reading of *Erec et Enide* in which one dimension of Erec's character is that of epic hero. Reread with the two miniatures of combat that it fulfills, the Joy of the Court episode, coming after the miniatures, provides an especially effective bridge from the epic of Garin de Montglane that precedes it to the epic of Ogier le Danois that follows.

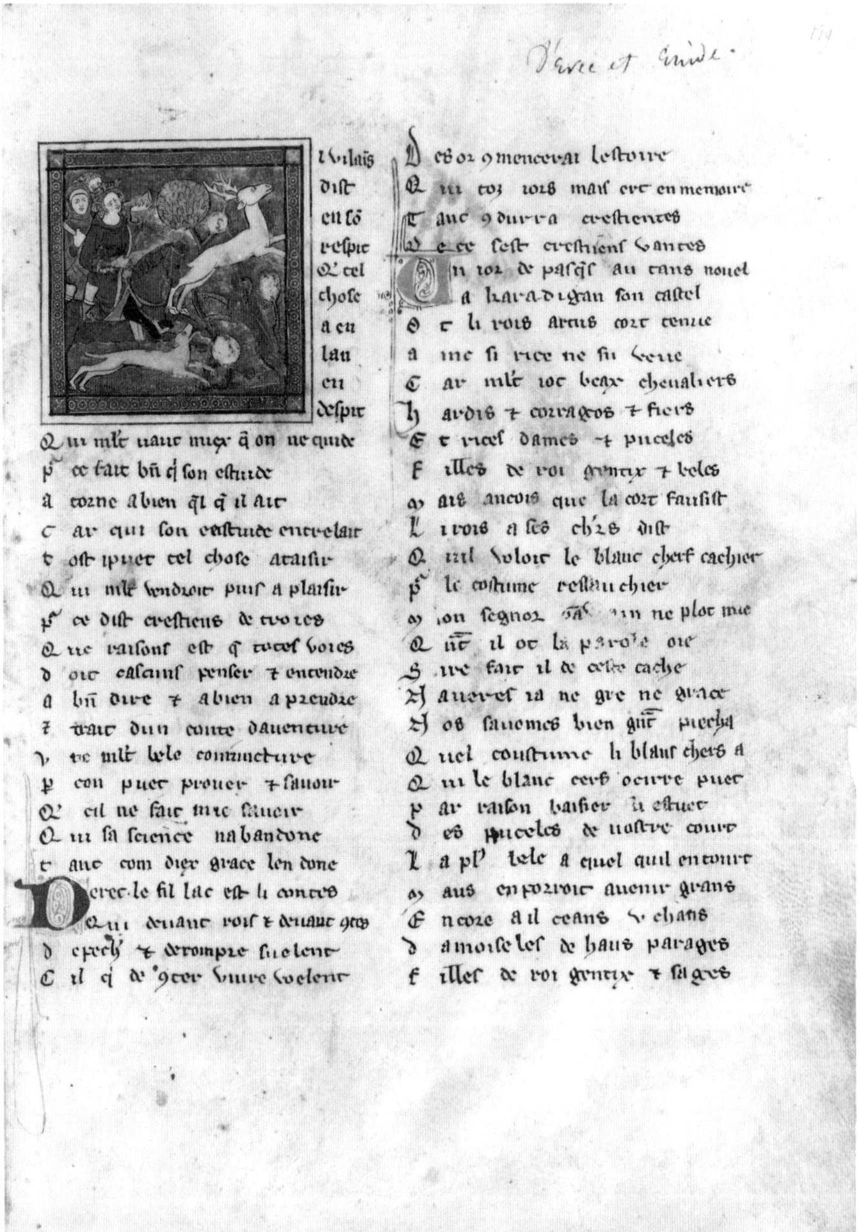

65: Hunt of the white stag, *Erec et Enide*
Paris, Bibliothèque Nationale, MS 24403, fol. 119

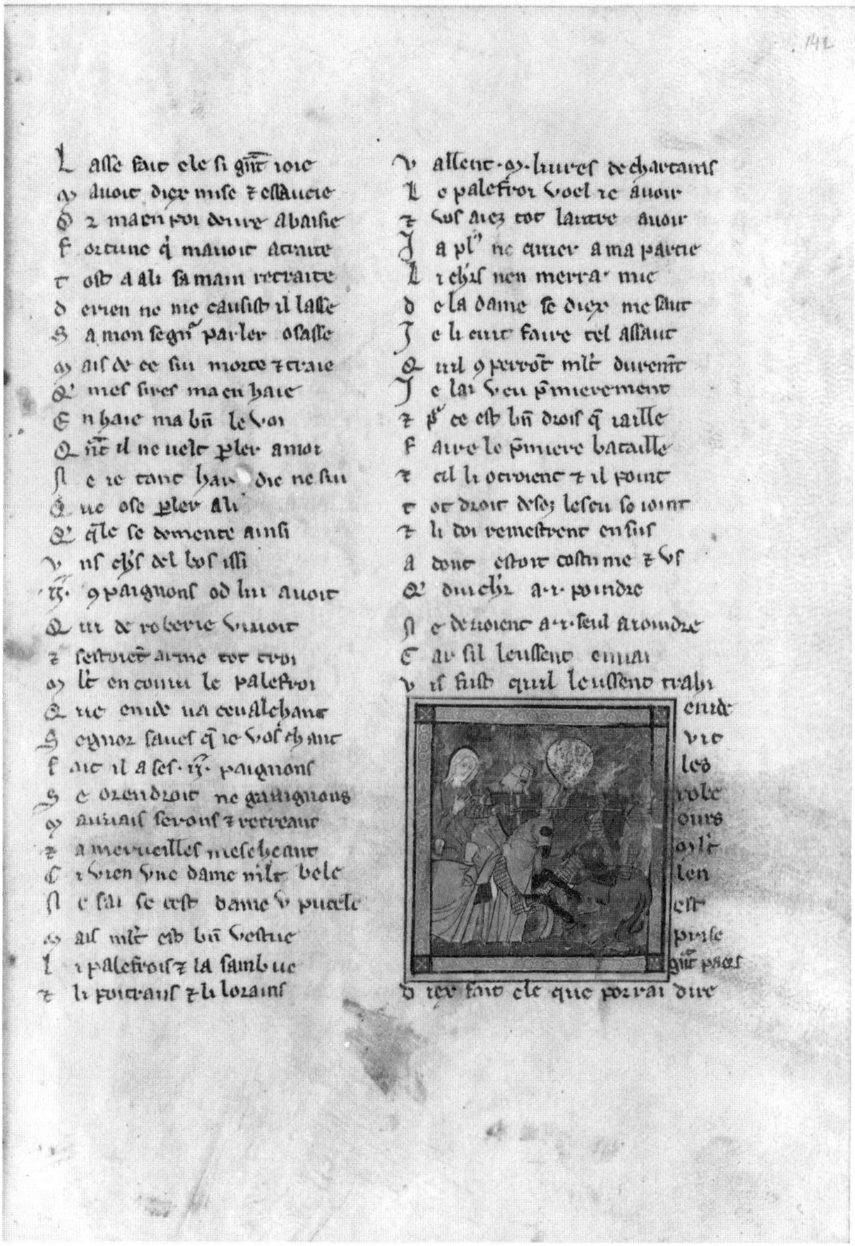

66: Erec defends Enide from three robbers, *Erec et Enide*
Paris, Bibliothèque Nationale, MS 24403, fol. 140v

67: Erec battles the giants, *Erec et Enide*
Paris, Bibliothèque Nationale, MS 24403, fol. 155

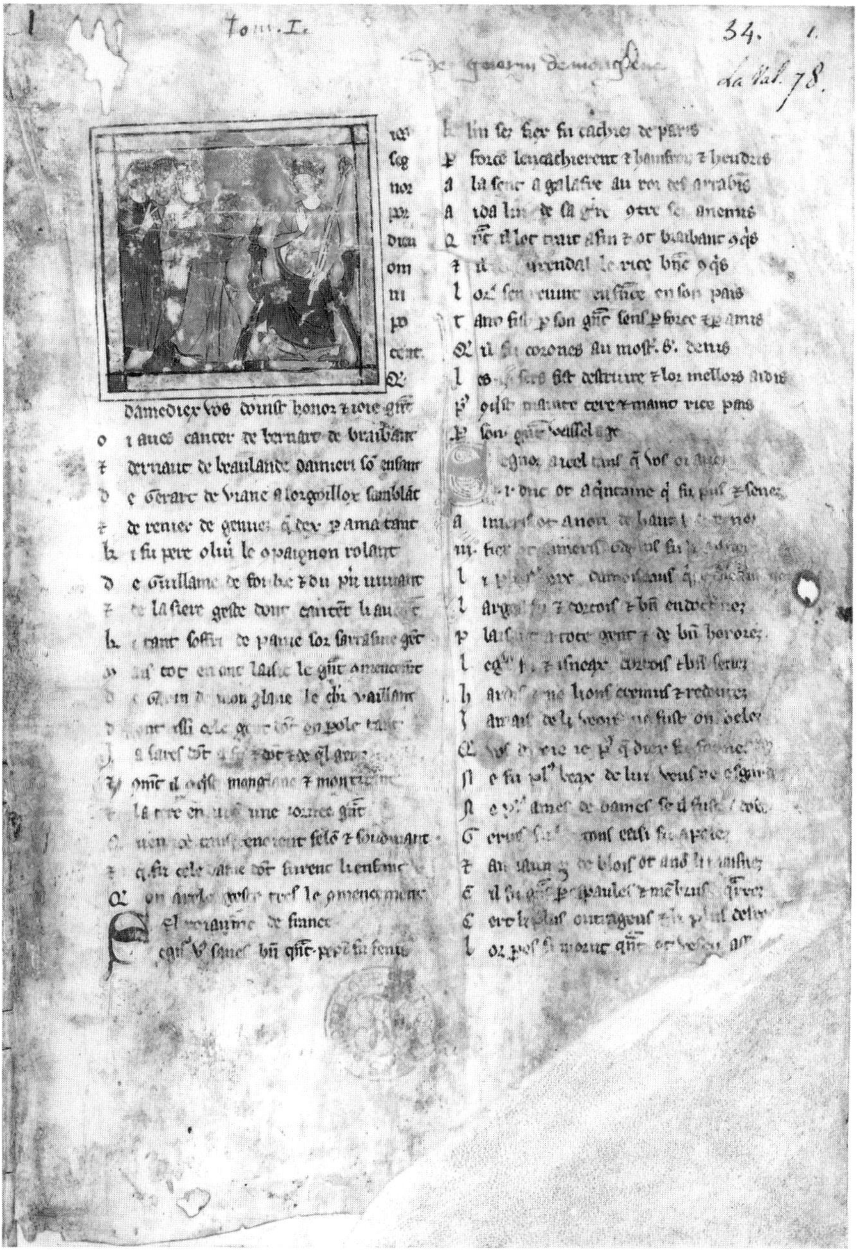

68: Garin and his brothers before Charlemagne, *Garin de Montglane*
Paris, Bibliothèque Nationale, MS 24403, fol. 1

69: Mabille on horseback with two knights, *Garin de Montglane*
Paris, Bibliothèque Nationale, MS 24403, fol. 19v

70: Robastre aids Garin in battle against Gaufroi, *Garin de Montglane*
Paris, Bibliothèque Nationale, MS 24403, fol. 47

71: Garin and Mabille in the forest with Perdigon, *Garin de Montglane*
Paris, Bibliothèque Nationale, MS 24403, fol. 64

72: Battle between Garin and Gaufroi, *Garin de Montglane*
Paris, Bibliothèque Nationale, MS 24403, fol. 90

73: Ogier and Caraheu depart for the island in preparation for battle, *Ogier le Danois*
Paris, Bibliothèque Nationale, MS 24403, fol. 188v

74: Game of chess between Baudouinet and Charlot, *Ogier le Danois*
Paris, Bibliothèque Nationale, MS 24403, fol. 199v

75: Ogier has Guy made a chevalier, *Ogier le Danois*
Paris, Bibliothèque Nationale, MS 24403, fol. 231v

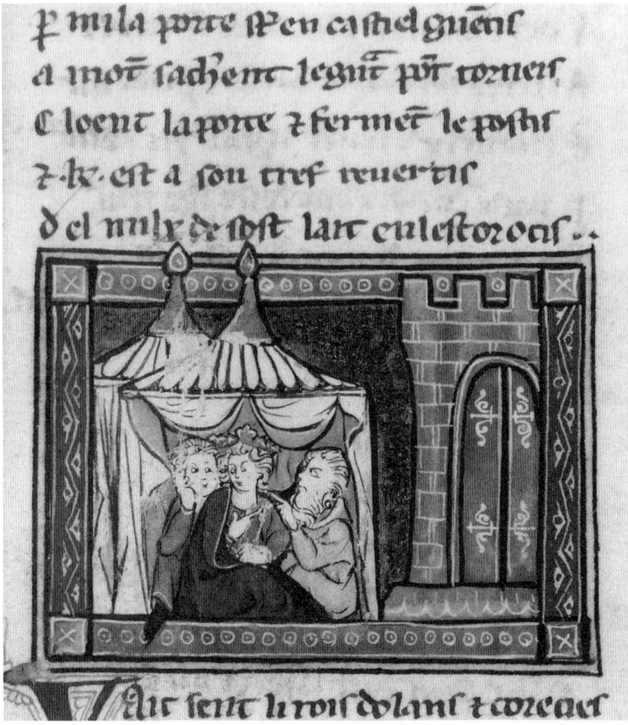

76: Ogier's encampment outside the walls, *Ogier le Danois*
Paris, Bibliothèque Nationale, MS 24403, fol. 234

77. Battle between the Lombards and the French, *Ogier le Danois*
Paris, Bibliothèque Nationale, MS 24403, fol. 239

78: Wooden dummies at Castelfort, *Ogier le Danois*
Paris, Bibliothèque Nationale, MS 24403, fol. 243v

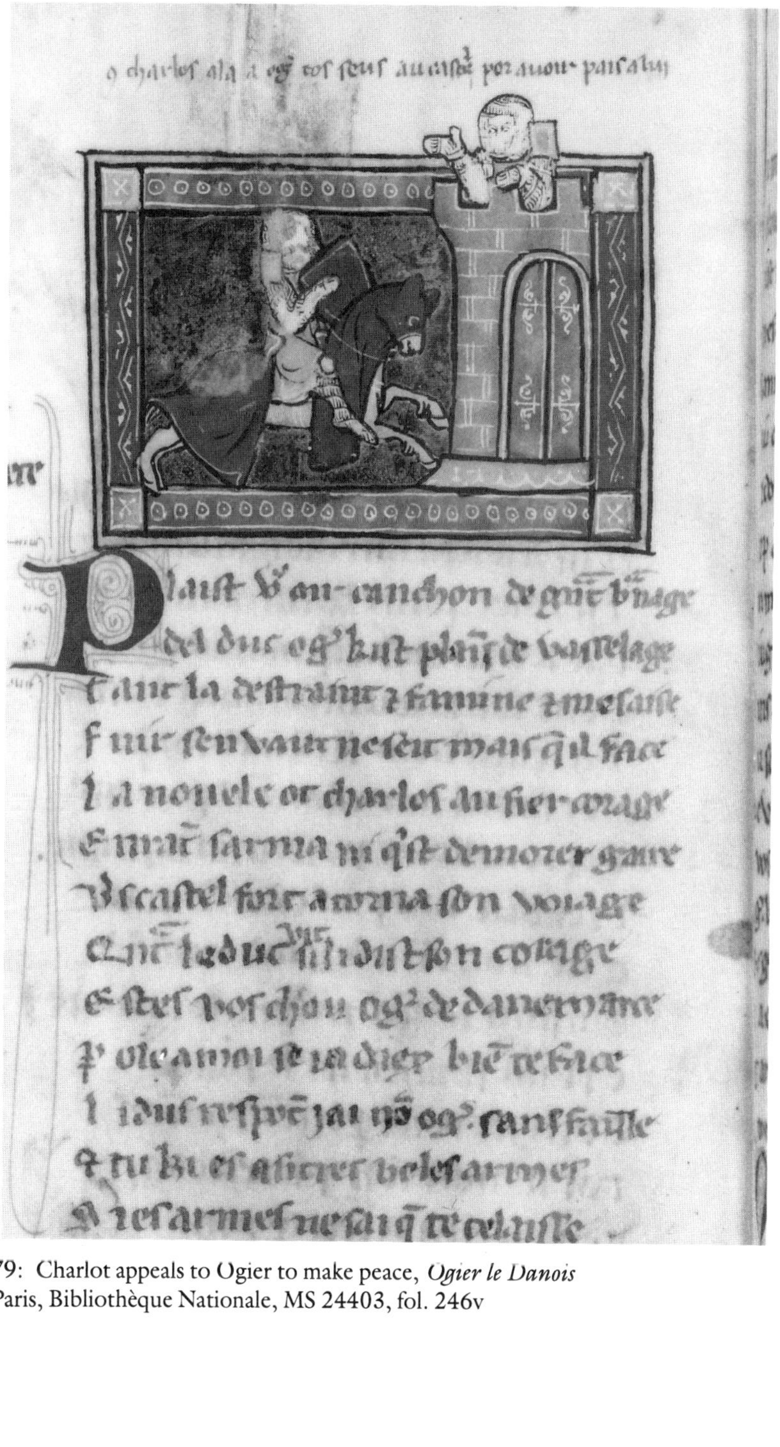

79: Charlot appeals to Ogier to make peace, *Ogier le Danois*
Paris, Bibliothèque Nationale, MS 24403, fol. 246v

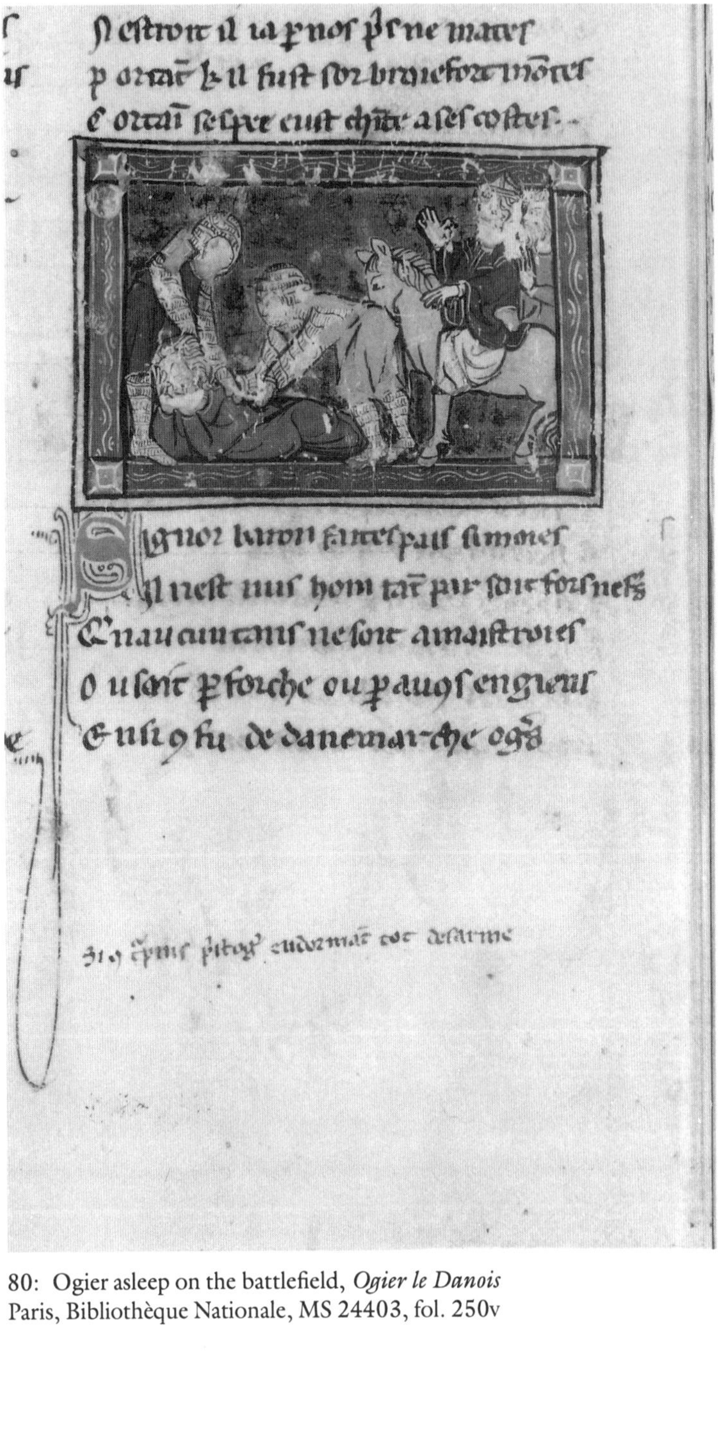

80: Ogier asleep on the battlefield, *Ogier le Danois*
Paris, Bibliothèque Nationale, MS 24403, fol. 250v

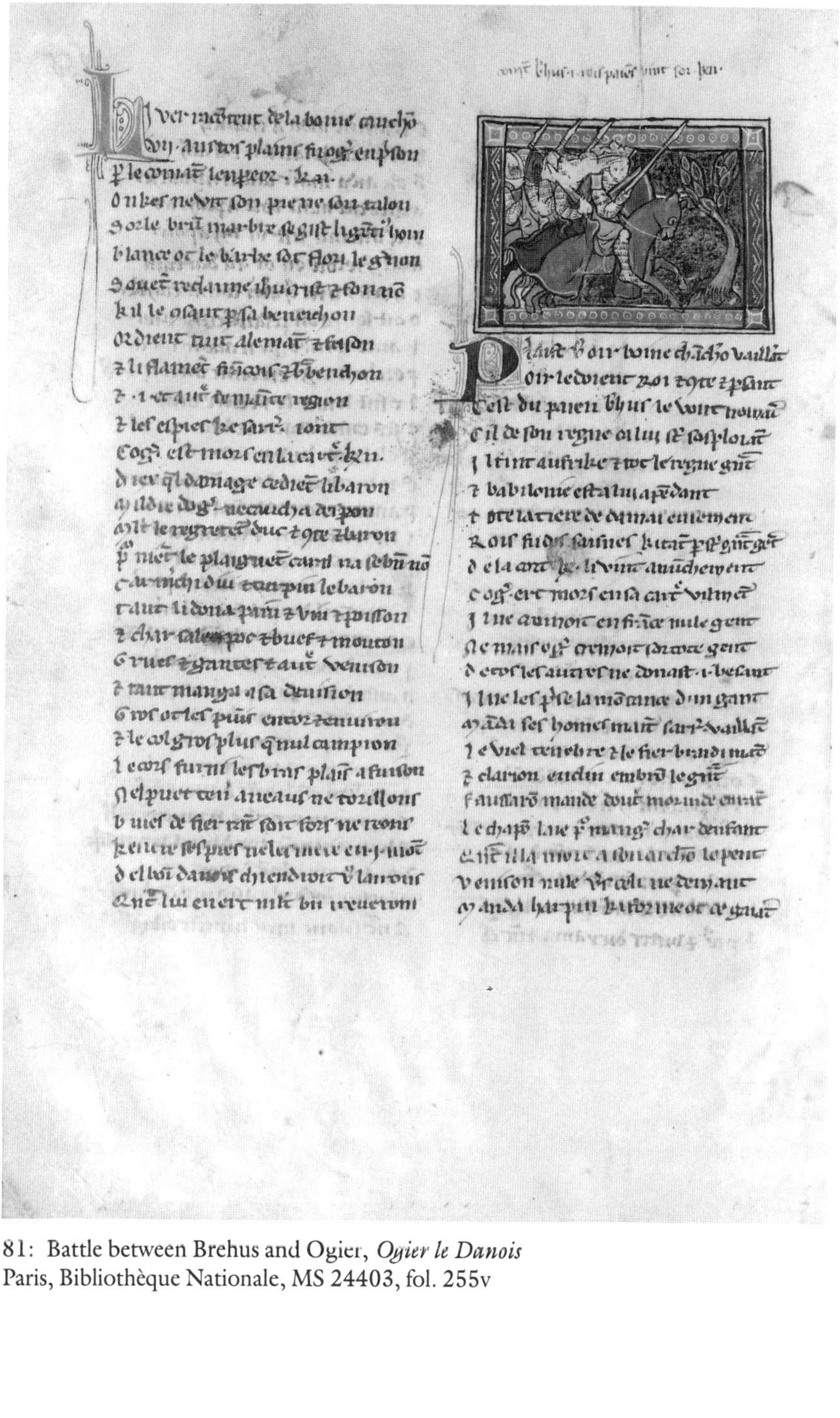

81: Battle between Brehus and Ogier, *Ogier le Danois*
Paris, Bibliothèque Nationale, MS 24403, fol. 255v

82: Ogier miraculously saved from murdering Charlot, and Ogier's battle with Brehus, *Ogier le Danois*
Paris, Bibliothèque Nationale, MS 24403, fol. 267

83: Penultimate battle, *Ogier le Danois*
Paris, Bibliothèque Nationale, MS 24403, fol. 274v

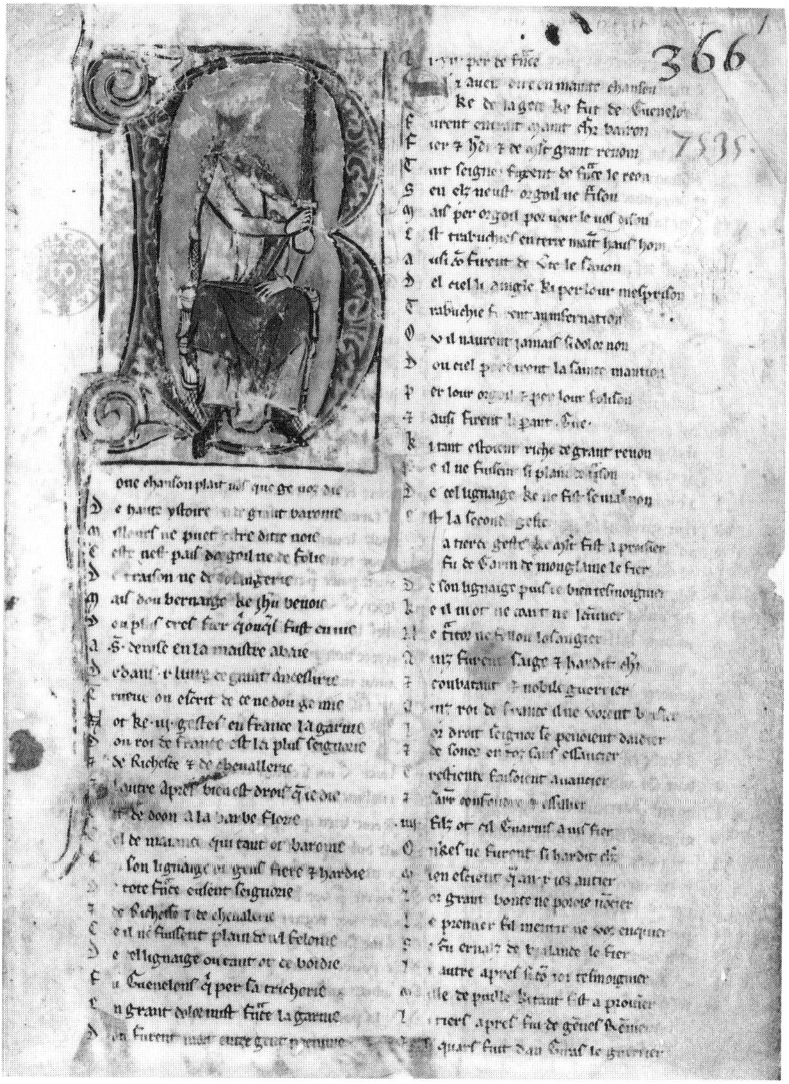

84: Standing king, *Cycle de Guillaume d'Orange*
Paris, Bibliothèque Nationale, MS 1448, fol. 1

Text and illustrations in *Garin de Monglane* constitute a sort of preamble that both reinforces and embellishes the reading of *Erec et Enide* as an epic that I have outlined. *Garin de Monglane* is the first of a series of three poems that trace the ancestry of William of Orange, a vassal of Charlemagne who, along with Roland, is one of the greatest epic heroes in the tradition of the chanson de geste.[8] In the pseudohistorical genealogy of epic, Garin and his wife, Mabille, begin a distinguished lineage that extends through William of Orange to King Louis le Debonaire, the successor of Charlemagne. They are great-grandparents of William of Orange, who is in turn grandson of their eldest son, Hernaut de Beaulande, and son of Aimeri de Narbonne. William himself is the father of Louis le Debonaire. In fact, when Erec extols the bravery of Thiebaut the Esclavon in the Joy of the Court, he refers to the epic cycle of William of Orange, for Thiebaut is a pagan king who was a powerful adversary of William and wounded him in battle.[9]

One of the characteristics of epic is that characters from one story reappear in other stories of the same cycle, and the cycle itself is composed of a series of gestes organized around the lineage or genealogy of a great hero. By implication, then, when *Erec et Enide* refers to heroes from the William of Orange cycle and is placed together in the manuscript with *Garin de Montglane,* a poem from this cycle, Chrétien's story could even be construed by its readers as a branch of the William of Orange cycle.

Forging further links between the two stories, the five miniatures accompanying *Garin de Monglane* present interesting parallels with the cycle of *Erec et Enide. Garin de Monglane* centers on Garin's siege and capture of the castle of Monglane, which is held by heathen enemies of France. Four of the miniatures focus in different ways on martial prowess, that is, on what I have considered to be the adventure of epic. Apart from an opening miniature depicting the appearance of Garin with his brothers at the court of Charlemagne (fig. 68), to which I will return, none of the subsequent events at the court that set the stage for the adventure are illustrated. For example, at the beginning of the story the empress Galienne falls in love with Garin, which enrages Charlemagne, who in turn jealously challenges Garin to a game of chess. If Garin wins he may have anything, even the kingdom of France. If he loses he will be killed. Not surprisingly, Garin wins the match. The emperor offers him France, but he declines, asking instead for Monglane. In spite of their importance to the narrative, these episodes are not illustrated. Instead, two miniatures focus, like those in the second section of *Erec et Enide,* on armed combat between protagonists on horseback (figs. 70 and 72). Like Eric, Garin and his forces vanquish their adversaries. For example, in the third miniature in the epic the giant Robastre joins Garin and his troops for the first major attack against Gaufroi, which, the epic recounts, they would have won except for the intervention of neighboring allies (fig. 70). In the last miniature in the epic, Garin's troops rout the forces of the duke in a decisive battle (fig. 72). It is difficult not to compare these warrior knights with Erec, since all are portrayed wearing similar costumes and engaged in like pursuits.

Like Enide, Garin's lover, Mabille, is relegated to a secondary, unimportant role. She appears once in the second miniature in the epic, on horseback, her radiant beauty hidden by her modest head covering, as the text specifies (fig. 69). It is difficult to be certain of the identity of the two figures who accompany Mabille and point toward her, but one might be the knight who grows jealous of Garin and the other could be the jongleur who praises her beauty. She appears again in the fourth miniature, where, just like Enide, she is shown helpless in a perilous situation, the attack by the enchanter Perdigon, from whom she is saved by Garin's skill in combat (fig. 71). After the battle at the conclusion of the story, the jubilant marriage of Garin and Mabille in a triple wedding ceremony with Berard and Robastre and their brides is not illustrated.

Following *Erec et Enide* in the Paris manuscript, *Ogier le Danois* continues the history of Charlemagne's vassals after the death of Garin de Monglane.[10] The chronological relation of the two stories is unmistakable: *Ogier le Danois* opens with Charlemagne grieving for Galienne, who caused the original feud between Charlemagne and Garin, and in the course of the story Ogier twice battles the son of Garin, Hernaut de Beaulande. As a sort of sequel to *Garin de Monglane, Ogier le Danois* likewise focuses on the expulsion of the pagans, first the Saracens from Italy and then the Babylonians from France. Single-handedly responsible for these resounding victories is the brutish foreigner Ogier, a vassal of the emperor and a legendary warrior like Garin. *Garin de Monglane* and *Ogier le Danois* can be understood as sequels that recount the gestes of Charlemagne's vassals. Stuck into the manuscript between these two chronologically related epics, *Erec et Enide* was most likely read by its thirteenth-century Picard audience as an intervening segment—a kind of geste of Erec—in this newly formulated trilogy.

Beginning and ending incompletely, the Paris text of *Ogier le Danois* lacks its opening and closing miniatures, but the twelve that remain, which concentrate on Ogier's prowess, further support the interpretation I have so far presented of the entire manuscript as a work that valorizes the knight as a warrior.[11] With the exception of the miniature of the chess match between Baudouinet and Charlot, at which the son of Charlemagne kills the son of Ogier (fig. 74), an event that triggers the ensuing conflict between Charlemagne and Ogier, the rest of the miniatures show Ogier engaged in various forms of combat.

In one miniature at the beginning of the story, Ogier makes his way to an island where Caraheu, a brave Saracen warrior, has challenged him to combat (fig. 73). Then, allied with the Lombards, to whom he flees after the murder of his son, he twice unsuccessfully fights the French (fig. 77). The next miniature illustrates Ogier's last major battle against the French, which occurs when he begins with three hundred men, is eventually down to just ten, and finally finds himself alone with his trusty horse Broiefort. In a charming vignette the text recites how he busily fetches water, heats the oven, bakes bread, cooks his meals, and even shoes his own horse the whole time that the French surround Castelfort. Suddenly Ogier has an idea. Cleverly, he fashions mannequins out of wood, puts beards on them with hair from Broiefort's mane, and dresses them in armor as false knights. By this ruse he deceives the French, who believe that numerous knights still defend Castelfort. The miniature shows the large fortified castle guarded by three dummy knights (fig. 78). (The reader of *Ogier,* who has just completed *Erec et Enide,* will be struck by the similarities between Castelfort and Bradiganz, the well-fortified feudal castle of King Evrain described in the Joy of the Court, a castle impervious to attack and self-sufficient in fruit, grain, and wine.) A sequence of miniatures of battle scenes follows, bringing the story to a conclusion: from Castelfort(?) Ogier rebuffs Charlot's offer of a truce (fig. 79); he then battles Brehus, the mighty pagan king of Babylon, on three different occasions (figs. 81, 82, and 83).

Naturally skilled arms and plainly undistracted by love, Ogier is thus the apotheosis of the knight as the perfect warrior, who most fully realizes the aptitude and achievements of Garin and Erec. Women are entirely absent in text and image in *Ogier le Danois.* In fact, they are progressively more marginalized in the sequence of three stories. The Paris anthology moves from the dynastic tale of Garin de Montglane, where women have a significant presence, to the royal romance of Erec with its marginalized heroine, to the blood-and-guts story of Ogier, where women have no place at all. Simultaneously brutish and clever, with only his horse for a companion, this last hero moves in an exclusively male world of epic adventure. Greater still than Thiebaut the Esclavon, Ospinel, or Fernagu—the intrepid pagan heroes Erec invokes in the Joy of the Court episode—Ogier, who handily vanquishes such pagans, emerges as "the bravest warrior of all whom we know."

THE PARTICULAR CONSTRUCTION OF THE PROGRAM OF TEXT AND ILLUSTRATION IN THE PARIS MANUSCRIPT RESPONDS IN PART TO THE CHANGING STATUS OF THE WARRIOR (*MILES*) RELATIVE TO THE nobility in thirteenth-century Picardy. Some unique features characterize chivalry in Picardy during the preceding period, particularly compared with the rest of northern France (Fossier 1987, 537–41). As a group, Picard warriors traditionally included both vassals, who might or might not be nobles (usually not), and soldiers, usually free men who received wages for their services. Above all, a warrior possessed technical aptitude and superior skills; he was not born into a certain class. This unusual composition of the warrior group in Picardy arose from the conjunction of two regional practices. First, the only service exacted for vassalage was military. The vassal owed the lord an *estage,* a variable period of military service at the castle (from one month to one year), rendered at the vassal's own expense and in full war regalia (Fossier 1987, esp. 668–73). Second, in Picardy the king had the option of conscripting free men for pay instead of calling up armed nobles for so-called host service as occurred in neighboring Flanders and Normandy (Fossier 1987, 2:669; 1988, 160–61). The special definition of the warrior class, as Fossier has noted, accounts for the relative absence of references to the habitual customs of chivalry, such as dubbing, among the nobility of Picardy before the end of the twelfth century (Fossier 1987, 2:659–65; 1976, esp. 112–14). An honorable occupation practiced by a skilled group of well-trained combatants, who mostly bore arms by choice, warfare was not historically the prerogative of the aristocracy.

Vast changes in Picard society during the thirteenth century brought about a significant redefinition of the warrior (Fossier 1987, 1976). The earlier, relatively homogeneous category of combatants who excelled at arms divided into two distinct groups—the knight who was a warrior and the soldier warrior. The first group, the noblemen, bore arms for honor and frequently took part in the ritual combat of tournaments. The emergence of this group has been traced to the early thirteenth century, when Picard nobles (*nobilis, vir nobilis*) began systematically to practice dubbing in preparation for bearing arms. Thus the established merit of the occupation combined with the prestige of class and the honor conferred by the quasi-religious ceremony to elevate the stature of the knight warrior. The second group, the mercenaries, fought for money and primarily engaged in real battles. During the thirteenth century, from the time of the battle of Bouvines in 1214, Picardy, long an area of royal conscription, became a zone of heavy recruitment, and so the presence of the mercenary was more keenly felt. It should be evident that, exercising their superior skill at actual combat, the noble heroes of the Paris manuscript—Garin, Erec, and Ogier—celebrate the historical, pre-thirteenth-century definition of the warrior, before the bifurcation of the warrior class, thus expressing a nostalgia for bygone days.

But at the same time that they recapture the historical persona of the Picard warrior, Garin, Erec, and Ogier may also speak to the contemporary crisis of the aristocracy. By this time the military function of the warrior had become a natural extension of the expanded ranks of the nobility, whose preoccupation with the social prestige of bearing arms is evident in the multiplication of honorific terms for the knight as warrior (e.g., *ecuyer*). Yet at the same time this group experienced serious socioeconomic upheaval. Members of the nobility were sometimes forced to sell off their lands to relieve their indebtedness. They began to divide the patrimony, which fragmented the lineage and further impoverished members of the family. And they suffered the effects of a severe agricultural crisis, which was intensified by the rise of towns. For this group the leisure activities of chivalry, especially bearing arms, had become a defense against social marginalization, but their shrinking resources meant there was little excess wealth for costly ceremonies like dubbing and for expensive equipment like armor, weapons, and horses. The very survival of knighthood became precarious. From this perspective, in the Paris manuscript the noble combatants, Garin, Erec, and Ogier, ascribe the idealized values of historical Picard warriors, engaged in real fighting instead of mock battle, to the faltering aristocracy of the thirteenth century.

Read in Picardy, portraits of combatants would have also evoked a sensitivity to the cost of warfare. For whatever value fighting was thought to have was somewhat undercut by its considerable expense, as the surviving documents suggest (Contamine 1984, esp. 65–115). A list of equipment for Picard knights includes, in 1143, a "valiant" horse with a saddle and bridle, a cape, a belt, a knife, a lance, and a tunic; and in 1217, a sword, two helmets, and two tunics (Fossier 1987, 2:670). Most costly were the mounts, especially since a knight was expected to have three horses—a war-horse, a palfrey, and a rouncy—and he was also expected to provide mounts for the three companions, usually squires, who accompanied him in battle (Contamine 1984, 96–97). Not counting upkeep, the price of a war-horse was seven to eight times that of an ordinary horse. Documents from the time of Philip the Fair intimate that the cost of a war-horse was an issue for soldiers, for they make provision for compensating knights for war-horses lost in battle (Contamine 1984, 97). Estimates of capital outlay for equipment run between six months' and one year's wages, which during less troubled times would have favored the landed knight over the paid soldier. When a Picard seigneur complained in 1280 about the feudal service he owed in *estage,* however, he objected not to the principle or to its duration, but to the fact that he had to report for duty fully armed as though for war, which presented a considerable expense (Fossier 1987, 2: 669). We should recall that, just like the Picard knights of the thirteenth century, Enide's father is described as a poor man because he has "been so involved in war" that he has spent all his money on arms.

A crippled economy, coupled with the increased expense of fighting, led to other transformations in warfare—how and by whom real battles were waged—during the thirteenth century. As early as the battle of Bouvines, footmen joined horsemen on the battleground, even if their participation does not initially seem to have had much impact.[12] A series of changes in the methods of warfare eventually culminated in the disappearance of mail-clad feudal horsemen in the fourteenth century. Although heavy cavalry survived through the fifteenth century, the threat posed by the infantry became important as early as the end of the thirteenth century. The infantry naturally did away with the expense of horses, but foot soldiers also began to wear lighter, and presumably cheaper, armor. Several technical changes likewise date from this era: conical helmets with visors replaced the flat-topped helmets with breathing grates, banded mail replaced chain mail, and plate armor supplemented chain mail (see Paluka 1972 and, for further references, Gaier 1979). The helmet and shield went out of use altogether by about 1350, when the remaining cavalry customarily dismounted for battle.

It was during these years near the end of the thirteenth century, in fact, that Philip the Fair inaugurated universal conscription, which mobilized heterogeneous forces throughout France (Contamine 1984, 87–88, 189). He simultaneously set up storehouses of weapons and arms to be distributed free of charge to the troops. The actual composition of armies thus gradually became even more mixed. Greater numbers of mercenaries, comprising cavalry and infantry, archers and crossbowmen, as well as groups of burghers, joined knights on the field of battle. The combination of mercenary and burgher troops, who fought for pay or for national pride, and the introduction of the infantry, who did not need horses, thus proclaimed the end of the feudal system and, with it, the demise of the celebration of the mounted knight.

The willful ignorance of the contemporary situation in the sequence of miniatures in the Paris manuscript suggests that there was an interest in preserving a view of the history of warfare and the role of the warrior that, by the time this manuscript was made, had been seriously compromised if it was not patently false. Not surprisingly, the miniatures display little of the social diversity or technological advances that characterized thirteenth-century warfare. Rather, Garin, Erec, and Ogier appear mostly as mail-clad knights, wearing their helmets and holding their shields and swords as they pose confidently astride their war-horses. Divergences from such representations are noteworthy. In *Garin de Monglane,* Robastre goes into combat with a club, presumably because he is a savage giant, whereas Garin, a noble warrior, wields a sword when he attacks Perdigon. Garin again wields a sword in the final battle as he vanquishes the pagans, whereas other combatants in this miniature, including the pagans, brandish spears. In *Ogier le Danois* the Danish hero inevitably sports a sword as he battles the Saracens, whereas they defend themselves with crude, old-fashioned spears. Indeed the sword of Ogier, as famous as that of Roland, even bears a name—Galant. From this sequence of miniatures it appears that the sword is the paramount weapon of the skillful warrior.

With this in mind, how are we to understand the miniatures of *Erec et Enide,* where Erec appears exclusively without a sword? He first fights the robbers and then the giants with the aid of just a lance like that customarily employed in jousting tournaments. That this is a choice made by the miniaturist seems evident because the text, here as elsewhere, does not specify a weapon. By this visual strategy Erec is presented as kind of alternative figure, as a knight who is more nobleman than warrior. Yet by implication—framed by stories and pictures of two knights as warriors and engaged in combat, not in love—Erec will become a successful combatant.

Informed by this perspective on the place of the knight as a warrior in Picard society, the pervasive image of the mounted horseman takes on yet another level of meaning. Clad in chain mail, decked out with a helmet, sporting a shield, and seated astride a war-horse, the knight in our romances valorizes the figure of the warrior at a time when his social status has become precarious and his professional services dispensable. The symbol of the mounted horseman, whether framed as a single image in manuscripts of *Le Chevalier au lion* and *Le Conte du Graal* or incorporated in a narrative as in the Paris compilation of *Erec et Enide* discussed here, simultaneously asserts the self-esteem of the knight as a warrior while it defends against his imminent marginalization.

Two miniatures in *Ogier le Danois* together provide an incisive conclusion to the compilation in the Paris manuscript. In a miniature that comes midway through the story, the importance of weapons resonates (fig. 80). Asleep on the field of battle, Ogier is caught unaware by Turpin; he is disarmed and subsequently imprisoned. Stripped of his armor and deprived of his war-horse, Ogier is of course ineffectual. The juxtaposition of his reclining figure and that of the archbishop Turpin, riding unarmed on a mule, makes Ogier's vulnerability even more manifest.

Though vulnerable without his arms, Ogier is the consummate warrior when properly equipped, because he knows how to use his equipment to best effect. In the penultimate miniature Ogier dismounts as he prepares to defeat the mighty pagan warrior Brehus, a detail not called for in the text (fig. 83). Sword raised high above his head, he expertly defends himself against the pagan troops who assault him from both sides. Effectively communicating Ogier's skill at combat, even in the face of his vulnerability as he stands surrounded on the field of battle, this miniature functions in another way as well. Ogier, the perfect warrior, employs the new form of fighting introduced at the end of the thirteenth century, which enables him finally to defeat the Saracens: he becomes a footman, a soldier of the infantry, at the very time when the infantry was becoming more prevalent in Picardy. Although the miniature of Ogier stripped of his armor midway through the Paris manuscript metaphorically admits to the precariousness of knighthood, the miniature of Ogier as a footman at the conclusion thus offers hope for a knighthood that is more in step with the times.

The message about the changing status of the Picard knight as a warrior presented in the Paris manuscript is set in a larger context in the program of illustration by the opening miniature (fig. 68). At the beginning of the entire manuscript, where it introduces *Garin de Monglane,* this miniature substitutes for a kind of donor scene or author portrait, whose conventions it adopts. It probably depicts Garin and his brothers before Charlemagne, thus alluding to a dream recounted at the beginning of the story. In the dream an angel appears to Garin, whose father, the duke of Aquitaine, is about to die, and advises him to abandon his duchy to his two brothers and return to the court of Charlemagne. The angel goes on to say that although Charlemagne will attempt to give Garin twenty fiefs, Garin should accept nothing but Monglane. In visual terms the miniature fixes the feudal relationship between Garin and Charlemagne, vassal and lord.

But providing an introduction to the entire manuscript as an anthology, the miniature also alludes to the feudal relationships between all three heroes and their sovereigns. Just as Garin, Erec, and Ogier are all combatants, defenders of the Christians, they are also all vassals of a sovereign. Garin and Ogier are vassals of Charlemagne, and Erec is a vassal of Arthur. It is important to remember that the stories of Garin and Ogier are as much about the troubled relationship of the heroes to Charlemagne as about their valiant deeds. That the rest of the miniatures in each of the three stories in the Paris manuscript so conspicuously ignore the feudal relationship, while they celebrate the valor of the heroes, is surely not insignificant. Relevant also is that in all three stories the heroes end up happily established on independent terrain (feudal fiefs for Garin and Ogier and an autonomous kingdom for Erec), where they dwell in harmonious accord with a benign and remote sovereign. Set up in the opening miniature, which serves as a kind of frontispiece to the manuscript, and embellished in the subsequent sequences of text and image we thus find a timely statement about the autonomy of provincial feudalism.

Picardy's special relationship with the monarchy helps to explain the larger historical perspective that underlies the Paris manuscript.[13] Because of its geographic position, bounded by Normandy to the west, Flanders to the north, and Ile-de-France to the south, Picardy presented a potential threat to the Capetian kings, who were eager to guard against an alliance of the Picards with the stronger Flemings and Normans. Beginning with the Treaty of Boves in 1186, in which Philip Augustus and the count of Flanders split Picardy between them, the Capetians sought to strengthen their control over the area. This process did not proceed without resistance. During the minority of Saint Louis between 1229 and 1236, Picard nobles joined with the count of Ponthieu in a revolt against royal authority. Ultimately such resistance was unsuccessful, however, perhaps because Picardy was made up of hundreds of relatively small counties and seigneuries, in contrast to Champagne, Normandy, and Flanders where there was a single strong count or duke. By the end of the century, thanks largely to measures initiated during the reign of Saint Louis, royal administration of Picardy was fully in place: officials appointed by the king replaced the authority of the sires in all administrative affairs.

By claiming a special relationship between the Picard warriors and the

Carolingian sovereign, the Paris manuscript offered a timely vehicle for reaffirming provincial feudalism. As a kind of legendary antitype for the Capetian monarchs, Charlemagne, like Arthur, was perceived as an ancestral model for the Picard nobles themselves, one who could potentially reemerge to endorse the now-threatened feudal customs.[14] Surely it is no accident that, just as Erec is compared to epic heroes in the text of *Erec et Enide,* Arthur is compared to "Caesar . . . and all the kings whose names you hear in stories and in epic songs" (vv. 6615–17).[15] In fabricating a glorious fictional past for the valorous Picard combatants, the Paris manuscript also offers a textual reconstruction of social hierarchy and dynastic descent.

THE OVERALL MESSAGE OF THE PARIS MANUSCRIPT AS IT EMERGES THROUGH AN ANALYSIS OF THE ANTHOLOGY AND ITS MINIATURES IN THE CONTEXT OF THE SOCIOPOLITICAL MILIEU OF THIRteenth-century Picardy foregrounds the sharp distinction between the genres of epic and romance—between essentially oral and written modes of literature.[16] As they are normally outlined, these distinctions revolve around the different roles perceived for the authors of the two genres, the divergent content of their works, and the unique characters of their audiences.[17] Epic is thought of as essentially anonymous. The teller of the tale, the minstrel or jongleur, is free to alter the verses, composed of *laisses similaires,* which are well suited to the commemorative, performed ritual of the historical past. Romance is understood to be fundamentally authorial. An author organizes events and characters, usually mythological, into a fictive narrative on which he or she imposes a moral interpretation. Whereas epic thus revives the past, where actual sovereigns play active roles in a series of haphazard events, romance constructs an imaginary situation with contrived encounters that focus on a love relationship, while an ideal sovereign may occupy the sidelines.

It is evident that in our manuscript neither the authorial nor the narrative distinction between the genres holds. All three texts emerge as anonymous creations (excepting Chrétien de Troyes's reference to himself in the introduction of *Erec et Enide*), and their content, primarily concerned with warfare, not love, shares more with epic than with romance. Nor is it possible to maintain a distinction between the hypothetical audiences. Whereas epic is understood as being performed orally before a diversified public, romance is generally thought of as more elite, composed for a literate, book-reading aristocratic society. Yet the survival of epic through the thirteenth century and into the fourteenth and its compilation in book form, coupled with what we have already surmised about the oral performance of romance, cautions against drawing the line too firmly between oral and literature cultures.

A number of features in the Paris copy point to a manuscript meant to be seen when read rather than heard while performed. For example, the intrusion of short descriptive rubrics only three-quarters of the way through the manuscript when none are present earlier cannot be fully explained, but it does suggest an attempt by the scribe to relate the images to a text designed for a certain style of reading. So too the scribe's attempt to draw out the lines of the octosyllabic verse in the transcription of *Erec et Enide,* putting more space between the letters and words, in order to harmonize the *mise-en-page* with the longer lines of the decasyllabic verse on the pages containing the two epics, suggests that he was grappling with the design of a page meant to be seen, not heard. These characteristics point to a culture that is moving away from performance, though it has not yet relinquished it altogether.

Pictures also play a role in signaling different genres of texts, as I have already suggested in discussing the image of the knight on horseback or, less frequently, the telling of a story at court, both taken to refer to Arthurian romance. In the Paris manuscript neither of these alternatives was used. Instead, the opening miniature of a seated king (fig. 68) aligns the manuscript with epic, frequently introduced by a miniature of a hieratically enthroned sovereign to underscore the dynastic character of the text and to lend authority to its tale, as in an anthology of chansons de geste in Paris (MS fr. 1448; fig. 84). As in the opening miniatures in romance, the absence of the image of the author in manuscripts of epic is conspicuous, a feature that harks back to oral culture, where the epic form originated and flourished.

Ironically, then, Chrétien's opening to *Erec et Enide,* where he refers to his fashioning of "a beautifully ordered composition" (*une molt bele conjointure*), has led some critics to suppose that by *conjointure* he meant the art of composition necessary to turn a tale of old-fashioned adventure, like epic, into a modern romance (Kelly 1970). Yet the salutory effect of *Erec et Enide* on the crisis of the aristocracy was framed in the Paris manuscript *not* by creating a "modern" tale, but by transforming a courtly romance into a historical epic.

CHAPTER FIVE

THE KNIGHT *Li Roi*

[Perceval] read [a letter] and learned that his uncle had died in his joy, and had wanted him not to stay at Cardueil but to return to be crowned and to rule his land and uphold his kingdom.

Manessier's Continuation to *Le Conte del Graal*[1]

NEARLY ALL THE NOTEWORTHY EVENTS IN *LE CONTE DEL GRAAL (PERCEVAL)* AND ITS CONTINUATIONS REVOLVE, IN ONE WAY OR ANOTHER, AROUND TWO ROYAL COURTS—THE COURT OF KING Arthur and that of the Fisher King. Following the opening sequence, when Perceval precipitously becomes a knight of Arthur's Round Table, the valiant adventurer seems always to be in transit, peripatetically departing from the court of one king in search of the court of the other. After brashly appropriating the armor of the Red Knight, Perceval sets out to show his worthiness, defending Blancheflor's castle of Beaurepaire from her enemies Engygeron and Clamadeu and avenging the girl whose ring he stole by defeating her lover, the Proud Knight of the Heath. In each instance, according to the custom of the day, he sends his vanquished prisoners to Arthur's court to surrender before the king they will henceforth serve. Remembering Perceval primarily as an impetuous youth dressed in rough Welsh garments, Arthur is eager to encounter again the now accomplished knight, whose heroism the returning captives so enthusiastically extol. When Gawain delivers Perceval, whom he interrupts musing over three drops of blood in the snow, to Arthur joyful celebration ensues among "the king, the queen, and the barons." This sequence of events—Perceval's hasty departure from court, his successful combat, the delivery of his prisoners, and his eventual return to court, where he often recounts his adventures to Arthur—is repeated many times in *Le Conte del Graal* and the continuations.

Perceval's persistent quest to rediscover the Grail castle, where he hopes to learn the secrets of the silver charger, the bleeding lance, and the Holy Grail, prompts his ceaseless wanderings. After five years, during which he sends some sixty worthy knights to Arthur's court, he learns from a wise hermit he meets on Good Friday that the reason he failed to ask the Fisher King the important questions concerning the charger, the lance, and the Grail is that he had sinned by causing the death of his mother. He simultaneously learns that the father of the Fisher King, the one who is "so spiritual that he needs no more in his life than the host that comes in the Grail," is, like the hermit, his uncle. In spite of the hermit's repeated injunctions to Perceval to worship God and to avoid "killing men like that," the rash young knight cannot resist the urge to fight, which prevents him from learning the secrets of the mysterious vessels. When Perceval is finally deemed worthy and reveals his identity, the Fisher King asserts: "All my land I bequeath to you. . . . I shall make you king, whatever the cost." Although Perceval initially forgoes his right to succession and returns instead to Arthur's court, where he recounts the conclusion of his adventures, the death of his uncle leads to his subsequent crowning. Arthur himself attends the coronation. Perceval then rules peaceably for seven years, after which he retires to a hermitage, where he spends the ten years until his death.

Two illuminated manuscripts present variants of the version of the story as I have just outlined it, featuring King Arthur and the Fisher King with unusual prominence (Paris, Bibliothèque Nationale, MSS fr. 1453 and 12577).[2] These manuscripts, which are both the latest and the most extensively illustrated copies of the Perceval story (each has fifty-two miniatures), share many other features. Each includes *Le Conte del Graal* along with three continuations, excluding that of Gerbert. Their texts are extensively altered and emended, often in similar ways, suggesting that they belong to the same family (Micha 1939, 237–39, 249, 382–86). Produced in Ile-de-France, almost certainly in Paris itself, between 1315 and 1325, even though the exact patrons remain unknown, they stand out as the only manuscripts among all of Chrétien's romances addressed to an audience in the royal capital.

On a superficial level this observation alone might help explain the more frequent appearance of kings in the illustrations of these manuscripts than in other copies. But the rereadings I propose here understand these two manuscripts as self-conscious responses to the political realities of early fourteenth-century France. By exalting models of political and spiritual kingship in the complementary roles of King Arthur and the Fisher King, these two manuscripts present, each in a slightly different way, a nostalgic view of a golden age of Capetian kingship. I will argue that, for their Parisian readers, they recast Perceval in the model of the last ideal Capetian monarch, Saint Louis, the just monarch and "most Christian king." I will also explore how the text, the illustrations, and the *mise-en-page* of the manuscripts raise important questions that help to explain the shift from verse to prose and at the same time explain why Chrétien was apparently no longer read by medieval audiences after the first quarter of the fourteenth century.

IN THE ILLUSTRATIONS IN THE FIRST PARIS COPY (MS FR. 1453), THE EXPANDED SEQUENCE OF MINIATURES DEVOTED TO KING ARTHUR IN *LE CONTE DEL GRAAL* UNDERSCORES HIS IMPORTANCE. Although incomplete at the beginning, which was most likely illustrated with a frontispiece, this manuscript opens with two miniatures showing Arthur at court. In the first Perceval approaches Arthur, "the king who makes knights," asking to be made a knight (fig. 85). In the second the vassal Yvonet present to the king the cup stolen by the Red Knight and retrieved by Perceval (fig. 86). Subsequent miniatures, as well as some textual interpolations, in *Le Conte del Graal* reinforce Arthur's important role in the adventures of his knights. For example, having vanquished Blancheflor's enemies, Perceval dutifully sends them to Arthur, as in the miniature of Clamadeu, which is followed in the text by an interpolated eulogy on Arthur's prowess (fig. 87) (Micha 1939, 383, vv. 2834–36). Then Perceval jousts with Kay while Arthur looks on, and immediately thereafter he arrives, accompanied by Gawain, at Arthur's court (fig. 88). *Le Conte del Graal* ends with King Arthur and Queen Guinevere majestically posed framing the figure of Lady Lore, who summons the court to Gawain's imminent joust with Guiromelant, which takes place at the beginning of the First Continuation (fig. 89). In the opening section of the manuscript, the conspicuous absence in the miniatures of both the Fisher King and the hermit (surprisingly, Perceval neither visits the Grail castle nor encounters the hermit) diverts the reader's attention from the spiritual aspect of Perceval's quest while calling attention to Arthur's relationship with his knights, including Perceval.

The nature of this relationship emerges with greater clarity in a sequence of miniatures illustrating the First Continuation. Nearly half the miniatures in this portion of the manuscript depict a relatively minor subplot, the conflict between Gawain and Bran de Lis (figs. 90 and 91). Following Arthur's arrangement of the marriage of Clarissant and Guiromelant and Gawain's visit to the Grail castle, Gawain stumbles across a beautiful pavilion in which he finds a girl who, offering herself to him, meets with no resistance. The girl's brother, Bran de Lis, hears of her seduction and, promising to avenge his sister, sets out to challenge Gawain to battle. They begin to fight but decide to postpone the battle until it can be fought before witnesses. Encountering Gawain later at the court of Arthur, Bran de Lis challenges him again. Gawain accepts the challenge, but the girl intervenes by pushing her five-year-old bastard son between the quarreling knights and having the child ask Bran de Lis not to kill his father. Bran de Lis kicks the boy aside, and Arthur rebukes him. Eventually Arthur himself intervenes to stop the fight and reconcile the adversaries.

Four miniatures illustrate this narrative: Bran de Lis parting from his sister at the pavilion; Bran de Lis and Gawain arming themselves for battle; Arthur enthroned with the child between Bran de Lis and Gawain; and Arthur enthroned as judge and arbitrator (figs. 90 and 91). Arthur appears enthroned in two other miniatures in the First Continuation, once as he receives the magic horn (likewise a minor episode) and again as he watches the swan boat sail by. It is noteworthy that, at least in the miniatures, Gawain, like Perceval, has yet to visit the Grail castle. The Grail castle is clearly regarded as secondary in importance to Arthur, presented here as a full-fledged monarch who is decked out in royal regalia, hieratically enthroned, and vested with the authority to judge and moderate, as he does even in private squabbles such as that between Gawain and Bran de Lis.

Red rubrics come before each picture and insist on Arthur's presence through the entire manuscript. These rubrics, along with their miniatures, punctuate the Perceval story, literally rewriting it with Arthur as the principal subject: for example, "Comment li cors fu presentez / Au roy artus devant ses barons; Comment li rois artus plora / Quant il vit lenfant que brandelis tu; Comment li rois ala veoir la nef" ("How the horn was presented / To King Arthur in front of his barons; How King Arthur cried / When he saw the child that Bran de Lis killed; How the king went to see the boat"). In the Second Continuation and the continuation by Manessier some miniatures, along with the rubrics, either assign Arthur a more primary role in the story or deviate from the story to include him, even when the text does not dictate his presence. For example, in the Second Continuation a series of jousts is designed to determine which knight is worthy of a special shield that has been brought to court. Although the jousts are not illustrated, the presentation of the shield to Arthur, enthroned in a pavilion, is represented, along with a rubric that focuses on the king ("Comment li escuier presente lescu / argent au roy artus enson paviellon" ["How the herald presents the shield / Of silver to King Arthur in his pavillion"] (fig. 92). Later, in Manessier's Continuation, when Gawain jousts with King Margon, Arthur watches from a bridge at the left, even though according to the author King Margon was a long way from Arthur's court, to which he later journeyed to present himself as the king's prisoner, the subject of the succeeding miniature ("Comment le roy magon se rent person au roy artus" ["How King Margon turned himself in as a prisoner to King Arthur"]) (figs. 93 and 94).

Given this emphasis on Arthur, it is hardly surprising to find that the king also figures prominently in the conclusion of the manuscript. Although eventually Perceval does visit the Grail castle (he still does not see the holy vessels) in a miniature at the end of the Second Continuation, and though he goes on to defeat the black hand in the chapel, to resist the devil who cleverly appears to him disguised as Blancheflor, and finally to see for the first time the Holy Grail carried by an angel in the penultimate miniature, his spiritual development is clearly not at issue here. Unique among the manuscripts of the Perceval story, this manuscript concludes instead with an image of Perceval's coronation (fig. 95). Arthur not only participates in the coronation (according to the text, he was one of twelve kings to attend the event), but he endorses it, as is evident in his gesture as he touches Perceval's crown just as the peers of France touch the king's crown in the French coronation rite, testifying that they uphold the king's authority as principal lawgiver throughout the realm (for comparable images, see Hedeman 1991, pls. 4–6). In this manuscript, then, Perceval comes of age not when he masters the martial arts or develops his spiritual ideals, but when he learns the qualities of kingship demonstrated by Arthur, especially the principles of justice.

The image of Perceval, like Arthur, as a just king whose wide authority extends over his immense kingdom recalls characteristics of thirteenth-century kingship, specifically those associated with the reign of Saint Louis (1226–70) (see esp. Hallam 1980 and Jordan 1979). Under Louis's reign, royal authority was for the first time effectively extended to the vast royal domains, thanks largely to a series of innovative initiatives by the king. In the provinces, Louis installed royal officials, *baillis* and *prevots,* who exercised judicial and financial authority on behalf of the Crown. For example, they collected fees, levied troops, and upheld justice in local courts. Safeguards were set in place to ensure the efficiency of this system. An ordonnance of 1256 obliged the king's officials to swear oaths promising good conduct, and *enquêteurs*—traveling agents for the king, often friars—were employed to collect complaints. This administrative system went a long way toward eliminating differences in regional law or custom, and it also discouraged arbitrary settlements such as family feuds and private wars. In fact another series of ordonnances issued between 1257 and 1261, unpopular among the regional nobility, explicitly forbade trial by battle, requiring all cases to come before royal courts of justice, whether convened locally or in Paris (Hallam 1980, 244).

With the refinement of the administrative system in the provinces came the establishment of a parliament in Paris over which the king presided. Reaching maturity in the first half of the fourteenth century, during the era when our manuscript was made, the success of the parliament was due in part to the revival of Roman law, which received new impetus under Louis, confirming his primary role as the individual empowered both to make new laws and to administer them personally. The revival of Roman law encouraged ideas not only of sovereignty but of nationalism, which were further nourished by the elaboration of royal rituals, the profusion of regalia, and the writing of official chronicles of the French "nation."

Read against this background, the Paris manuscript seems to locate the mythical kingdom of Arthur in a setting remarkably reminiscent of the kingdom of France under Saint Louis. Arthur's imposing presence as he receives prisoners, observes battles, and mediates between adversaries is not unlike Louis's presence felt throughout the French realm. His direct intervention among his knights—for example, in resolving the differences between Bran de Lis and Gawain—may be understood as comparable to Louis's attempts to limit trial by battle. His regal persona, enthroned and hieratically presented, conveys the image of the monarch as preeminent sovereign of the realm, much as contemporary sources acknowledged Louis to be. The particular stance of Arthur at the coronation of Perceval, where he imitates the gesture of the barons at the coronation rite and thereby symbolically affirms the king's authority over the baronial territories, effectively sums up these views. My rereading of the Perceval story based on its miniatures acquires even greater force when we take into account how considerably it departs from a reading based on the text, which consistently marginalizes Arthur, who is at best a harmless, passive agent in a community where his knights are the dynamic instigators.

Miniatures in the second Paris copy (MS fr. 12577) present a somewhat different view of kingship by stressing the importance of the Fisher King at the same time that they offer an analogous view of King Arthur. In an opening frontispiece depicting four moments at the beginning of the romance, Perceval encounters the five knights; he rides off with his javelins; his mother dies; and he kills the Red Knight (fig. 96). This sequence conspicuously skips over his appearance at the court of Arthur. A subsequent single-column miniature illustrates his joust with Engygeron before he visits the court of the Fisher King in the third miniature in the manuscript (fig. 97). In this miniature the Fisher King appears twice, once on the left where he greets Perceval, to whom he gives the sword, and once on the right where he is seated enthroned with a queen at a table while the Grail and the lance pass before them. The importance of this miniature is signaled by its extending across the entire page, breaking the two-column rhythm of the text. Giving the miniature a quasi-independent status, the extensive rubrics that accompany it in effect even substitute for the preceding relevant textual passages. Next King Arthur and Queen Guinevere welcome Perceval back to court as an accomplished knight in a miniature that portrays Perceval's first appearance at Arthur's court. Finally, in another double-column miniature, the penultimate illustration of *Le Conte del Graal,* Perceval encounters a group of penitent lords and ladies before arriving at the hut of the hermit on Good Friday, when he receives guidance on how to remedy his spiritual deficiencies (fig. 98). This entire sequence not only centers on Perceval's spiritual quest for the Grail castle, where the pious Fisher King resides, but serves to suppress altogether the more foolish aspects of his initial attainment of chivalry.

Arthur's role, alongside that of the Fisher King, is not unlike that in the first Paris manuscript. In a striking miniature at the beginning of the First Continuation, Arthur and Guinevere ceremoniously watch the joust between Gawain and Guiromelant (fig. 99). Then Arthur himself leads a siege at the Proud Castle, and subsequently the rich soldier is delivered to Arthur as a captive (fig. 100). In the Second Continuation, the unnamed knight whom Perceval vanquishes in a tent is also sent to Arthur. Unique among all the manuscripts, this copy presents Arthur waging war against King Carras, a relatively minor episode in the text but one of the few instances in the narrative when Arthur exercises an active role, as with a large army of knights he besieges Carras's castle for two months until Carras surrenders (fig. 101).

Even more than in the first Paris manuscript, the rubrics in this one rewrite the story to focus on Arthur: "Ci devise comment le roy artus est devant le chastel orgueilleux"; "comment le riche soldier fu livrez au roy artus"; "Ci devise i. tournoiement que li roie artus fist fere"; "Ci devise comment li rois artus ala a aquavalon pour assiegie le roy cahars." ("Here is described how King Arthur is in front of the Proud Castle"; "How the Rich Soldier was delivered to King Arthur"; "Here is described a tournament that King Arthur had made"; "Here is described how King Arthur went to Aquavalon to besiege King Cahars.") Often these rubrics break with the double-column format of the rest of the text to spread, like the miniatures they accompany, over two columns, a layout that creates the effect of an independent story in which Arthur's role progressively unfolds from rubric to rubric and from miniature to miniature.

The importance of the Fisher King also persists through the continuations. Among the illuminated manuscripts of the Perceval story, this copy is the only one to include a particular sequence of miniatures in the Second Continuation that begins with Perceval's visit to his sister and concludes with his second visit to the Grail castle. First Perceval meets his sister, and they visit his mother's grave. Then he encounters the girl on the mule, who promises to show him the way to the Grail castle. She leads him across the ivory bridge, to the tournament at the Proud Castle, to the knight with the marble tomb, and eventually to the Tree Child before Perceval arrives at the table of the Fisher King, where he again sees the mysterious vessels pass before him. This miniature of the third visit to the Grail castle (Gawain visits the Fisher King in the First Continuation) reinforces the importance of the recurring episode.

Yet ultimately the destiny of the Perceval who visits the Grail castle is not as a lettered cleric who eventually withdraws from the active world, but as a chosen ruler like King Arthur and the Fisher King, as the last miniature implies. Found only in the Mons manuscript of the Perceval story, the subject of this miniature, Perceval and Hector healed by the Holy Grail, seems at first an odd choice for a conclusion (fig. 102). The episode it illustrates precedes most of the events that are generally considered to be climaxes in the text of the story. Illustrated in other manuscripts, these events include the courageous killing of Partinal, which is Perceval's final test; his last visit to the Fisher King, to whom he delivers the head of his enemy Partinal; his final recounting of the story at Arthur's court; his subsequent coronation as heir to the Fisher King; and his eventual retirement with the Grail to a hermitage (e.g., figs. 17, 61, and 95). Instead our miniature illustrates the conclusion of the battle between Perceval and Hector, another knight of the Round Table, whom Perceval does not recognize as they engage in near mortal combat. Unconscious from their serious wounds, the two knights lie on the ground while a "royal angel," as the text specifies, holding the Holy Grail circles them to heal their wounds.

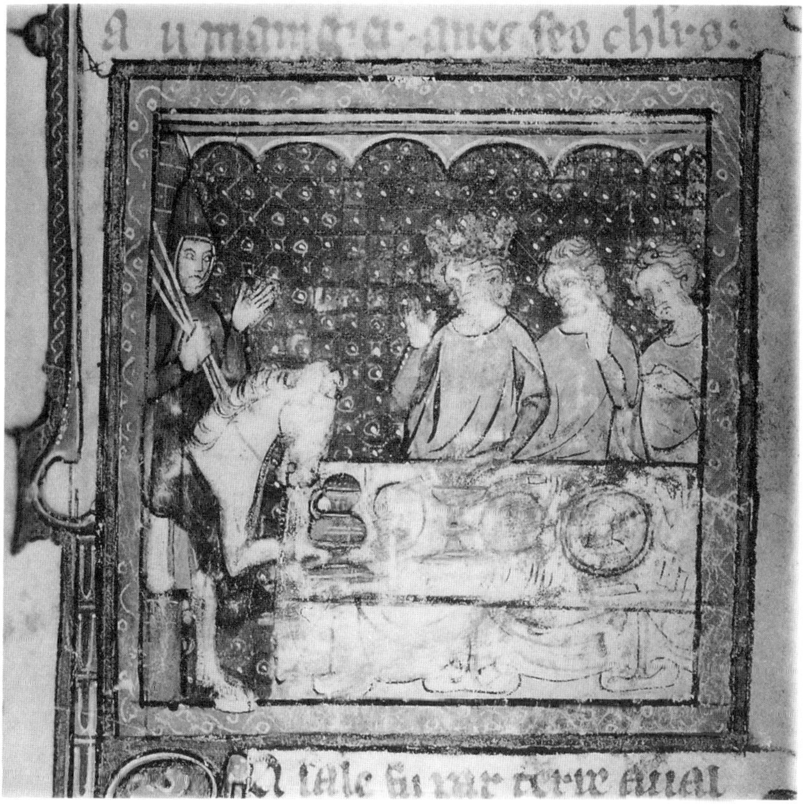

85: Perceval at the court of King Arthur, *Le Conte del Graal*
Paris, Bibliothèque Nationale, MS fr. 1453, fol. 6

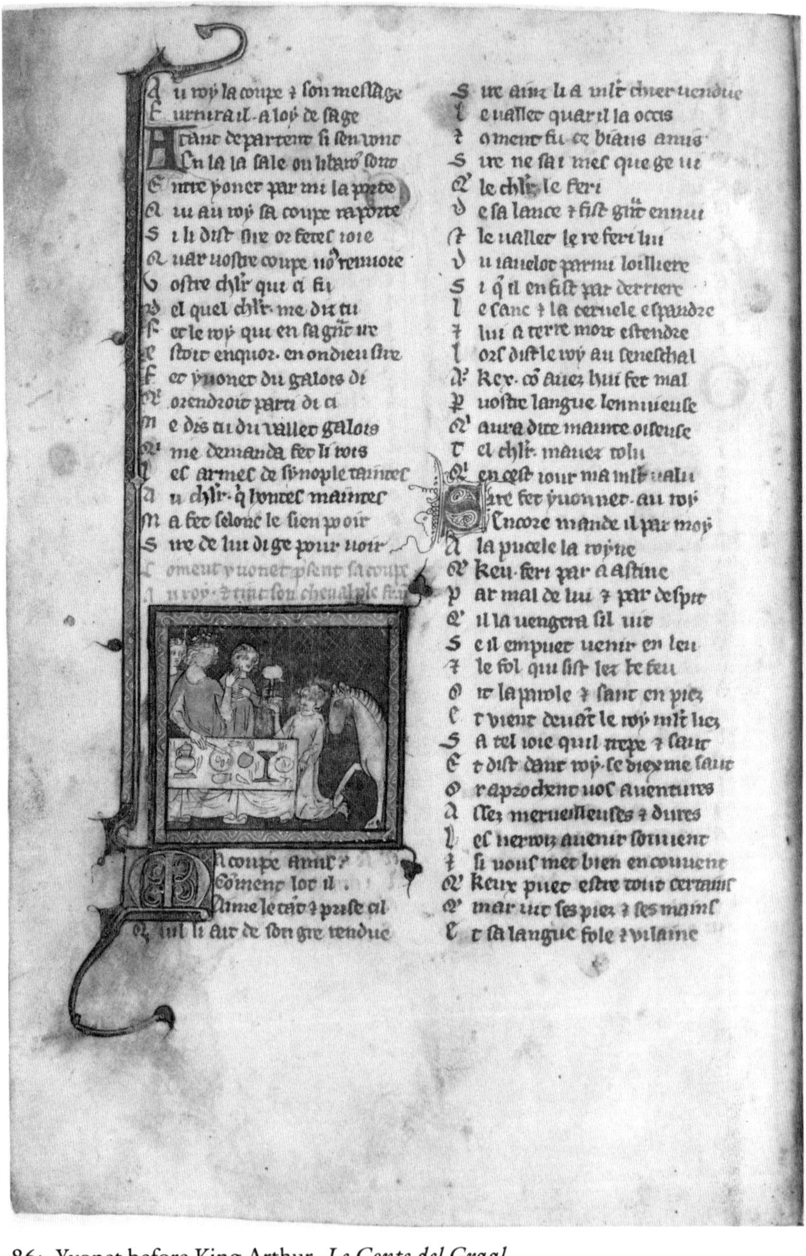

86: Yvonet before King Arthur, *Le Conte del Graal*
Paris, Bibliothèque Nationale, MS fr. 1453, fol. 8

87: Clamadeu before King Arthur, *Le Conte del Graal*
Paris, Bibliothèque Nationale, MS fr. 1453, fol. 20

88: Perceval jousts with Kay, *Le Conte del Graal*
Paris, Bibliothèque Nationale, MS fr. 1453, fol. 30

89: King Arthur and Queen Guinevere with Lady Lore, *Le Conte del Graal*
Paris, Bibliothèque Nationale, MS fr. 1453, fol. 65

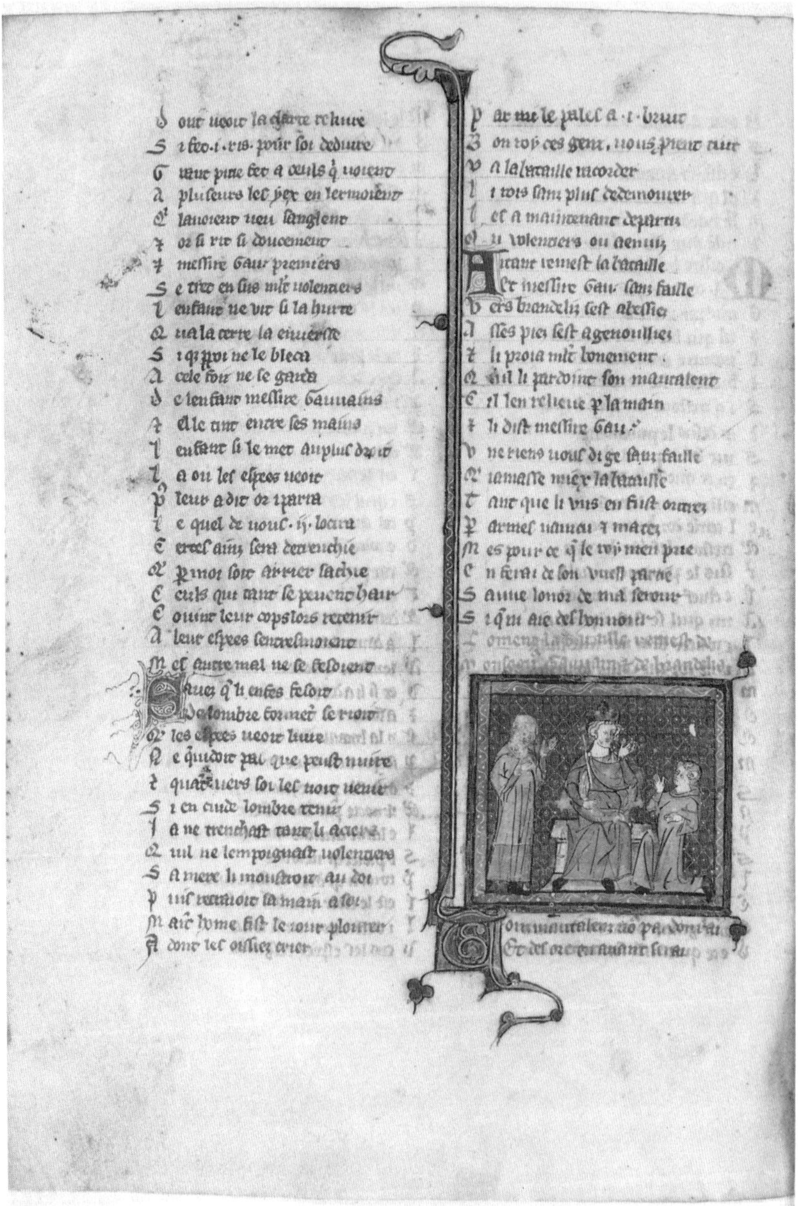

90: King Arthur between Bran de Lis and Gawain, First Continuation
Paris, Bibliothèque Nationale, MS fr. 1453, fol. 102v

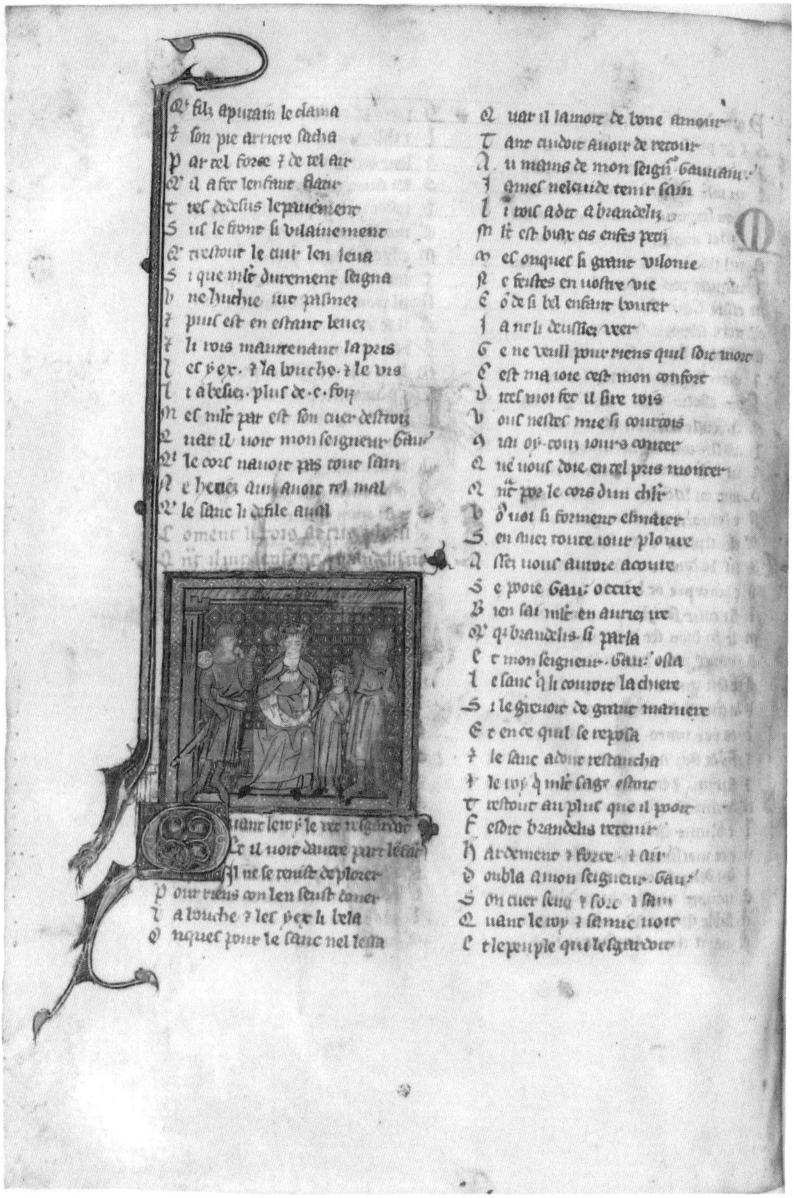

91: King Arthur as judge, First Continuation
Paris, Bibliothèque Nationale, MS fr. 1453, fol. 103v

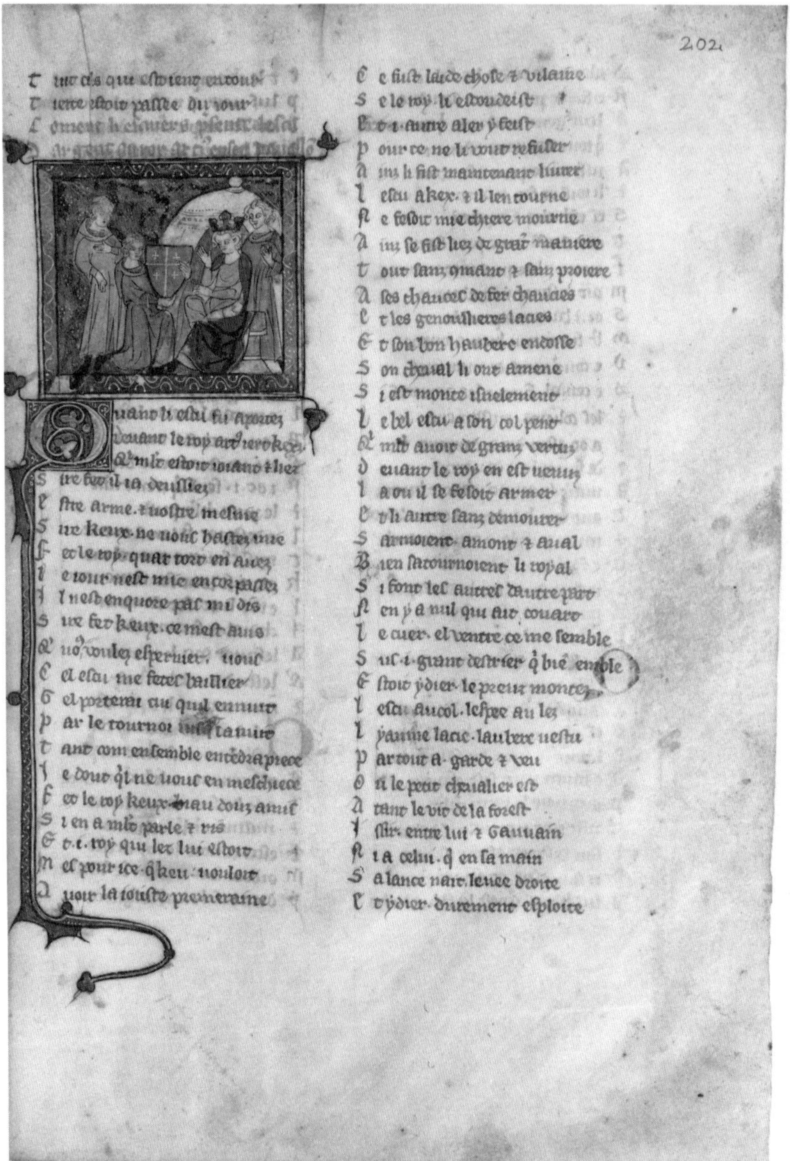

92: The herald presents a shield to King Arthur, Second Continuation
Paris, Bibliothèque Nationale, MS fr. 1453, fol. 202

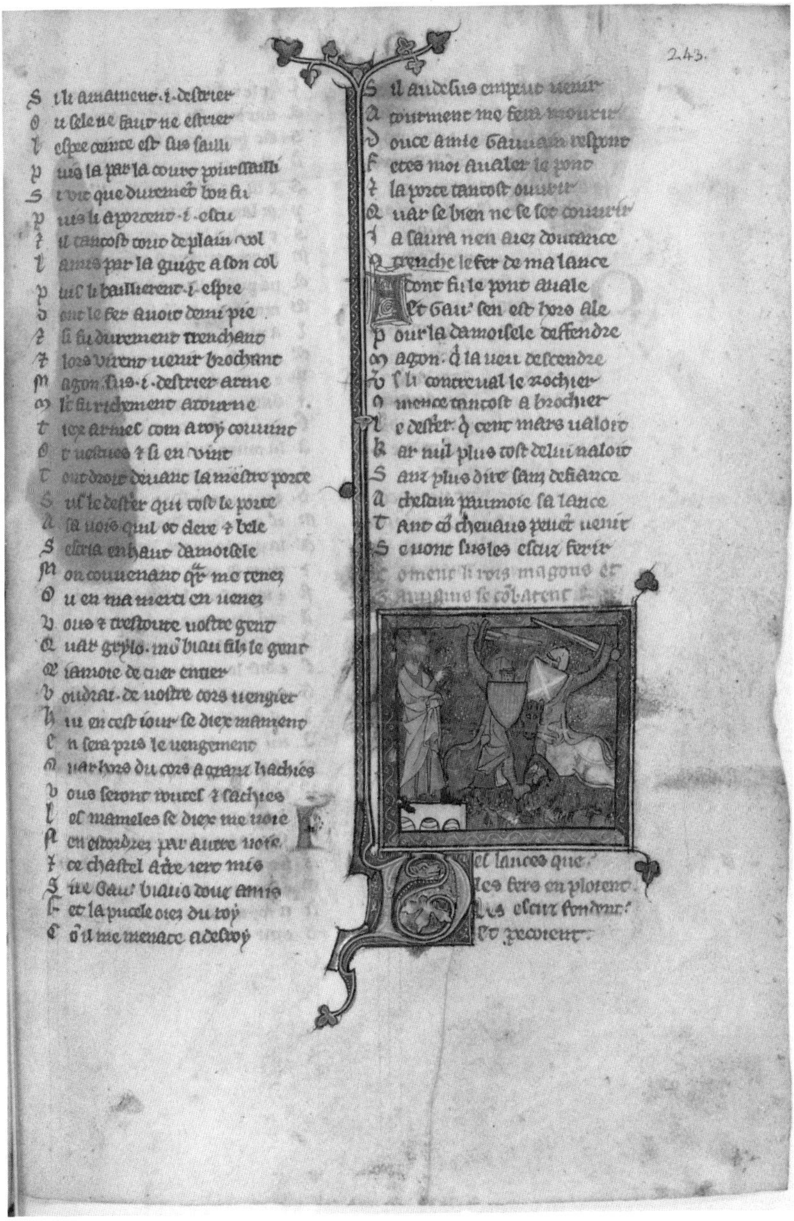

93: Gawain jousts with King Margon in front of King Arthur, Manessier's Continuation
Paris, Bibliothèque Nationale, MS fr. 1453, fol. 243

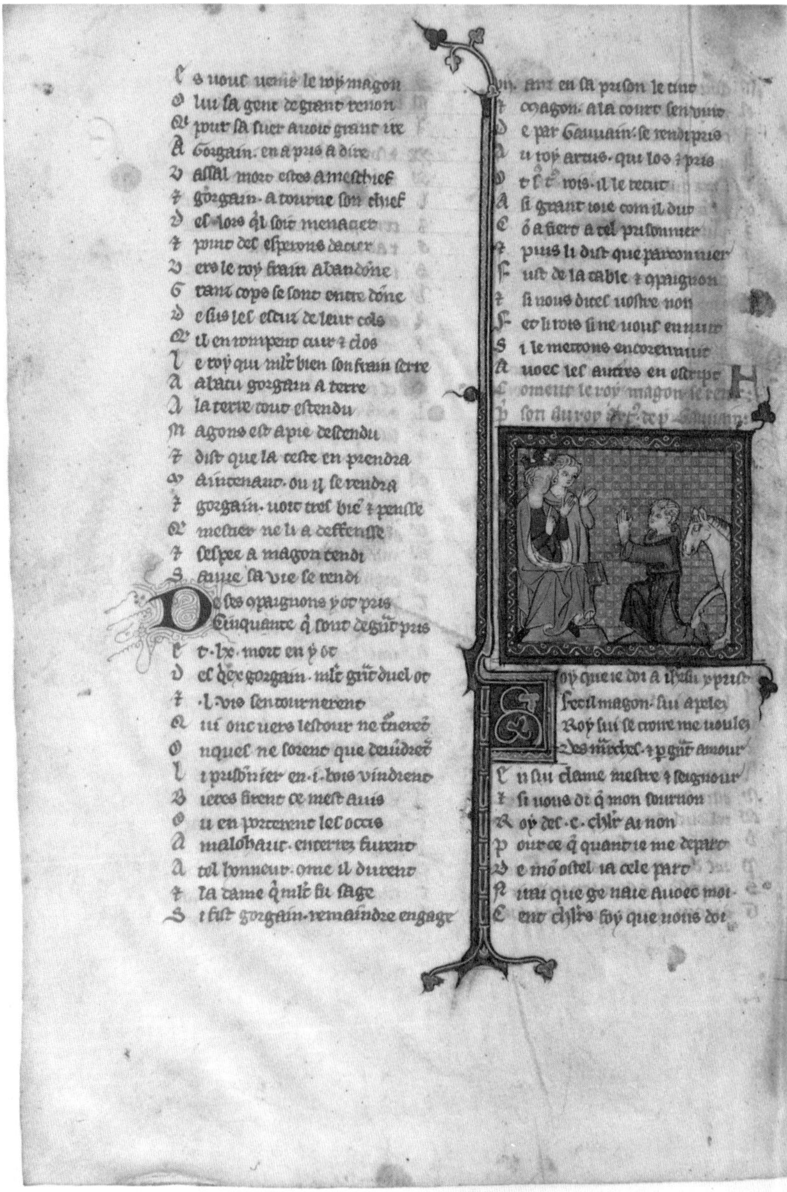

94: King Margon gives himself up as a prisoner to King Arthur, Manessier's Continuation
Paris, Bibliothèque Nationale, MS fr. 1453, fol. 245v

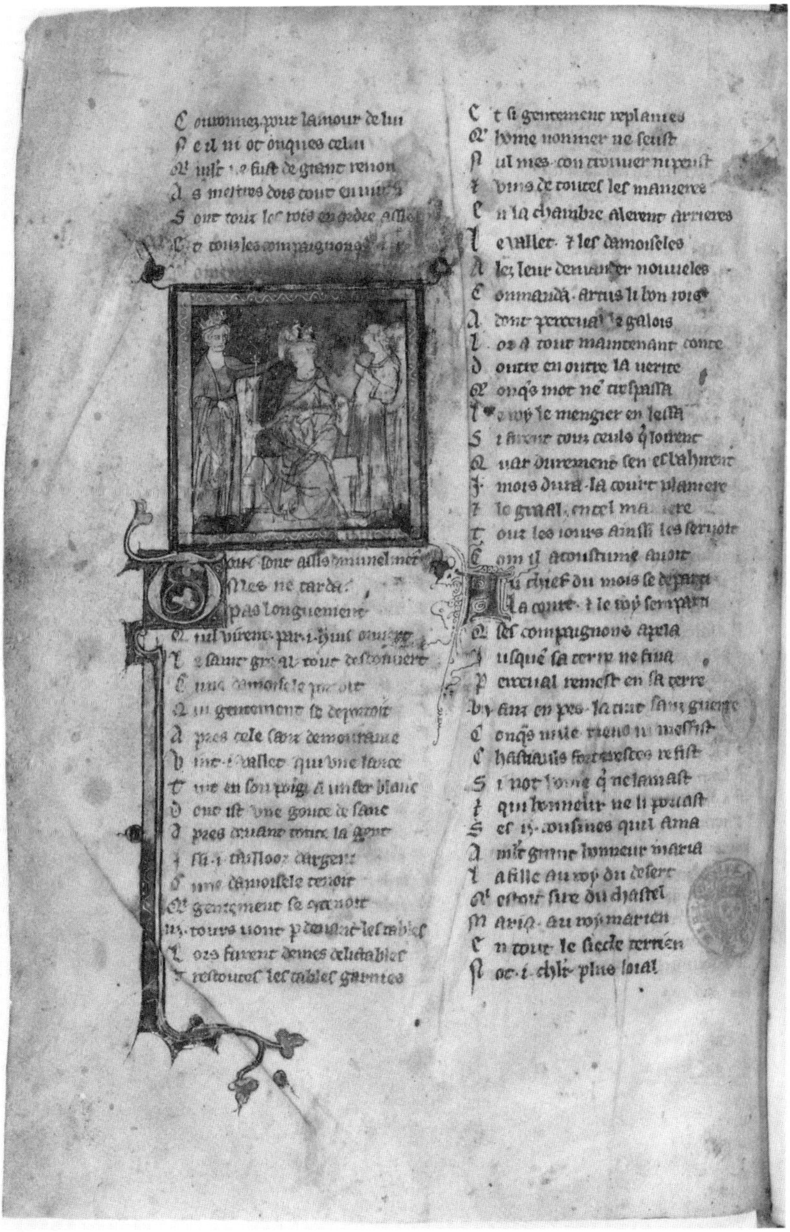

95: Coronation of Perceval, Manessier's Continuation
Paris, Bibliothèque Nationale, MS fr. 1453, fol. 288v

96: Frontispiece, *Le Conte del Graal*
Paris, Bibliothèque Nationale, MS fr. 12577, fol. 1

97: Perceval at the Grail castle with the Fisher King, *Le Conte del Graal*
Paris, Bibliothèque Nationale, MS fr. 12577, fol. 18v

98: Perceval encounters the penitents, *Le Conte del Graal*
Paris, Bibliothèque Nationale, MS fr. 12577, fol. 36

99: Gawain and Guiromelant joust, *Le Conte del Graal*
Paris, Bibliothèque Nationale, MS fr. 12577, fol. 61

100: King Arthur besieges the Proud Castle, First Continuation
Paris, Bibliothèque Nationale, MS fr. 12577, fol. 125v

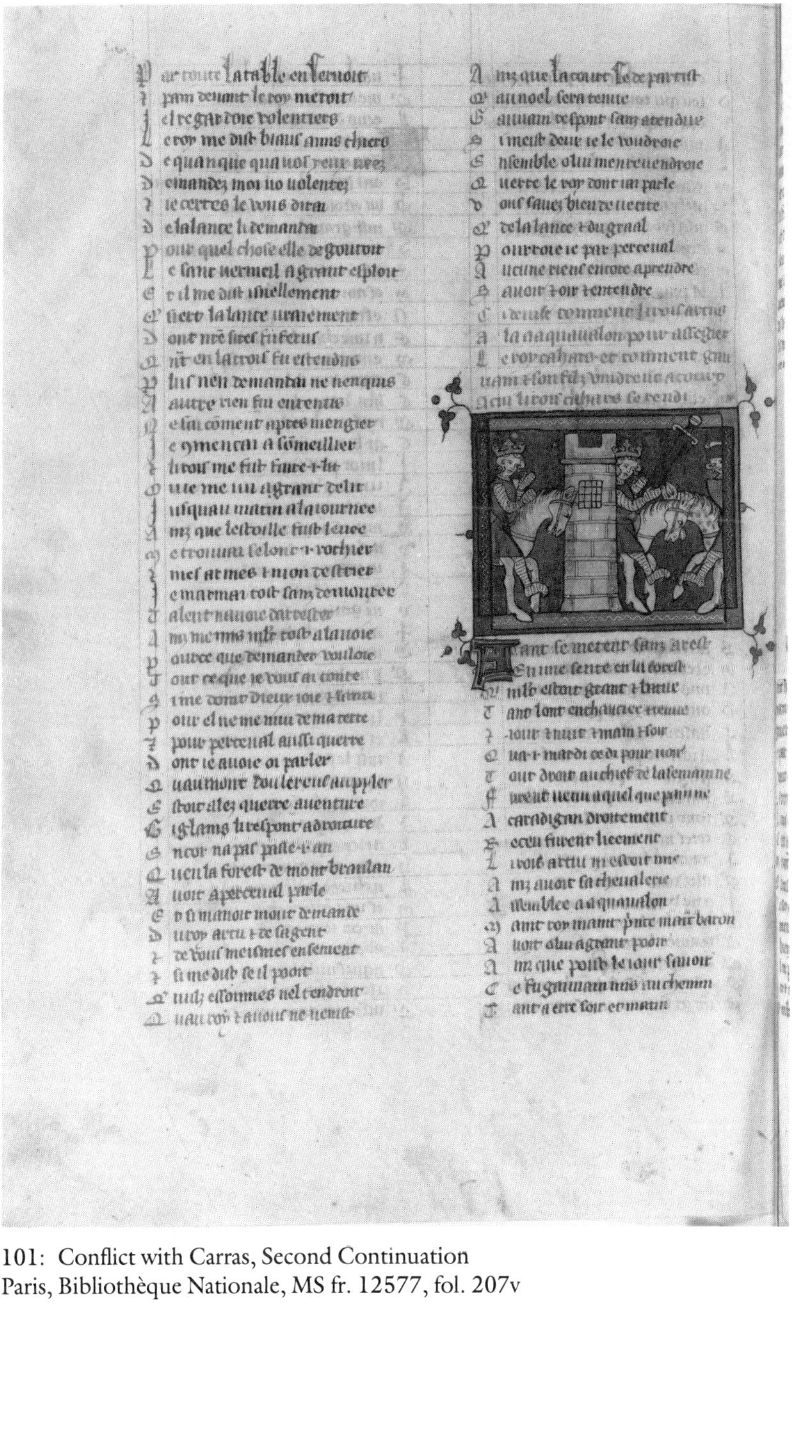

101: Conflict with Carras, Second Continuation
Paris, Bibliothèque Nationale, MS fr. 12577, fol. 207v

102: Perceval and Hector healed by the Grail, Manessier's Continuation
Paris, Bibliothèque Nationale, MS fr. 12577, fol. 265v

103: Gawain on the perilous bed, *Le Conte del Graal*
Paris, Bibliothèque Nationale, MS fr. 12577, fol. 45

104: Frontispiece, Robert de Boron, *L'Estoire del Saint Graal*
Paris, Bibliothèque Nationale, MS fr. 749, fol. 1

It cannot be an accident that Perceval is coupled with Hector at the conclusion of this manuscript, for not only is Hector one of the knights of Arthur's Round Table, but he is also a prince of Troy, from which the French kings were said to be descended through Francio. According to legend, which received "official" confirmation in chronicles originating in Ile-de-France at precisely this time, France was founded by a prince who fled Troy and planted a golden bough on Gallic soil.[3] Some versions of the legend even identify that prince as Hector, son of King Priam and heir to his kingdom. In the miniature, then, Perceval and Hector are linked as types of rulers in what becomes a nationalistic fusion of ancient history with Arthurian romance. The presence of the Grail angel, who also alludes to the French kings' divinely sanctioned right to rule as the "most Christian kings," further underscores their privileged status as rulers. They enjoyed this status in part because of the ceremonial apparatus associated with their rule—for example, the holy ampoule that contained the celestial balm with which they had been anointed since the time of Clovis. This miniature thus presents an unusual, though fitting, conclusion to the Perceval story. In the Arthurian community—understood here as an extension of France's glorious past—Perceval, like Hector, becomes one of the types of French kingship. Like the Capetian kings descended from Clovis, Perceval and Hector stand for a kingship that is divinely sanctioned, suggested here by the Grail angel who miraculously heals their wounds and so enables Perceval to visit the Grail castle and assume the rule of the Fisher King's realm.

If nationalistic myths of origin are bound up in the pictorial conclusion to the Paris manuscript, the miniature cycle taken in its entirety pays tribute to a specific French king, Saint Louis, the "most Christian king." Written and read in the royal capital in the years following the death of Saint Louis, the Paris copy readily evokes a comparison between the Fisher King's castle with its holy vessels and Saint Louis's Sainte Chapelle with the relics of the Passion housed therein. Not so much a church as a reliquary, the Sainte Chapelle, built within the palace complex and dedicated by Saint Louis in 1248, was actually a monumental shrine for the crown of thorns, acquired from Constantinople in 1239, for part of the true cross, purchased in 1241, and for other holy relics (Grodecki, n.d.). By the time the Paris manuscript was written, the platter, the lance, and the Grail in the Perceval story had come to be equated, largely through the circulation of the prose romances, with the charger that served Christ at the Last Supper, the lance that pierced his side at the Crucifixion, and the cup he drank from and that later held his blood. Along with the principal relics of the Sainte Chapelle, the lance, among the three relics in the Perceval story, also appears in contemporary accounts of its treasures (Jordan 1979, 108, n. 14), thus reinforcing the analogy between the royal chapel and the Grail castle.

But in this manuscript there is also much in the character of Perceval to remind the reader of Louis. As in MS fr. 1453, Arthur persists as a model of political strength and judicial authority who wages war and adjudicates disputes. In this respect he recalls the virtues of Louis, which he teaches to the young Perceval. Arthur is joined in the second Paris manuscript by two other male models, the hermit and the Fisher King. In the hermit's character we find Louis's commitment to Christian virtues—humility, charity, and asceticism. In the Fisher King's character we find Louis's religious devotion, including its ostentatious display (the analogy between the Sainte Chapelle and the Grail castle). Even Perceval's unswerving quest to learn the meaning of the holy vessels, which turns his tale into a long pilgrimage, is not unlike Louis's enthusiastic participation in the crusade. Through his quest Perceval eventually achieves a balance between the secular and the spiritual, to become an ideal ruler who, if not canonized like Louis, is clearly divinely appointed, seated at the right hand of God in paradise.

Louis had been dead for more than a quarter of a century when the Paris manuscripts were written, but the memory of his reign endured (for the following, see Hallam 1980, 273ff.). Especially promoted by Philip IV, the Fair (r. 1285–1314), a rapidly developing cult of Louis culminated in 1297 in his official canonizing by Pope Boniface VIII. Philip subsequently had a reliquary made for Louis's skull and distributed fragments of his bones. By the beginning of the fourteenth century, official accounts of Louis's life, biographies composed in the vernacular, monasteries dedicated to him, representational cycles of his miracles and virtues in frescoes and stained glass, and even a religious office served to popularize his political accomplishments and, more notably, to insinuate that his piety was the very cornerstone of French royal prestige (Gousset and Avril 1990, 89–93). Although the program in our manuscripts does not present the same sort of homage to Louis as these semibiographical cycles—and I do not insist on the absolute fusion of Perceval and Louis—the Parisian manuscripts, originating in the same milieu, illustrate another aspect while at the same time confirming the prestige of the saintly king.

The stability and peace enjoyed under Louis's reign gradually eroded. Louis was succeeded by Philip III (r. 1270–85), a weak ruler whose uneventful reign was filled with intrigue (Langlois 1901). Although Philip IV was a more powerful monarch, serious problems plagued his reign. War in

Gascony and Flanders, two provinces that had always resisted royal rule, led to the baronial movement of 1314–15. This movement consisted of leagues of local noblemen, particularly in northern France and Flanders, who opposed excessive taxation and administrative centralization and also sought to restore age-old liberties such as the rights to hold tournaments, wage private wars, and conduct trial by battle. Other crises included a crucial standoff between Pope Boniface VIII and Philip IV over the king's determination to tax the clergy. Then, in the beginning of the fourteenth century a sustained period of cooler and wetter weather ruined crops and produced food shortages, only partially alleviated by a brief recovery in 1318. Dramatic price fluctuations exacerbated increasing problems with the economy.[4] The succeeding short reigns of Philip's three sons, Louis X (1314–16), Philip V (1316–22), and Charles IV (1322–28), did little to counter these crises (Hallam 1980, 273–324). When Charles IV died without male heirs, the kingdom thus faced not only civil war but a dispute over succession, which provoked the Hundred Years' War. Small wonder that Louis's reign came to be seen in nostalgic terms as an idealized golden age.

If the set of historical circumstances I have just outlined helps to explain the idiosyncratic readings of the Paris versions, it nevertheless leaves largely unresolved an important question regarding their place in the entire manuscript tradition. It is curious that these two copies represent the latest illuminated versions of Chrétien's romances. In fact, among the unillustrated manuscripts there is only one that is thought to date later, specifically in the second half of the fourteenth century.[5] There are no versions whatever extant from the fifteenth century, even though the genre of romance remained very much in vogue, and there are no early printed examples. Chrétien's works virtually vanished until nineteenth-century editors went back to the manuscripts to revive them. Why did Chrétien de Troyes go out of fashion? Can we suppose that changing times account for the conspicuous absence of his illuminated manuscripts after the first quarter of the fourteenth century? Or might we hypothesize that, though the twelfth-century romances of Chrétien de Troyes had been recast to address concerns of the northern nobility and the urban populace between the latter half of the thirteenth century and the opening decades of the fourteenth, they no longer served the needs either of regional feudalism or of centralized monarchy in Valois France? I think not.

Of course Chrétien's stories did survive in the many prose versions of Arthurian romance they inspired. Starting with Robert de Boron's trilogy *Li livres dou Graal,* composed initially in verse about 1200 and shortly thereafter translated into prose, numerous revised redactions of the stories circulated, including *Joseph d'Arimathie,* the Didot *Perceval,* and *Perlesvaus.* Then between 1215 and 1230 the five romances that constitute the massive Vulgate cycle, also known after its probably spurious author, Walter Map, as the "pseudo-Map" cycle, were composed: *L'Estoire del Saint Graal, Merlin, Lancelot du Lac, Queste del Graal,* and *La Mort Artu.*[6] Virtually complete by about 1230, the prose cycles subsequently were repeatedly copied and densely illustrated. In fact the proliferation of illustrated prose versions during those very years when the manuscript tradition of Chrétien de Troyes declined suggests pointedly that the two trends may be interrelated. Another look at the Paris copies helps us understand how. I believe that the latest manuscripts of the romances, especially MS fr. 12577, show in their text and images a resistance to verse that eventually gave way to the predominance of prose.

The shift from verse to prose in Old French has been well documented and widely studied.[7] Originating around 1200 principally in northern France, where most of our manuscripts of Chrétien's works also originate, the earliest prose romances (*romans*) appeared in two forms: historical chronicles and Arthurian tales. A self-conscious reference to the power of prose occurs in a frequently cited prologue by Nicolas de Senlis, who in 1202 translated into French the Latin text known as the *Chronicle of Turpin* or *Pseudo-Turpin,* an account of Charlemagne's reign falsely attributed to the archbishop Turpin. Nicolas asserts that, though many of his readers will have already heard the story sung or told aloud, "no rhymed tale is true," and so he will put the story into "rhymeless French."[8] An anonymous colophon to the prose *Perlesvaus,* written about 1200, seems to share Nicolas's disquietude about the fictive qualities of verse when it claims that the story, translated from the Latin, is "true from beginning to end."[9] Verse is unanimously discredited as hearsay in both sorts of writing.

In historical chronicles, the favored status of prose coincides with the use of these texts to legitimize the social and political aspirations of a small group of French aristocrats, the Picard and Flemish lords (this is the argument of Spiegel 1984, 1993). But the contemporaneous rejection of verse in Arthurian romance seems less readily explained. I have argued here that the manuscript versions of Chrétien's verse mask similar social and political uncertainties among a related group of northern aristocrats. In itself, even if fictitious, verse thus apparently posed no obstacle to social expression. Far from it. Rather, in the Arthurian tales the favored status of prose arises when they serve to validate the legend of the Grail as a tangible sign of the incarnation of Christ or, in the case of the Paris manuscript, as testimony to divine kingship.[10] For this purpose Arthurian romances employed the form of writing—prose—used for sacred "true" texts such as the Bible.

The Paris manuscript's particular reliance on rubrics suggests that prose may already have been the preferred linguistic form for Arthurian romance. Not all manuscripts of Chrétien's stories employ rubrics. In fact, I have already linked those that do not more to a culture of orality, where readers still understand the manuscripts partly through their memories of performance. In the Paris manuscript, however, rubrics not only accompany each miniature but summarize the verse text in lengthy, often self-sufficient prose narratives. For example, at the conclusion of *Le Conte del Graal* a rubric describes in extensive detail the action portrayed in the double-column miniature that illustrates the episode of Gawain and the perilous bed: "Ci divise comment mesire Gauvain se coucha ou lit perillieus, l'escu au col, et comment on traioit a li saietes, qu'il ne savoit, dont il venoient. Et estaoient fichiees en son escu. Et apres ce j. lyon issi d'une chambre, a qui il se combati, et tant avint, que le lyon fu ocis, et demoura j. de ses piez dehors l'escu et l'autre par dedens" ("Here is described how Sir Gawain slept on the perilous bed, his shield around his neck, and how he was shot full of arrows, not knowing whence they came. And how they stuck in his shield. And after that, a lion came out of a room, and he battled it, and how it happened that the lion was killed and left one of its paws [embedded] in his shield and the other [paw] outside"). In nine lines of succinct prose, with phrases directly appropriated from the verse, the rubric recounts an episode that stretches over fifty-three lines of melodic verse. In fact, the reader of the verse learns very few additional details not found in the prose.

Not only the length of the rubric but its placement gives it a status independent of the verse text (fig. 103). Transcribed in two columns, one after the other, the rubric comes immediately before the miniature, which in turn breaks the verse text just at the moment when, after the ferryman departs, Gawain reclines on the perilous bed (below the miniature the text reads, "A tant hors du plaes sen ist" ["He went away"]). When we try to comprehend all the parts of the page—the prose rubric, the miniature, and the verse text—we realize how disjunctive this reading is. On one hand, to read the rubric and look at the miniature, we must ignore the natural sequence dictated by the two-column format, specially suited to the short lines of verse. On the other hand, to read the relevant verse text we must start below the picture in one column, continue at the top of the second column, then skip nearly half a page—the space occupied by the rubric and the miniature—to resume the text below the miniature. There are even more extreme examples of such disjunctive reading in this manuscript. In the episode of the combat between Gawain and Guiromelant, among other examples, the rubric deviates entirely from the two-column format of the manuscript and extends, like the picture, across both columns (fig. 99). The conclusion seems inescapable: the unit composed of the prose rubric with its miniature intervenes to substitute for any other reading of the text. Understood in this way, the verse remains in the manuscript merely as a kind of outmoded referent to the original text rather than as an integral part of the reading process.

Taken together, the rubrics in the Paris manuscript could even be considered to present a kind of "derhyming" (*dérimage*) of the verses of Chrétien and his continuators—a composite, if abridged, translation into prose comparable to the prose redactions made from Robert de Boron's *Li livres dou Graal.*[11] My argument concerning the relation of the Paris manuscript to prose gathers further support from the observation that it contains the Long Redaction of the First Continuation, a version almost twice the length of the Short Redaction of the text and one that, composed last, is also thought to be furthest from oral models (Tobbini-Roblin 1989; *Continuations* 1949–83).

But the break with verse is perhaps most striking in the language of the rubrics, which employ distinctive rhetorical strategies, discursive modes of description, and a presentation thought to be characteristic of prose (Godzich and Kittay 1987, 7, 18–21, 22, 37, passim). In our example of Gawain and the perilous bed, the language of the rubric functions as a written intermediary between the reader and the text to summarize or describe the narrative ("Ci devise" ["here is described"]). It also circumscribes the space and time of discourse and action ("Et apres ce" ["and after that"] and "et tant avint" ["how it happened that"]). How different this language is from the language of rubrics in other manuscripts that are more closely related to performance is evident when we notice that they more frequently employ rhetorical strategies that a jongleur reciting the text might use, such as naming the thing or person ("Perceval" or "Messire Gauvain"), rather than summarizing the narrative for silent reading. They also include phrases that more directly recall performance, such as "ci vient li contes a perceval . . . gauvain," or "li contes disent" ("here the stories come to Perceval . . . "or" the stories say"). The idea that in the Paris manuscript action and the discourse associated with it now clearly occur only within the book instead of outside it in performance is reinforced by other rubrics explicitly specifying the manuscript as the locus of the story ("Ci endroit devise" ["In this place is described"]) and quite distinct from those in other manuscripts where the performed story is still understood to be the locus for the picture ("li contes disent"]. To put it another way, the rubrics seem to evolve from oral remarks or asides uttered by a performer before a live audience to descriptive tags or legends added by a scribe to help the reader grapple with the disparate elements now brought together on the page.[12]

The book thus subsumes, and then transforms, elements formerly left to the oral and gestural space of performance, which included the book as a repository of the text, as a sort of prop, but certainly transcended it. Initially not only the recited text but other elements as well—both aural (like rubrics) and visual (like images)—are incorporated into the book, which is no longer dependent on an external performer. Then, just as the text shifts to prose in the manuscript, the rubrics also evolve, likewise developing different discursive strategies.

In claiming that the Paris manuscript presents a prosification of the Arthurian tale that helps us understand the dysfunction of verse, I will take my argument one step further to include a discussion of the miniatures. Just as we read verse and prose texts differently because of their distinctive cultural and cognitive components, so we perceive certain kinds of pictures differently. I suggest that there are the equivalents of "verse" miniatures and "prose" miniatures, pictures more suited to one or the other kind of reading of the text. The growing uneasiness with verse, most acutely observed in the Paris manuscript though also evident in other copies of Chrétien's works, brought with it a disquietude about certain types of pictures. The birth of prose romance thus entails not only new discursive strategies but revised pictorial ones.

A fresh look at the illustrations in the Paris manuscript, compared with illustrations in other manuscripts of Chrétien, focuses on certain features that, in general terms, distinguish the sorts of miniatures accompanying prose and verse. As independent pictures rather than historiated initials, the Paris miniatures stand apart from the text they illustrate. Occupying the entire width of a two-column page, the miniatures, like many of their accompanying rubrics, thus altogether ignore the shorter line required by verse. In contrast, in verse romance the very nature of the historiated initial, situated in a single column, formed with the first letter of the opening word of a passage, and often illustrated with a mimetic image of that word, associates it inextricably with the text in a material and cognitive sense.

The construction of prose miniatures also differentiates them from miniatures more commonly found in verse, in that miniatures in prose works are often static, whereas those in verse texts are more directional. (We might compare this effect to the presence of punctuation in prose, which breaks the text into units, and its absence in verse [evident in the verse text and prose rubrics of the Paris copy].) Certain studies on reading suggest that the silent reader in the later Middle Ages assimilated a text rather differently than does today's reader, working piecemeal and often reading and rereading several passages on one page instead of reading the book through from beginning to end (Saenger 1982; Saenger and Heinlen 1991). In pictorial terms the static character of a prose miniature can be observed in the picture illustrating the combat of Gawain and Guiromelant, which shows the two combatants coming together in the center of the picture—the page—at the junction of the two compartments. They are framed on the left by the onlookers accompanying Guiromelant and on the right by the king and queen. The words of the rubric above stand in direct visual relation to the details of the picture below, fixing—freezing—the rapport between the text and its image. Many other miniatures in the Paris manuscript include details of the composition that link the left and right compartments, unifying them on the page and functioning as a kind of pictorial closure quite distinct from the open-ended momentum in verse manuscripts. In contrast, the omnipresent mounted knight repeatedly rides into the verse text from left to right.

In a sense the miniatures in prose romance, like the rubrics, are descriptive in the full meaning of the word; they summarize the story. There is no need for such complete description in the text or miniatures in verse romance because the jongleur tells the story while the actors enact it; the pictures simply refer to moments in a performative situation, providing memory aids to a tableau that exists outside the book instead of summarizing the story. The hieratic character of the miniatures in prose instead follows the conventions of religious illustration.[13] Just as prose adopts the sacred language of truth, it adapts forms of illustrating truth, the Word revealed, that derive from biblical illustration. These disparate pictorial features might be thought of as analogous to the so-called liberty of verse and constraint of prose (Cerquiglini 1977, 34).

The dysfunction of verse and the preference for prose, which help account, I claim, for the disappearance of Chrétien de Troyes's works from the medieval repertory of romance, also had unexpected consequences for the development of the author portrait. I have already commented on the absence of conventional author portraits in Chrétien's works. Indeed, the closest we come is the historiated initial of Marie de Champagne that introduces *Le Chevalier de la charrette* in the "Guiot" copy of Chrétien's collected works (fig. 41). Through her gesture, Marie instructs Chrétien (absent from the miniature) to tell (not write) the story and thus gives visual form to the opening verses of the romance. I have, however, proposed that in many of the manuscripts of Chrétien's romances the recurring opening image—the historiated initial of the knight on horseback— functions as a kind of author portrait, in part by alluding to the oral deposition of the story at the court. Paradoxically, then, the singular author who for modern critics is named as the creator of the entire genre of Arthurian romance, and who explicitly identifies himself in several of his works, is pictorially absent from the corpus of his works.

Turning to the prose romances, whose authorship is often highly disputed, we find quite the opposite situation—specifically, the insistent intrusion of the author in the pictures. Typical of many such manuscripts is a thirteenth-century copy of Robert de Boron's *L'Estoire del Saint Graal* (Paris, Bibliothèque Nationale, MS fr. 749). Robert de Boron was a Burgundian knight who, between 1191 and 1212, wrote a trilogy of verse romances, *Li livres dou Graal,* which was shortly thereafter, perhaps as early as 1210, translated into prose.[14] His collective account puts the Grail, the cup of the Last Supper and the vessel used by Joseph of Arimathea at the Crucifixion to catch the last drops of Christ's blood, in the context of a pious legend. Robert thus bridges the gap between the early story of the Grail in apostolic times and the quest for the Grail in the time of King Arthur. For Robert, as well as for the authors of the Vulgate cycle, the stories of Chrétien served as sources for Christianizing the legend. A triple-compartment miniature that introduces the Paris copy of Robert's works takes up the full width of the page, like miniatures in the two latest versions of Chrétien's works, and it is followed by a historiated initial (fig. 104).

This pictorial sequence illustrates the long prologue to the prose text.[15] In the first compartment there appears an image of the Trinity, with which the romance opens, for the author's doubts about the Trinity are to be dispelled by "the little book" ("j. livre qui nestoit pas plus grans en tous endrois que le palme d'un home") given to him by Christ himself, who wrote it with his own hand. In the second compartment the hermit author, kneeling before a small chapel, reads from the little book, which afterward he locks up in the chapel where the host is kept. Alas, the book disappears. In the third compartment the hermit, having fallen asleep after a series of adventures, is awakened from a dream by Christ, who appears once more to instruct him to make a copy of the little book. Below the miniature, the historiated initial that incorporates the first words of the prose text depicts the author writing the book.

The textual and pictorial preoccupation with the author and the book in the prose romances is directly related to the sacred character of the narrative as the Word revealed, like the Bible. The writing author in the historiated initial is not unlike the writing evangelists of earlier author portraits, who receive divine inspiration, which they merely transcribe with their instrument, the pen. That the identity of the author is not always altogether clear—in the prologue the translator (or *dérimeur*) of Robert de Boron dwells on the reasons he will not reveal his identity—is in line with what critics point to as the effacement of the author in prose narrative (Cerquiglini 1977, 47–48). Yet for our purposes what is important is not this effacement but the emphasis on *an* author and *the* book, which situates the prose romances squarely in written rather than oral culture.

In a relatively well circumscribed area of northern France that came to include Paris, a social crisis thus coincided with the collapse of an essentially oral culture. For groups of loosely linked feudal families, the tales of the verse romances—Chrétien's stories—served as a diversion at the same time that they reinforced threatened social and economic values of diverse members of this group. For the centralized Capetian monarchy, when written language itself became the very basis for constructing power that was divinely sanctioned, romance like history became linked with truth and had to be recast to reflect its derivation from the Bible, mostly written in prose. In the end one of the most interesting points about the illuminated manuscripts of Chrétien de Troyes is how, in their profound ambivalence about cognitive processes, they seem to stand on the threshold of these two cultures, one oral, the other written.

References to these two cultures are bound up in the last continuation of *Le Conte del Graal.* Manessier, after referring to the sourcebook that preserves the true story of the Grail, concludes his continuation with the provocative couplet, "All those who travel the road will still see the story there sealed in parchment" ("Que li rois Artus seella. / Encor le puet on veoir la, / Tot seelle en parchemin, / Cil qui errent par le chemin").[16] By referring to the sourcebook on which his story depends, Manessier echoes the topos of the "little book" (the divine Word) of Robert de Boron. Yet by describing it as sealed in parchment he employs the language of orality, in which a seal witnesses an oral transaction. Then in a much richer, more subtle metaphor that hinges on a pun in his concluding couplet, *par le chemin* and *parchemin,* he equates the traveling knight with the reader, on one hand, and the road or journey of the knight-reader with the process of *seeing* (hearing, watching, reading) the tale on the other. For Manessier, and I believe for Chrétien, the quest takes place in the present, in the here and now that constitutes the tale. This is what changes with prose romance. In it the quest, taking place in the past and future, is about revelation, and the story can only lead the way.

NOTES

References to works by Chrétien de Troyes are made here by the editor's name and the date of the edition; these works are included in the reference list under "primary sources" by the author's name and the date. Other works, both primary and secondary, are cited here and in the text by author (or title) and date, as listed in the references.

Introduction

1. "Tot seellé en parchemin, / Cil qui errent par le chemin": *Continuations* 1949, 5:343, vv. 42667–68.

2. For the author's life see Frappier 1957 and, with further bibliography, Kelly 1976.

3. For the former view, see Frappier 1982, 4; for the latter, Holmes and Klenke 1959, 51.

4. Available in a useful prose translation, Comfort and Owen 1914; Staines 1990; and in critical editions by Roques, ed. (1952–73). Except when otherwise noted, passages quoted and verse numbers are from these editions.

5. For the manuscript tradition, see Micha 1939; for a list of additional manuscripts and fragments, see Nixon in Busby et al. 1993; the forty-fourth fragment is published in Verbeke, Janssens, and Smeyers 1987, no. 4.23, p. 251.

6. For manuscripts of the lays, see Hoepffner 1927; for the fables, Keidel 1909.

7. For example, Philippe de Beaumanoir, *Jehan et Blonde*, one manuscript; *La Manekine*, one manuscript; Jean Renart, *Roman de l'Escoufle*, one manuscript and one fragment; *Guillaume de Dole*, one manuscript; Gerbert de Montreuil, *Roman de la Violette*, two manuscripts; *Joufroi de Poitiers*, one manuscript; *Hunbaut*, one manuscript; see *Grundriss* 1968, 4, 1:400–453; 4, 2, passim.

8. Paris, Bibl. Nat., MSS fr. 24403 and 1376.

9. Paris, Bibl. Nat., MS fr. 794; Princeton University Library, Garrett MS 125.

10. Paris, Bibl. Nat., MS fr. 1433; Princeton University Library, Garrett MS 125.

11. Paris, Bibl. Nat., MSS fr. 12576, 1453, 12577; Mons, Bibl. Mun., MS 331/206; and Montpellier, Bibl. de l'Ecole de Médecine, MS H 249. The Montpellier manuscript does not figure in this study.

12. Turin, Bib. Nat., cod. G. II.9, including the text of *Cligès* in a compilation; Clermont, Bibl. Mun., MS 248, including only the text of *Perceval;* see Micha 1939, 58–59, 56.

13. London, Brit. Lib., Harley MS 978; see Hoepffner 1927.

14. See the study of reception by Schmolke-Hasselmann 1980.

15. Foerster, ed. (1884–99, 1965); Foerster's and Hilka's editions are based on a composite text of the manuscripts.

16. Hilka, ed. (1932, 1966); most of Hilka's editions form part of Foerster's editions (see preceding note).

17. See above, note 4. Roques's editions are based on a transcription of the "Guiot" manuscript, Bibl. Nat., MS fr. 794.

18. Gerbert de Montreuil 1922–75.

19. *Continuations* 1949–83.

20. See especially "The Transformation of the Aristocracy: France at the Beginning of the Thirteenth Century," in Duby 1977, 178–85, as well as other essays in that volume.

21. Picardy in the thirteenth century has best been studied by Fossier 1976, 1983, 1987, and 1988.

22. Köhler 1974 (first published in German in 1956); for a reassessment of Köhler, see Maddox 1991.

23. For this view of sealing, see Clanchy 1979, 248.

Chapter One

1. "Molt le tint chier, molt l'anora, / De letres bien l'endoctrina, / Grant cure et grant entente i mist. / Tant s'en pena et entremist, / Tant li plot et tant s'i delite / Qu'au tierz an le fist acolite, [*T:* Que clerc le fist et acolite] / Souzdïacre et dïacre aprés": *Continuations* 1949–83, 5 : 340–41, vv. 42569–75.

2. See *Continuations* 1949–83 and, with additional bibliography, *Grundriss* 1968, 4, 1 : 354–61, and 2 : passim.

3. See Corley 1987, 64–67, for a summary of the question of authorship; and *Continuations* 1949–83, vol. 4.

4. Gerbert de Montreuil 1922–75; and *Continuations* 1949–83, vol. 5.

5. Described by Micha 1939, 46–47; Loomis and Loomis 1938, 90–91, fig. 204; Hilka, ed. (1932, 6); Busby 1988, 44; and edited with this manuscript as the base text by Roach, ed. (1956).

6. Gerbert's Continuation appears also in Paris, Bibl. Nat., MS nouv. acq. fr. 6614, fols. 119–97v; see Micha 1939, 51.

7. Described and edited by Van Hamel, ed. (1885), although this manuscript was not known to Van Hamel; and Potvin 1863, esp. 43–56 and 19.

8. For another interpretation of the frontispiece, with a misidentification of its subjects, see Dragonetti 1980.

9. For the French, see Lecoy, ed. (1973–75); and for the English translations, Cline, trans. (1983).

10. English translations of the continuations are from Bryant, trans. (1982).

11. See Van Hamel, ed. (1885), with descriptions of the manuscripts: Paris, Bibl. Nat., MSS fr. 12594 and 24307, are compiled with the *Testament de Jehan de*

Meung and the *Voie d'enfer et de paradis,* xv–xvi; Paris, Bibl. de l'Arsenal, MS 3518, is compiled with the *Miracles de la Vierge,* xxii; and MS fr. 25545 is compiled with the *Roman de la Chastelaine de Vergi,* xvii–xviii.

12. For example, Paris, Bibl. Nat., MS fr. 24307, illustrated with an author portrait, cited by Van Hamel, ed. (1885), xv.

13. See "The Transformation of the Aristocracy: France at the Beginning of the Thirteenth Century" and "The Nobility in Medieval France" in Duby 1977, 94–111 and 178–85.

14. For a brief discussion of this practice with original texts, see Fossier 1983, 27–28, after the Cartulaire-Chronique du prieuré Saint-Georges d'Hesdin.

15. Roques, ed., *Erec et Enide* (1952–73), 203.

16. *Continuations* 1949–83, 5:340.

17. Fol. 1: "Ce livre appartient a Monseigneur de la Hargerie, qui l'a preste a Madame de Contay qui a promis lui rendre."

18. See Chastel 1881–87, 3:250 (F. de Raisse), and La Morlière 1642 (de Contay).

19. On the territory of Blancfosse, not far from Amiens, see Fossier 1987, 1: 303, 2:512, n. 194, 2:686, n. 241.

20. There are two saints named Firmin, both bishops of Amiens; see Réau 1958, 3:500:502.

Chapter Two

For an earlier version of this chapter, see Hindman 1991.

1. "De ce que li rois devisa / tote la corz mialz l'en prisa, / car molt i voloient aler / li baron et li bacheler": Roques, ed. (1952–73), 21, vv. 673–76; translation from Cline, ed., (1975) 19.

2. See "Youth in Aristocratic Society of Northwestern France in the Twelfth Century," in Duby 1977, 112–22; Flori 1975; and for the various medieval meanings, Godefroy 1880–1938, 1:545–46.

3. On Paris, Bibl. Nat., MS fr. 1433, see Loomis and Loomis 1938, 100–101; Micha 1939, 44; Foerster, ed. (1884–99), vii; Jonin 1958, 15; Porcher 1955, 29; and Woledge 1986, 1:4. With the exception of Porcher, who based his analysis on the illustrations, all scholars place the manuscript in Picardy based on its dialect. I thank Alison Stones for informing me that she believes the manuscript might be localized in Tournai. On Princeton, Univ. Lib., Garrett MS 125, see McGrath 1963a, 583–94, and 1963b; Rahilly 1973, 1974, 1978; Rushing 1991–92.

4. Woledge 1969. In royal fief lists, the vavasor appears at the very base of the feudal hierarchy, according to Baldwin 1986.

5. Roques, ed. (1952–73), 24–25, vv. 785–87: "Qu'an ne puet pas dire la some / de prode fame et de prodome, / des qu'il s'atorne, a grant bonte."

6. See "Youth," "The Transformation of the Aristocracy in France at the Begin-

ning of the Thirteenth Century," and "The Diffusion of Cultural Patterns in Feudal Society" in Duby 1977, 171–85; and "Remarques sur la littérature généalogiques en France au XIe et XIIe siècles" in Duby 1973, 287–98.

7. For a study of the manuscripts and a partial edition, see Smeets, ed. (1955, 1985, 1991), and McGrath 1963b. Gautier's continuator, Pierre de Riés, writing after about 1280, again in Picardy, more explicitly linked Judas Maccabees with knighthood in a related work called *La Chevalerie de Judas Macabé.*

8. On Judas Maccabees in medieval art and literature, see Loomis and Loomis 1938, 39ff., and Schroeder 1971.

9. See Rushing 1991–92 for a different discussion of the importance of the marriage episode in the Princeton manuscript.

10. Roques, ed. (1952–73), 64, vv. 2083ff. On the feudal control over a widow's or heiress's marriage, which continued in the thirteenth century, see Brundage 1987, 438–39.

11. See especially Krueger 1985; Frappier 1969, 72–76; Halligan 1970; and Uitti 1973, 183–213.

12. See Brundage 1987; and on the twelfth century, Leclercq 1983 and Duby 1978, 1983.

13. See, for example, the prominence of cases of cruelty in marriage as noted by Brundage 1987, 455.

14. For a French translation of the chronicle see Lambert d'Ardres 1973, 143–44.

15. For the passage in *Erec et Enide,* see Roques, ed. (1952–73), 1, vv. 19–22: "d'Erec, le fil Lac, est li contes, / que devant rois et devant contes / depecier et corronpre suelent / cil qui de conter vivre vuelent." For the passage in *Le Chevalier au lion,* see Roques, ed. (1952–73), vv. 5356–71.

16. *Romance of Hunbaut* 1984, 81, vv. 3048–53: "La pucele est contre els levee / Si tost conme venir le[s] voit. / O li sis puceles avoit / Et chevaliers desi a dis / d'un roumant oënt uns biaus dis, / La pucele le faissoit lire." The unique manuscript of Hunbaut is contained in an unillustrated compilation, written in Picard dialect, that also includes three works by Chrétien—*Erec et Enide, Le Chevalier au lion,* and *Le Chevalier de la charrette*—along with other octosyllabic Arthurian romances such as *L'Atre périlleux,* thus reinforcing the thesis that these manuscripts functioned similarly in similar sociogeographic milieus. On the manuscript (Chantilly, Musée Condé, MS 472), see Micha 1939, 39.

Chapter Three

1. "Bien largement encor deus ans / Que ne porent avoir enfans, / . . . / Tant que Dex les a porveü / Si que la dame ençainte fu. / Grant joie en ont tout cil eü, / Qui lor seignor aiment de rien": *Bliocadran* 1976, 85–86, vv. 55–61.

2. See Micha 1939, 57–58; Faider and Faider-Feytmans 1931, 352; Potvin, ed.

(1865–71); Potvin 1863; *Continuations* 1949–83, 1:xxiii–xxiv and passim; and Verbeke, Janssens, and Smeyers 1987, 207–9.

3. On date and localization based on heraldry, see Potvin, ed. (1865–71), 3:1; based on dialect, see *Elucidation* 1931, 26–27; based on style, see Stones 1970, 246.

4. *Elucidation* 1931, 101, vv. 478–81, actually part of eight lines from Chrétien's original prologue: "Chrestiens qui entent et paine / A reimoier le mellor conte / Par le comandement le conte / Qui soit contes en court roial."

5. In this case the interpretations of both Potvin, ed. (1865–71), 2:2, and Thompson (*Elucidation* 1931), 67–78 would be essentially correct; the former took them as the seven heroes (although the mounted figure cannot be Arthur), and the latter as the seven stories told by knights at court.

6. For a transcription of all the rubrics in the Mons manuscript, see Potvin 1863, passim.

7. "Et aprés çou vos jüerront / Que la terre vos garderont / A oés vo fil, se vos volés / Qu'il en sera sires clamés, / Et tout a seignor le tenront, / Come seignor le garderont": *Bliocadran* 1976, 101, vv. 557–62.

8. Also independent of the other textual redactions is a twenty-two-line opening to the Second Continuation that, in conformity with the historiated initial, describes Perceval riding in the forest; for the passage, see *Continuations* 1949–83, 4:3, 5.

9. Lille, Archives Départementales du Nord, MS 10 H 323; see Bruchet 1928, 206, and Loisne 1903, with plates. For further illustrations, some in color, see Warlop 1975–1:64, 87, 97, 147.

10. For this view see especially "The Structure of Kinship and Nobility: Northern France in the Eleventh and Twelfth Centuries" and "French Genealogical Literature: The Eleventh and Twelfth Centuries" in Duby 1977, 134–48 and 149–57. see also Genicot 1975.

11. Paris, Bibl. Nat., MS fr. 6978; the genealogy is published in *Chroniques Anglo-Normandes* 1936–40, 3:vi–xxxvi.

12. Ibid., 3:xi: "Artus, rois de Bretaigne, donna et otria francement et entirement a home noble, Legier, conte de Bouloigne, Amiens, Teroane et Tournais; liquels Legiers fu li premiers quens de Bouloigne, liquele estoit apelee Hautemure."

13. From the *Metalogicon,* quoted by Clanchy 1979, 202–3; see also Stock 1984 for a particularly useful discussion of the overlap between orality and literacy.

Chapter Four

1. "Mes une grant mervoille voit / qui poïst faire grant peor / qu plus riche conbateor, / ce fu Tiebauz li Esclavons, / ne nus de ces que or savons, / ne Opiniax, ne Fernaguz": Roques, ed. (1952–73), 174 vv. 5724–29.

2. See Bezzola 1947; Maddox 1978; Luttrell 1974; and with further bibliography, Burgess 1984.

3. Described by Micha 1939, 50–51, 219–21, 262–63, and Eusebi (Raimbert de Paris 1963, 9); reproduced by Bezzola 1947, pl. 8, and Loomis and Loomis 1938, 100, fig. 258. On the text, Micha claims, "Ce ms. est la copie peu retouchée, mais exécuté sans grand soin, d'un mauvais modèle" (221).

4. I have not considered Paris, Bibl. Nat., MS fr. 1376, the only other illustrated manuscript of the text, which includes a historiated initial of the hunt of the white stag introducing *Erec et Enide;* see Micha 1939, 42–43. Rebound at a later date with *Le Roi Florimont,* MS fr. 1376 is, for Micha, of Burgundian origin.

5. Micha (1939) dates the manuscript thirteenth to fourteenth century and notes merely that the text is "très teinté de picard"; I thank Alison Stones for her suggestions on date and localization, which I have followed here.

6. Struck by the unusual combination of texts in the Paris manuscript, which he found "disconcerting," Micha, puzzling over the manuscript's audience, speculated that the readers must have had very diverse tastes to be pleased by three such dissimilar works (1939, 262–63).

7. With the following exceptions: MS fr. 1374, an anthology that includes, among others, *Cligès* and two chansons de geste—Girard de Vienne and *Le Roman de Florimont* by Aymon de Varennes (cf. Micha 1939, 42); and MS fr. 12603, an anthology that includes *Le Chevalier au lion* along with *Les Enfances Ogier le Danois* by Adenet le Roi and *Le Roman de Fierabras* (cf. Micha 1939, 49–50). It was more common to compile romances of Chrétien with antique romances or other Arthurian tales. It was not unusual, however, for epics to be compiled with other romances: e.g., MS fr. 368, the cycle of William of Orange with Partenopeu de Blois, among other texts.

8. There is no modern edition of *Garin de Monglane,* pending the one promised by Hendrickson 1989, 203–15, esp. 215, n. 5. According to Hendrickson, the Paris manuscript is the most authoritative version of the text. He has published prolegomena to an edition of a fragment of 15,048 lines at Princeton (Garrett MS 125) in Hendrickson 1975. On the manuscript tradition and a summary of the story, see also Gautier 1878–92 1:240 and 4:126–71. Gautier records three manuscripts of Garin, to which Hendrickson added the Princeton fragment, making a total of four.

9. On Thiebaut the Esclavon in the William of Orange cycle, see Wathelet-Willem 1975, 1:591–92. See Roques, ed. (1952–73), 239 and 242, for identifications of Fernaguz, "héro de chanson de geste," and Ospiniax, "roi de Babylone, dans une chanson de geste perdue."

10. On *Ogier le Danois,* see Eusebi, in Raimbert de Paris 1963; Barrois, in Raimbert de Paris 1842; Gautier, 1878–92, 3:52–63, 240–57, and 1:236; and Le Gentil 1957. Gautier, then Eusebi, records five manuscripts of *Ogier le Danois.* The epic character Ogier may be identical with a certain Antcharius, whose historical role at Charlemagne's court is documented.

11. The manuscript lacks vv. 1–112 at the beginning, vv. 12004–12346 at the end, and has one lacuna, vv. 10681–11424, according to Eusebi (Raimbert de Paris 1963, 9).

12. On the evolution of the foot soldier and the battle of Bouvines, see Oman 1898, 457–80.

13. For an interpretation of the writing of history motivated by related sociopolitical circumstances, see Spiegel 1986, 1987, and 1993.

14. On the relation between ancestry and epic, see Bloch 1983, 92–127.

15. Cesar, l'empereres de Rome, / et tuit li roi que l'en vos nome / an diz et an chançons de geste": Roques, ed., *Erec et Enide* (1952–73), 201, vv. 6615–17. Chrétien's sporadic references to epic and epic heroes have instead been understood as revealing his recognition of the inadmissibility of transferring characters from the genre of epic to that of romance; see Jauss 1963, esp. 70.

16. See especially the series of articles by Curtius 1950, 307, who proposed abandoning the old distinction between the genres and claimed that these all were chivalric romances, distinguished by their subjects—national, antique, Eastern, or Celtic. For contemporary distinctions between the genres, however, see Bodel 1906, vv. 6–11, in which Jean Bodel distinguishes between the *vain et plaisant* Arthurian tales and the *voir* French ones.

17. For a summary of the criticism and bibliography, see Victorio and Payen 1988.

Chapter Five

1. "Il les lut et trueve sanz faille / Que del siecle finés estoit / Ses oncles, qui molt covoitoit / Qu'a Corbenic, n'i sejornast, / Venist et si se coronast": *Continuations* 1949–83, 5:337, vv. 42452–56.

2. See Micha 1939, 44–45, 47–49, and Holland 1854, 201–3 (for a transcription of the rubrics in MS fr. 12577); Loomis and Loomis 1938, 101–2, figs. 263–66 (on MS fr. 12577); described by Hilka, ed. (1932), vi; and *Continuations* 1949–83, 1:xxvi–xxvii, xxix–xxx. Some of the miniatures are reproduced in Bryant, trans. (1982), 144, 145, 160, 161.

3. This myth was popularized in the *Grandes Chroniques de France* (1920), 1: 9–12, where Francio, "fiuz d'Ector," is credited with founding the city of Sicambria in France.

4. On the economic and political crises, see Duby 1968 and Perroy 1949.

5. London, Heralds College, Arundel MS 14, dates in the second half of the fourteenth century according to Micha 1939, 61.

6. On the prose romances, with further bibliography, see Reiss, Reiss, and Taylor 1984.

7. See especially Godzich and Kittay 1987, Kittay 1988, Spiegel 1993, Jodogne 1963, and Clanchy 1979.

8. "Nus contes rimes n'est verais": see Woledge and Clive 1964, esp. 27–29.

9. "Vraie des le commencement desqu'en la fin": quoted in Woledge and Clive 1964, 39–40.

10. For a related argument, see Chasse 1985 and the articles in *Perspectives médiévales* (1977), esp. Poirion and Cerquiglini, and Robert de Boron 1981, 7–11.

11. Robert de Boron 1981, xv, xix, and passim.

12. On the further evolution of rubrics in prose romancees, see Baumgartner 1985.

13. For the relation between religious and secular illustration, see especially Stones 1977.

14. Robert de Boron 1981; Bogdanow 1966; and for a list of the manuscripts in prose, see Woledge 1954, 69–70, 82–83; *Lestoire del Saint Graal* 1908.

15. *Lestoire del Saint Graal* 1908, 3–12; for a related series of illustrations (denser) in two dated manuscripts, see Loomis and Loomis 1938, fig. 217 (Bonn, MS 526, dated 1286), and fig. 216 (Paris, BN, MS fr. 342, dated 1274), in which King Henry appears before Map, commanding him to write the book.

16. *Continuations* 1949–83, 5:343, vv. 42665–68.

REFERENCES

Printed Primary Sources

Anonymous of Bethune. 1904. *Chronique française des rois de France.* Ed. Léopold Delisle. In *Recueil des historiens des Gaules et de France,* 24:750–75. Paris.

L'Atre périlleux. 1936. Ed. B. Woledge. Classiques français du Moyen Age 75. Paris: Champion.

Bliocadran: A Prologue to the "Perceval" of Chrétien de Troyes. Edition and Critical Study. 1976. Ed. Lenora D. Wolfgang. Beihefte zur Zeitschrift für Romanische Philologie 150. Tübingen: Max Niemeyer.

Bodel, Jean. 1906. *Jean Bodels Sachsenlied.* Ed. F. Menzel and E. Stengel. Part 1. Ausgaben and Abhandlungen 99. Marburg.

Chrétien de Troyes. 1865–71. *Perceval le Gallois, publié d'après le manuscrit de Mons.* Ed. Charles Potvin. 6 vols. Société des Bibliophiles Belges Séant à Mons 21. Mons.

———. 1884–99. *Sämtliche erhaltene Werke.* Ed. W. Foerster. Halle; reprint Amsterdam, 1965.

———. 1914. *Arthurian Romances.* Trans. W. W. Comfort, intro. and notes D. D. R. Owen. London: Everyman's Library.

———. 1932. *Der Percevalroman (Li Contes del Graal).* Ed. A. Hilka. Halle; reprint 1966.

———. 1952–73. *Les Romans de Chrétien de Troyes.* Ed. Mario Roques. CFMA. Paris: Champion. *Erec et Enide,* vol. 80, 1952; *Cligès,* ed. A. Micha, vol. 84, 1957; *Le Chevalier de la charrette,* vol. 86, 1958; *Le Chevalier au lion (Yvain),* vol. 89, 1960; *Le Conte du Graal (Perceval),* vol. 100, 1973.

———. 1956. *Le Roman de Perceval, ou Le Conte du Graal.* Ed. William Roach. TLF. Geneva: Droz.

———. 1973–75. *Le Conte du Graal.* Ed. F. Lecoy. 2 vols. CFMA. Paris: Champion.

———. 1975. *Yvain, or The Knight with the Lion.* Trans. Ruth Harwood Cline. Athens: University of Georgia Press.

———. 1982. *Perceval: The Story of the Grail.* Trans. Nigel Bryant. Cambridge: D. S. Brewer.

———. 1983. *Perceval, or The Story of the Grail.* Trans. Ruth Harwood Cline. Athens: University of George Press.

———. 1990. *The Complete Romances of Chrétien de Troyes.* Trans. David Staines. Bloomington: Indiana University Press.

Chroniques Anglo-Normandes: Recueil d'extraits et d'écrits relatifs à l'histoire de Normandie et d'Angleterre pendant les XIe et XIIe siècles. 1936–40. 3 vols. Rouen: Edouard Frère.

Continuations: The Continuations of the Old French Perceval of Chrétien de Troyes. 1949–83. Ed. William Roach. 5 vols. Philadelphia: University of Pennsylvania Press and American Philosophical Society.

The Elucidation: A Prologue to the Conte del Graal. 1931. Ed. A. W. Thompson. New York: Publications of the Institute of French Studies; reprint Slatkine, 1982.

Gautier de Belleperche. 1955. *La Chevalerie de Judas Macabé.* Ed. Jean Robert Smeets. Assen.

———. 1991. *La Chevalerie de Judas Maccabee de Gautier de Belleperche (et de Pieros du Riés): Ms. Berlin Staatsbibliothek, Hamilton 363.* Ed. Jean Robert Smeets. 2 vols. Assen: Van Gorcum.

———. 1985. *Le Fragment de la Chevalerie de Judas Machabee de Gautier de Belleperche: Contenu dans le manuscrit Garrett 125 de la Princeton University Library.* Ed. Jean Robert Smeets. Leiden: Hakucki Press.

Gerbert de Montreuil. 1922–75. *La Continuation de Perceval.* Ed. Mary Williams and Marguerite Oswald. 3 vols. CFMA. Paris: Champion.

Les Grandes Chroniques de France. 1920. Ed. J. Viard. Paris: SHF.

Lambert d'Ardres. 1973. *Histoire intellectuelle de l'Occident médiéval.* Ed. Jacques Paul. Paris: Armand Paul.

Lestoire del Saint Graal. 1908. Ed. Oscar H. Sommer. In *The Vulgate Version of the Arthurian Romances,* 8 vols. Washington, D.C.: Carnegie Institution; reprint New York, 1969.

Mimes français du XIIIe siècle. 1910. Ed. Edmond Faral. Paris: Champion.

Panegyriques des comtes de Hainaut et de Hollande Guillaume I et Guillaume II. 1863. Ed. C. Potvin. Mons: Masquillies et Dequesne.

Raimbert de Paris. 1842. *La Chevalerie d'Ogier de Danemarche par Raimbert de Paris.* Ed. J. Barrois. 2 vols. Romans des Douze Pairs de France 8. Paris: Techener.

———. 1963. *La Chevalerie d'Ogier de Danemarche.* Ed. Mario Eusebi. Testi e Documenti di Litteratura Moderna 6. Milan: Istituto Editoriale Cisalpino.

Rencluse of Molliens. 1885. *Li Romans de Carité et Miserere, du Renclus de Moiliens.* Ed. A. G. Van Hamel. 2 vols. Bibliothèque de l'Ecole des Hautes Etudes 61–62. Paris.

Robert de Boron. 1981. *Le Roman du Graal: Manuscrit de Modène par Robert de Boron.* Ed. Bernard Cerquiglini. Paris: Union Générale d'Edition.

The Romance of Hunbaut: An Arthurian Poem of the Thirteenth Century. 1984. Ed. Margaret Winters. Davis Medieval Texts and Studies 4. Leiden: E. J. Brill.

Secondary Works

Adolf, Helen. 1943. "A Historical Background for Chrétien's *Perceval.*" *Proceedings of the Modern Language Association* 58:597–620.

Baldwin, John. 1986. *The Government of Philip Augustus: Foundations of French*

Royal Power in the Middle Ages. Berkeley and Los Angeles: University of California Press.

Baumgartner, Emmanuele. 1985. "Espace du texte, espace du manuscrit: Les manuscrits du *Lancelot-Graal.*" In *Ecritures, II,* ed. Anne-Marie Christin, 95–119. Paris: Le Sycomore.

———. 1991. "Robert de Boron et l'imaginaire du livre du Graal." In *Arturus Rex, Acta Conventus Lovaniensis 1987,* vol. 2, ed. W. Van Hoecke, G. Tournoy, and W. Verbeke, 259–68. Mediaevalia Lovaniensia, ser. 1, studia 17. Louvain: Leuven University Press.

Bedos Rezak, Brigitte. 1982. "Les Sceaux au temps de Philippe Auguste." In *La France de Philippe Auguste: Le temps des mutations. Actes du Colloque international organisé par le C.N.R.S., Paris, 29 septembre–4 octobre 1980,* ed. Robert-Henri Bautier, 721–36. Paris: Editions du CNRS.

———. 1986. "The Social Implications of the Art of Chivalry: The Sigillographic Evidence (France 1050–1250)." In *The Medieval Court in Europe,* ed. Edward R. Haymes, 142–75. Houston German Studies 6. Munich: Wilhelm Fink.

———. 1988. "Medieval Seals and the Structure of Chivalric Society." In *The Study of Chivalry: Resources and Approaches,* ed. Howell Chickering and Thomas Seiler, 313–72. Kalamazoo, Mich.: Medieval Institute Publications.

Bezzola, Reto. [1947]. *Le Sens de l'aventure et de l'amour (Chrétien de Troyes).* Paris: La Jeune Parque.

Bloch, R. Howard. 1983. *Etymologies and Genealogies: A Literary Anthology of the French Middle Ages.* Chicago: University of Chicago Press.

———. 1991. *Medieval Misogyny and the Invention of Western Romantic Love.* Chicago: University of Chicago Press.

Bogdanow, Fanni. 1966. *The Romance of the Grail.* Manchester: Manchester University Press.

Bozoky, Edina. 1985. "De la parole au monument: Marquer la mémoire dans la littérature Arthurienne." In *Jeux de mémoire: Aspects de la mnémotechnie médiévale,* ed. Bruno Roy and Paul Zumthor, 74–75. Paris: Vrin.

Brault, Gerard J. 1972. *Early Blazon: Heraldic Terminology in the Twelfth and Thirteenth Centuries with Special Reference to Arthurian Literature.* Oxford: Clarendon Press.

Brownlee, Marina S., Kevin Brownlee, and Stephen G. Nichols, eds. 1991. *The New Medievalism.* Baltimore: Johns Hopkins University Press.

Bruce, James Douglas. 1928. *The Evolution of Arthurian Romance from the Beginning down to the year 1300,* 2d ed., 2 vols. Göttingen, Vanderhoeke and Ruprecht.

Bruchet, Max. 1928. *Archives Départementales du Nord: Répertoire numérique.* Vol. 1, *Fonds Bénédictins et Cisterciens I H à XXXV H.* Lille: Imprimerie L. Danel.

Brundage, James. 1987. *Law, Sex, and Christian Society in Medieval Europe.* Chicago: University of Chicago Press.

Burgess, Glyn S. 1984. *Chrétien de Troyes "Erec et Enide."* London: Grant and Cutler.

Burns, E. Jane. 1985. *Arthurian Fictions: Rereading the Vulgate Cycle.* Columbus: Ohio State University Press.

Busby, Keith. 1988. "The Illustrated Manuscripts of Chrétien's *Perceval.*" *Zeitschrift für Französische Sprache und Literatur* 98:41–52.

———, ed. 1993. *Towards a Synthesis? Essays on the New Philology.* Amsterdam: Rudopi.

Busby, Keith, Terry Nixon, Alison Stones, and Lori Walters, eds. 1993. *Les Manuscrits de Chrétien de Troyes.* Amsterdam: Rodopi.

Cerquiglini, Bernard. 1977. "Sur la prose du *Joseph d'Arimathie:* Forme et statut de la parole." *Perspectives Médievales* 3:43–48.

Chasse, Dominique. 1985. "La Mise en mémoire des informations narratives: Le système du vers et le système de prose." In *Jeux de mémoire: Aspects de la mnémotechnie médiévale,* ed. Bruno Roy and Paul Zumthor, 57–64. Paris: Vrin.

Chastel de la Howarderies, P.-A. du. 1881–87. *Notices généalogiques tournaisiennes dressées sur titres.* 3 vols. Tournai: Vasseur-Delmee.

Clancy, Michael T. 1979. *From Memory to Written Record: England 1066–1307.* London: Edward Arnold.

Contamine, Philippe. 1984. *War in the Middle Ages.* Trans. Michael Jones. London: Basil Blackwell.

Corley, Corin F. V. 1987. *The Second Continuation of the Old French Perceval: A Critical and Lexicographical Study.* Texts and Dissertations 24. London: Modern Humanities Research Association.

Curtius, E. R. 1950. "Über die altfranzösische Epik IV." *Romanische Forschungen* 62:294–349.

Demay, Germain. 1873. *Inventaire des sceaux de la Flandres.* 2 vols. Paris: Imprimerie Nationale, 1873.

Dragonetti, Roger. 1980. *La Vie de la lettre au Moyen Age: Le Conte du Graal.* Paris: Seuil.

Duby, Georges. 1968. *Rural Economy and Country Life in the Medieval West.* Trans. Cynthia Postan. London: Edward Arnold.

———. 1973. *Hommes et structures du Moyen Age.* The Hague: Mouton.

———. 1977. *The Chivalrous Society.* Trans. Cynthia Poston. Berkeley and Los Angeles: University of California Press.

———. 1978. *Medieval Marriage: Two Models from Twelfth-Century France.* Trans. Elborg Forster. Baltimore: Johns Hopkins University Press.

———. 1982. "The Culture of the Knightly Class: Audience and Patronage." In *Renaissance and Renewal in the Twelfth Century,* ed. Robert L. Benson and Giles Constable, with C. Lanham, 249–62. Cambridge: Harvard University Press.

———. 1983. *The Knight, the Lady, and the Priest: The Making of Modern Marriage in Medieval France.* Trans. Barbara Bray. New York: Pantheon.

———. 1985. *William Marshall: The Flower of Chivalry.* Trans. Richard Howard. New York: Pantheon.

Duggan, Joseph J. 1989a. "Oral Performance of Romance in Medieval France." In *Continuations: Essays on Medieval French Literature and Language in Honor of John L. Grigsby,* ed. Norris J. Lacy and Gloria Torrini-Roblin, 51–61. Birmingham, Ala.: Summa Publications.

———. 1989b. "Performance and Transmission, Aural and Ocular Reception in the Twelfth- and Thirteenth-Century Vernacular Literature of France." *Romance Philology* 42:49–58.

Faider, Paul, and Mme Faider-Feytmans. 1931. *Catalogue des manuscrits de la Bibliothèque publique de la ville de Mons.* Universiteit te Gent, Werken Uitgegeven door de Faculteit der Wijsbegeerte en Letteren 65. Paris: Champion.

Flori, Jean. 1975. "Qu'est-ce qu'un *bacheler?* Etude historique du vocabulaire dans les chansons de geste du XIIe siècle." *Romania* 96:290–314.

Fossier, Robert 1974. *Chartes de coutume en Picardie (XIe–XIIIe siècle).* Collection de Documents Inédits sur l'Histoire de France 10. Paris: Bibliothèque Nationale.

———. 1976. "La Noblesse picarde du temps de Philippe le Bel." In *La Noblesse au Moyen Age, XIe XVe siècles,* ed. P. Contamine, 105–127. Paris: Presses Universitaires de France.

———. 1983. *Le Moyen Age en Picardie: Textes choisis et présentés.* Amiens. Centre Régional de Documentation Pédagogique.

———. 1987. *La Terre et les hommes en Picardie jusqu'à la fin du XIIIe siècle.* 2d ed. Publications de la Faculté des Lettres et Sciences Humaines de Paris-Sorbonne, Série Recherches 48–49. Paris: Béatrice-Nauwelaerts.

———. 1988. *Histoire de la Picardie.* 2d ed. Toulouse: Privat.

Foulet, Lucien. 1950–51. "Sire messire." *Romania* 71:1–48, 180–221; 72: 31–77, 324–67, 479–528.

Frappier, Jean. 1957. *Chrétien de Troyes: L'Homme et l'œuvre.* Connaissance des Arts 50. Paris: Hatier Boivin.

———. 1969. *Etude sur "Yvain, ou Le Chevalier au lion" de Chrétien de Troyes.* Paris: Société d'Edition d'Enseignement Supérieur.

———. 1972. *Chrétien de Troyes et le mythe du Graal: Etude sur "Perceval, ou Le Conte du Graal."* Paris: Société d'Edition d'Enseignement Supérieur.

———. 1982. *Chrétien de Troyes: The Man and His Work.* Trans. Raymond J. Cormier. Athens: Ohio University Press.

Gaier, Claude. 1979. *Les Armes.* Typologie des Sources du Moyen Age Occidental 34. Turnhout: Brepols.

Gallais, P. 1972. *Perceval et l'initiation.* Paris: Sirac.

Gautier, Léon. 1878–92. *Les Epopées françaises.* 2d ed. 4 vols. Paris: V. Palmé.

Genicot, Léopold. 1961. "Noblesse et principautés en Lotharingie du XIe au XIIIe siècle." In *Scrinium Lovaniense: Mélanges historiques Etienne van Cauwenberge,* 191–206. Université de Louvain, Recueil de Travaux d'Histoire et de Philologie, ser. 4, fasc. 24. Louvain: Publications Universitaires.

———. 1975. *Les Généalogies.* Typologie des Sources du Moyen Age Occidental 15. Turnhout: Brepols.

Godefroy, Frédéric. 1880–1938. *Dictionnaire de l'ancienne langue française.* 10 vols. in 11. Paris.

Godzich, Wlad, and Jeffrey Kittay. 1987. *The Emergence of Prose: An Essay in Prosaics.* Minneapolis: University of Minnesota Press.

Gousset, Marie-Thérèse, and François Avril. 1990. *Saint Louis roi de France: "Livre des faits de monseigneur Saint Louis."* Paris: Chêne.

Green, D. H. 1986. "The Reception of Hartmann's Works: Listening, Reading, or Both?" *Modern Language Review* 81:257–68.

Grodecki, Louis. n.d. *La Sainte Chapelle.* Paris.

Grundriss der romanischen Literaturen des Mittelalters. 1968. Ed. Jean Frappier and Reinhold Grimm. Vol. 4, pts. 1–2, *Le Roman jusqu'à la fin du XIIIe siècle.* Heidelberg: Karl Winter.

Hadju, R. 1980. "The Position of Noblewomen in the Pays des Coutumes, 1100–1300." *Journal of Family History* 5:122–44.

Hallam, Elizabeth M. 1980. *Capetian France, 987–1328.* New York: Longman.

Halligan, G. J. 1970. "Marriage in Chrétien's *Yvain.*" *Journal of the Australian Universities Language and Literature Association* 34:264–85.

Hedeman, Anne D. 1991. *The Royal Image: Illustrations of the "Grandes Chroniques de France," 1274–1422.* Berkeley and Los Angeles: University of California Press.

Hendrickson, William. 1975. "Un nouveau fragment de *Garin de Monglane.*" *Romania* 96:163–92.

———. 1989. "*Garin de Monglane* and *La Chanson de la Croisade Albigeiose:* A Comparative Old French-Occitan Study." In *Continuations: Essays on Medieval French Literature and Language in Honor of John L. Grigsby,* ed. Norris J. Lacy and Gloria Torrini-Roblin, 203–15. Birmingham, Ala.: Summa Publications.

Hindman, Sandra. 1991. "King Arthur, His Knights, and the French Aristocracy in Picardy." *Yale French Studies,* special ed., *Contexts: Style and Values in Medieval Art and Literature,* 114–33.

———. 1994. "Perceval à l'image de Saint Louis: Vers une nouvelle lecture des manuscrits parisiens de Chrétien de Troyes." *Bulletin de Bibliophile.* In press.

Hoepffner, Ernest. 1927. "La Tradition manuscrite des *Lais* de Marie de France." *Neophilologus* 12:1–10, 85–96.

Holland, Wilhelm. 1854. *Chrestien von Troies, eine literaturgeschichtliche Untersuchung.* Tübingen.

Holmes, Urban T., and M. Amelia Klenke. 1959. *Chrétien, Troyes, and the Grail.* Chapel Hill: University of North Carolina Press.

Hult, David. 1986. "Lancelot's Two Steps: A Problem in Textual Criticism." *Speculum* 61:836–58.

———. 1988. "Reading It Right: The Ideology of Text Editing." *Romanic Review* 79:74–88. Reprinted in Brownlee, Brownlee, and Nichols 1991.

———. 1989. "Steps Forward and Steps Backward: More on Chrétien's *Lancelot.*" *Speculum* 64:307–16.

Hunt, Tony. 1979. "Chrétien de Troyes: The Textual Problem." *French Studies* 33: 257–71.

Huot, Sylvia. 1987. *From Song to Book: The Poetics of Writing in Early French Lyric and Lyrical Narrative Poetry.* Ithaca: Cornell University Press.

Jauss, Hans R. 1963. "Chanson de geste et roman courtois au XIIe siècle (Analyse comparative du *Fierabras* et du *Bel Inconnu*)." In *Chanson de geste und Höfischer Roman: Heidelberger Kolloquium 30. Januar 1961,* 61–77. Studia Romanica 4. Heidelberg: Carl Winter.

Jodogne, Omer. 1963. "La Naissance de la prose française." In *Bulletin de la Classe des Lettres et des Sciences Morales et Politiques,* 5:296–308. Brussels: Palais des Académies.

Jonin, P. 1958. *Prolegomènes à une édition d'Yvain.* Annales, n.s., 19. Aix-en-Provence: Faculté des Lettres.

Jordan, William. 1979. *Louis IX and the Challenge of the Crusade: A Study in Rulership.* Princeton: Princeton University Press.

Keen, Maurice. 1984. *Chivalry.* New Haven: Yale University Press.

Keidel, George. 1909. "The History of French Fable Manuscripts." *Publications of the Modern Language Association of America* 24:208–12.

Kelly, Douglas. 1970. "The Source and Meaning of *Conjoincture* in Chrétien's *Erec* 14." *Viator: Medieval and Renaissance Studies* 1:179–200.

———. 1976. *Chrétien de Troyes: An Analytic Bibliography.* London: Grant and Cutler.

Kittay, Jeffrey. 1988. "Utterance Unmoored: The Changing Interpretation of the Act of Writing in the European Middle Ages." *Language in Society* 17, no. 2: 209–30.

Köhler, Erich. 1974. *L'Aventure chevaleresque: Idéal et réalité dans le roman courtois. Etudes sur la forme des plus anciens poèmes d'Arthur et du Graal.* Trans. Eliane Kaufholz, preface Jacques Le Goff. Paris: Gallimard.

Krueger, Roberta L. 1985. "Love, Honor, and the Exchange of Women in *Yvain:* Some Remarks on the Female Reader." *Romance Notes* 25:302–17.

———. 1988. "Desire, Meaning, and the Female Reader: The Problem in Chretien's *Charette.*" In *The Passing of Arthur: New Essays in Arthurian Tradition,* 31–51. New York: Garland.

———. 1993. *Women Readers and the Ideology of Gender in Old French Romance.* Cambridge: Cambridge University Press.

La Morlière A. de. 1642. *Antiquitez, histoires et choses plus remarquables de la ville d'Amiens.* Paris: Cramoisy.

Langlois, C. V. 1901. *Saint Louis, Philippe le Bel, les dernier Capétiens directs.* Paris.

———. 1925. *La Vie en France, d'après quelques moralistes du temps.* Paris: Hachette.

Leclercq, Jean. 1983. *Le Mariage vu par les moines au XIIe siècle.* Paris: Cerf.

Le Gentil, Pierre. 1957. "Ogier le Danois, héros épique." *Romania* 78:199–233.

Lejeune, Rita. 1954. "La Date du *Conte del Graal* de Chrétien de Troyes." *Le Moyen Age* 60–53–58.

Lock, Richard. 1985. *Aspects of Time in Medieval Literature.* New York: Garland.

Loisne, C. de. 1903. "Les Miniatures du cartulaire de Marchiennes." *Bulletin Archéologique,* 476–89.

Loomis, Roger Sherman, and Laura Hibbard Loomis. 1938. *Arthurian Legends in Medieval Art.* New York. Modern Language Association of America.

Luttrell, Claude. 1974. *The Creation of the First Arthurian Romance.* London: Edward Arnold.

Maddox, Donald. 1978. *Structure and Sacring: The Systematic Kingdom in Chrétien's "Erec et Enide."* Lexington, Ky.: French Forum.

———. 1991. *The Arthurian Romances of Chrétien de Troyes: Once and Future Fictions.* Cambridge: Cambridge University Press.

McGrath, Robert. 1963a. "A Newly Discovered Illustrated Manuscript of Chrétien de Troyes' *Yvain* and *Lancelot* in the Princeton University Library." *Speculum* 38:583–94.

———. 1963b. "The Romance of the Maccabees in Mediaeval Art and Literature." Ph.D. diss., Princeton University.

Micha, Alexandre. 1939. *La Tradition manuscrite des romans de Chrétien de Troyes.* Publications Romanes et Française 90. Paris: Champion; reprint Geneva: Librairie Droz, 1966.

Nichols, Stephen G. 1988. "Editor's Preface." *Romanic Review* 79:1–3.

Niemeyer, Dariva H. 1969. "The Writer's Craft: *La Joie de la Cort.*" *L'Esprit Créateur* 9, no. 4:286–92.

Noonan, John T., Jr. 1973. "Power to Choose." *Viator: Medieval and Renaissance Studies* 4:419–34.

Oman, Charles. 1898. *A History of the Art of War: The Middle Ages from the Fourth to Fourteenth Century.* New York: G. P. Putnam's Sons.

Ong, Walter S. 1982. *Orality and Literacy: The Technologizing of the Word.* New York: Methuen.

Pakula, Marvin H. 1972. *Heraldry and Armor of the Middle Ages.* New York: A. S. Barnes.

Parkes, Malcolm B. 1973. "The Literacy of the Laity." In *Literature and Western Civilization,* vol. 2, *The Mediaeval World,* ed. David Daiches and Anthony Thorlby, 555–77. London: Aldus.

Pastoureau, Michel. 1980. "Remarques sur les armoiries de Gauvain." In *Mélanges Charles Foulon,* 2 vols., 229–36. Rennes: Institut de Français.

———. 1983. *Armorial des chevaliers de la Table Ronde.* Paris: Léopard d'Or.

Payen, Jean-Charles. 1981. "La 'Mise en roman' du mariage dans la littérature française des XIIe et XIIIe siècles: De l'évolution idéologique à la typologie des genres." In *Love and Marriage in the Twelfth Century,* ed. Willy van Hoecke and Andries Welkenhysen, 218–35. Mediaevalia Lovaniensia, ser. 1, studia 8. Louvain: Leuven University Press.

Perroy, Edouard. 1949. "Les Crises du XIV siècle." *Annales, E.C.S.* 4:167–82.

Poirion, Daniel. 1977. *Perspectives Médiévales* 3:3–6.

Porcher, Jean. 1955. *Les Manuscrits à peintures en France du XIIIe au XVIe siècles.* Paris: Bibliothèque Nationale.

Potvin, Charles. 1863. *Bibliographie de Chrestien de Troyes: Comparaison des manuscrits de Perceval le Gallois. Un manuscrit inconnu. Chapitres uniques du manuscrit de Mons. Autres fragments inédits.* Paris: A. C. Herold.

Rahilly, Leonard J. 1973. "Le Manuscrit Garrett 125 du *Chevalier de la charrette* et du *Chevalier au lion:* Un nouveau manuscrit." *Romania* 94:407–10.

———. 1974. "La Tradition manuscrite du *Chevalier de la charrette* et le manuscrit Garrett 125." *Romania* 95:395–413.

———. 1978. "La Tradition manuscrite de *Chevalier au lion* et le manuscrit Garrett 125." *Romania* 99:1–30.

Réau, Louis. 1958. *Iconographie de l'art chrétien.* 3 vols. Paris: Presses Universitaires de France.

Reid, T. B. W. 1976. "Chrétien de Troyes and the Scribe Guiot." *Medium Aevum* 45:1–19.

Reiss, Edmund, Louise Horner Reiss, and Beverly Taylor. 1984. *Arthurian Legend and Literature: An Annotated Bibliography.* Vol. 1, *The Middle Ages.* New York: Garland.

Runte, Hans R. 1989. "Initial Readers of Chrétien de Troyes." In *Continuations: Essays on Medieval French Literature and Language in Honor of John L. Grigsby,* ed. Norris J. Lacy and Gloria Torrini-Roblin, 121–32. Birmingham, Ala.: Summa Publications.

Rushing, James A., Jr. 1991–92. "The Adventures of the Lion Knight: Story and Picture in the Princeton *Yvain.*" *Princeton University Library Chronicle* 53: 31–49.

Saenger, Paul. 1982. "Silent Reading: Its Impact on Late Medieval Script and Society." *Viator: Medieval and Renaissance Studies* 13:367–414.

Saenger, Paul, and Michael Heinlen. 1991. "Incunable Description and Its Implication for the Analysis of Fifteenth-Century Reading Habits." In *Printing the Written Word: The Social History of Books, circa 1450–1520*, ed. Sandra Hindman, 225–58. Ithaca: Cornell University Press.

Schmolke-Hasselmann, Beate. 1980. *Der Arthurische Versroman von Chrestien bis Froissart.* Tübingen: Niemeyer.

Scholz, Manfred Günther. 1980. *Hören und Lesen: Studien zur primären Rezeption der Literature im 12. und 13. Jahrhundert.* Wiesbaden: Steiner.

Schroeder, Horst. [1971]. *Der Topos der 'Nine Worthies' in Literatur und bildender Kunst.* Göttingen: Vandenhoeck und Ruprecht.

Spiegel, Gabrielle. 1983. "Genealogy: Form and Function in Medieval Historical Narrative." *History and Theory* 22:43–53.

———. 1984. "Forging the Past: The Language of Historical Truth in the Middle Ages." *History Teacher* 17:267–88.

———. 1986. "*Pseudo-Turpin*, the Crisis of the Aristocracy and the Beginnings of Vernacular Historiography in Medieval France." *Journal of Medieval History* 12:207–23.

———. 1987. "Social Change and Literary Language: The Textualization of the Past in Thirteenth-Century Old French Historiography." *Journal of Medieval and Renaissance Studies* 17:129–48.

———. 1993. *Romancing the Past: The Rise of Vernacular Prose Historiography in the Thirteenth Century.* Berkeley and Los Angeles: University of California Press.

Stanger, Mary. 1957. "Literary Patronage at the Medieval Court of Flanders." *French Studies* 11:214–29.

Stanton, Amida. 1939. "Gerbert de Montreuil as a Writer of Grail Romance: An Investigation of the Date and the More Immediate Sources of the Continuation of *Perceval*." Ph.D. diss., University of Chicago.

Stock, Brian. 1983. *The Implications of Literacy: Written Language and Models of Interpretation in the Eleventh and Twelfth Centuries.* Princeton: Princeton University Press.

———. 1984. "Medieval Literacy, Linguistic Theory, and Social Organization." *New Literary History* 16:13–29.

Stones, Alison. 1970. "The Illustrations of the French Prose Lancelot in Belgium, Flanders and Paris, 1250–1340." Ph.D. diss., University of London.

———. 1976. "Secular Manuscript Illumination in France." In *Medieval Manuscripts and Textual Criticism*, ed. Christopher Kleinhenz, 83–102. North Carolina Studies in the Romance Languages and Literature, Symposia 4. Chapel Hill: University of North Carolina Press.

———. 1977. "Sacred and Profane Art: Secular and Liturgical Book-Illumination in the Thirteenth Century." In *The Epic in Medieval Society, Aesthetic and Moral Values*, ed. Harold Scholler, 100–112. Tübingen: M. Niemeyer.

———. 1991. "Arthurian Art since Loomis." In *Arturus Rex, Acta Conventus Lo-*

vaniensis 1987, vol. 2, ed. W. Van Hoecke, G. Tournoy, and W. Verbeke, 21–76. Mediaevalia Lovaniensia, ser. 1, studia 16. Louvain: Leuven University Press.

Sturm-Madox, Sara. 1982. "The *Joie de la Cort:* Thematic Unity in Chrétien's *Erec et Enide.*" *Romania* 103:513–28.

Torrini-Roblin, Gloria. 1989. "Oral or Written Model? Description, Length, and Unity in the *First Continuation.*" In *Continuations: Essays on Medieval French Literature and Language in Honor of John L. Grigsby,* ed. Norris J. Lacy and Gloria Torrini-Roblin, 143–59. Birmingham, Ala.: Summa Publications.

Uitti, Karl. [1973]. *Story, Myth, and Celebration in Old French Narrative Poetry, c. 1050–1200.* Princeton: Princeton University Press.

Uitti, Karl, with Alfred Foulet. 1988. "On Editing Chrétien de Troyes: Lancelot's Two Steps and Their Context." *Speculum* 63:271–92.

Vance, Eugene. 1986. *Mervelous Signals: Poetics and Sign Theory in the Middle Ages.* Lincoln: University of Nebraska Press.

Van Coolput, Colette-Anne. 1985–86. "Por deviser comment: L'Evolution de la formule dans le *Tristan en prose.*" *Tristania* 11:10–20.

Vandermaesen, M. 1980. "Vlaanderen en Henegouwen onder het Huis van Dampierre, 1244–1384." In *Algememe Geschiedenis der Nederlanden,* 2:399–440. Haarlem.

Verbeke, Werner, Joset Janssens, and Maurtis Smeyers, eds. 1987. *Arturus Rex.* Vol. 1, *Catalogus, Koning Artur en de Nederlanden: La matière de Bretagne et les anciens Pays-Bas.* Mediaevalia Lovaniensia, ser. 1, studia 16. Louvain: Leuven University Press.

Vial, Guy. 1978. "L'Auteur de la deuxième continuation du *Conte del Graal.*" *Travaux de Linguistique et de Littérature* 16:519–30.

Victorio, Juan, and Jean-Charles Payen. 1988. *L'Epopée.* Typologie des Sources du Moyen Age Occidental 49. Turnhout: Brepols.

Vitz, Evelyn Birge. 1986. "Rethinking Old French Literature: The Orality of the Octosyllabic Couplet." *Romanic Review* 77:307–21.

———. 1990. "Chrétien de Troyes: Cler ou ménestrel. Problèmes des traditions orale et littéraire dans les cours de France au XIIe siècle." *Poétique* 8:23–42.

Walters, Lori. 1985. "Le Rôle du scribe dans l'organisation des manuscrits des romans de Chrétien de Troyes." *Romania* 106:303–25.

Warlop, Ernest. 1975–. *The Flemish Nobility before 1300.* Trans. J. B. Ross and H. Vandermoere. 4 vols. Kortrijik: G. Desmet-Huysman.

Wathelet-Willem, Jeanne. 1975. *Recherches sur la Chanson de Guillaume: Etudes accompagnées d'une édition.* 2 vols. Bibliothque de la Faculté de Philosophie et Lettres de l'Université de Liège, fasc. 210. Paris: Société d'Edition "Les Belles Lettres."

West, G. D. 1971–72. "Grail Problems, I: The Grail Family in the Old French Verse Romances." *Romance Philology* 25:53–73.

Woledge, Brian. 1930. *L'Atre périlleux: Etude sur les manuscrits, la langue et l'importance littéraire du poème avec un spécimen du texte.* Paris: E. Droz.

———. 1954. *Bibliographie des romans et nouvelles en prose française antérieurs à 1500.* Geneva: Librairie Droz.

———. 1969. "Bons vavasseurs et mauvais sénéchaux." In *Mélanges Rita Lejeune,* 2 vols., 2:1263–77. Gembloux: Editions J. Duculot.

———. 1986. *Commentaire sur Yvain (Le Chevalier au lion) de Chrétien de Troyes.* 2 vols. Publications Romanes et Françaises 170–71. Geneva: Librairie Droz.

Woledge, Brian, and H. P. Clive. 1964. *Répertoire des plus anciens textes en prose française depuis 842 jusqu'aux premières années du XIIIe siècle.* Publications Romanes et Françaises 79. Geneva: Librairie Droz.

Zink, Michel. 1985. *La Sujectivité littéraire autour du siècle de Saint Louis.* Paris: Presses Universitaires de France.

Zumthor, Paul. 1972. *Essai de poétique médiévale.* Paris: Editions du Seuil.

———. 1981. "Intertextualité et mouvance." *Littérature* 41:8–16.

———. 1984. *La Poésie et la voix dans la civilisation médiévale.* Paris: Presses Universitaires de France.

INDEX